KU-132-703

# Tall Ships
# and
# Master Mariners

R.J. Cunningham
K.R. Mabee

*Simon Graham's sextant*

# Tops'l
# Books

©1985 Copyright Cunningham, Robert, Mabee, Ray

British Library CIP Data

Cunningham, R.J.

Tall ships and master mariners.
1. Merchant marine – Maritime Provinces –
History – 19th century
I Title II Maybee R.
387.5'09715 HE770

ISBN 0 906397 13 8

## CAUTION

No part of this publication may be photocopied, or otherwise
reproduced, without the Publisher's permission: Breakwater Books
Ltd., 277 Duckworth Street, St. John's, Newfoundland, A1C 1G9.

# TALL SHIPS
# AND
# MASTER MARINERS

# ACKNOWLEDGMENTS

The authors are grateful for the assistance provided by a number of individuals and organizations. In addition to a wide range of reading and investigation, the scope of the topic called for the examination of materials located in many distant centres. Canada Council provided funds for necessary research assistance.

Ray W. Guy, of Musgrave Harbour, Newfoundland, searched the extensive and unique merchant marine records held by Memorial University of Newfoundland. A naval officer in World War II, he was at ease with his assignment and turned in highly competent reports. Yvonne Pigott, of Halifax, Nova Scotia, a graduate student, searched records in Halifax, Fredericton and Saint John, and uncovered valuable data. Mary Pain of London, England, conducted a search at the Public Records Office and related sources there, finding, among other things, Simon Graham's application for a Master's Certificate of Competency. Leo Dube of Dorchester, New Brunswick, retired craftsman with seatime under sail, examined the New Brunswick press for shipping notes of the period and assisted with technical points.

Wally Zinck, of Chester, Nova Scotia, one-time mate of *Bluenose II,* Harold Lister of Moncton, New Brunswick, Captain Norman Rees-Potter of Sackville, New Brunswick, forty years a Master Mariner, and Captain Clary Williams, LLD, of Pool's Cove and St. John's, Newfoundland, provided important insights into seafaring. Roland Graham Jardine of Richmond Hill, Ontario, a descendent of Simon Graham, and John Corey of Havelock, New Brunswick, who has a collection of Graham's books were very helpful. Cynthia McCausland of Virginia Beach, Virginia, also a descendent, obtained a photograph of Simon Graham's sextant for us.

Advice, criticism and other help were provided by Jocelyn LeBel and Roger Nason of Historic Resources Administration, Frederiction, New Brunswick; A. Gregg Finley, of the New Brunswick Museum in Saint John, New Brunswick; Douglas Lochhead and Bill Godfrey, both professors at Mount Allison University, Sackville, New Brunswick; Douglas How of St. Andrews, New Brunswick, and Peter Fleiger of Northport, Nova Scotia. Keith Ingersoll, then of Historic Resources Administration, Fredericton, New Brunswick, was particularly generous with his time and was most helpful.

Gratitude is also expressed to the Maritime History Group of Memorial University, St. John's, Newfoundland; Mount Allison University, Sackville, New Brunswick; National Maritime Museum, Greenwich, England; New Brunswick Museum, Saint John, New Brunswick; Provincial Archives of New Brunswick, Fredericton, New Brunswick; Provincial Archives of Prince Edward Island, Charlottetown, Prince Edward Island; Public Archives of Canada, Ottawa, Ontario; Public Archives of Nova Scotia, Halifax, Nova Scotia; and the Public Records Office, London, England.

# CONTENTS

# FOREWORD

Some time ago the authors acquired two folio manuscripts of ships' logs kept by one Simon Graham, a master mariner, between 1833 and 1855. The logs recounted details of more than 80 voyages, most across the Atlantic Ocean, some around the legendary Cape Horn. Interspersed between records of seafaring were numerous quaint poems written by Graham to while away lonely hours in ships' cabins.

The chuckles inspired by occasional readings of the strange old rhymes found in the folios gradually gave way to a kind of sympathetic wonder at the lonely life they reveal. Simon Graham looked to Richibucto in the Colony of New Brunswick as his home, despite the fact that he was seldom there. Cryptic references suggest that the mariner resented his long absences but was unable to tear himself free of the ocean's grip. An air of mystery seemed to surround his life of which only part was evident through the logs.

Brief moments of high drama — shipwreck, death, birth, mutiny and even piracy — came cutting across the tedium of seafaring. Slowly it was realized that the sea had begun to ensnare the readers of the logs just as surely as it had taken the writer of them years before. Simon Graham's words were then examined more intently and with a new respect for what they had to say.

A close reading and analysis of the log books proved problematic. The handwriting was good yet it was not easy to read. The ink had faded and some areas were nearly obliterated by waterstain. The language, that of a seaman out of the distant past, was one that had to be learned by the authors. Some usages were archaic and others, it developed, came from the lowland Scots dialect. Difficulties were compounded by phonetic spelling, often quite imaginative, which caused every unfamiliar word to be suspect when it was finally deciphered beneath a magnifying glass.

It was necessary to know what Simon Graham did when he brailed up; how strong a "duble reeft gaill" might be; why he sometimes came to with the best bower and, at other times, needed only the other, — whatever bowers were! A library of books to do with the sea was quickly assembled but it was soon discovered that few were as informative as they purported to be. Some, in fact, contradicted others on quite simple matters. None was complete in its coverage of the period and areas that concerned Captain Graham's seafaring.

Accordingly it became clear that if the logs were to be understood, a systematic interpretation would have to be made using books, newspapers, records and dictionaries of the era. More than the language of seamanship, the significance of such remarks as these begged to be explained: "saw a round-starned (sic) brig" and "passed a ship with two topgallant yards on eatch (sic) mast." In the event, the two examples quoted led to exploring the changing shapes of hulls and sails through the period.

Such directions of search opened into others. To comprehend seamanship it proved necessary to know the vessels. That demanded a knowledge of construction which rested on materials, the times, the shipbuilding locations, the people, their tools and so on. Few aspects proved distinct; generally, they were closely related and interdependent. Separately and collectively they had to be considered along with the histories of several very different social-economic areas. Nor could one part of Simon Graham's life be examined and the rest be left as if without relevance.

This book is the outcome of research undertaken. It is by no means exhaustive of its subject because, although many areas of search were rewarding, others proved fruitless.

J.C.
K.R.M.

## CHAPTER 1

# The Gilded Penny

The vigour of shipbuilding in nineteenth century British North America has always been regarded with some astonishment, although the shape of the phenomenon has never been clearly defined. Local writers have tended to associate the industry with regional enterprise and few historians concerned with broader panoramas have paid much attention to the scene. A significant aspect may thereby have been overlooked. When Nelson's fleet won the last of several important naval battles at Trafalgar in 1805, Britain began a century of almost undisputed leadership in ocean commerce. The period was one of immense growth in British industry and empire. Many factors contributed and may have been necessary to this growth, among them the ready availability of the bottoms required for the conduct of trade. These vessels, without which Britain's maturation might never have been realized, for more than half a century, came largely from British North America.

An ever-critical shortage of shipbuilding materials before the manufacture of iron plate would have precluded such eminence for Britain, but King Alfred, founder of the British Navy, had foreseen long before how precarious his kingdom's independence would be if ever her scant woodlands failed to yield ships' timbers. He caused trees to be marked to show those that might be felled for ordinary use and those to be left for defence. The practice continued through the centuries and even extended the Crown's mark, the Broad Arrow, into the forests of North America. Notwithstanding such husbandry, at the time of Trafalgar Britain had barely enough native timber for her navy and none for merchantmen. She was, then, fortunate to have colonies embracing the great woodlands of Acadia and the St. Lawrence River.

When appraising the areas from which Britain drew timbers and vessels it is important to bear in mind how small their total population was and how sparsely it was distributed along coasts and rivers. Settlements were far removed from the British Isles and, considering the difficulties of communication at the time, nearly as remote from one another. One business could fail in one part of the world while another, not to learn of the event for months, happily continued valueless contracts.

Owing to a shortage of suitable timbers handy to her ports, Newfoundland was not part of the great shipbuilding endeavour, but she was just as important to Britain as the timber colonies for another reason. The outports of the island were Britain's most valued source of seamen beyond the old country's shores. As Sir Winston Churchill once said, Newfoundland fishermen were the best small-boatmen in the world. Innumerable schooners were built and operated in the fishing trade of the old colony, whalers and sealers were based there and naval vessels called regularly at St. John's.

Although many fine ships and barques were built in Prince Edward Island, that province did not have the timber resources to make it a great provider of vessels or materials for Britain. Instead, like Newfoundland, the Island's inhabitants were schooner men. They fished and farmed; and they traded around the shores of the Atlantic Provinces, into the Gulf of the St. Lawrence and down to the Caribbean.

The thirteen provinces south of Nova Scotia were important suppliers of ships and timbers to Britain before the American Revolution.[1] Even afterwards, in times of friendly relations, American-built vessels augmented Britain's Merchant Marine. Canadian shipping lists compiled after Confederation show a surprisingly large number of American hulls registered at ports like Saint John and Halifax even at that late date.

Acceptance of colonial vessels into the British merchant fleet before 1776 brought considerable reward later for both Britain and the United States. Emigrant British shipbuilders established in the American colonies had to innovate designs suited to local waters. One of the more successful was the schooner, devised by Captain Robinson of Gloucester, Massachusetts, in 1713. Its rig led to variations such as brigantines and barquentines. The clean lines which evolved with the schooner must have influenced the clipper hull 130 years later. Americans retained some marine oddities in the midst of all their novel craft, nevertheless.

One of them was the row-galley, a stylized representation of which appears in the arms of New Brunswick. Captain John Gorham showed the Union Flag around the Bay of Fundy and up the St. John River in two row-galleys, the *Anson* and *Warren*, in 1748. Americans had similar craft in service in the Revolutionary War and in the War of 1812. In New Brunswick, Joseph Cunard named a barque *Ouzel Galley* in 1845 and Louise Manny in *Ship-building in Bathurst* wondered over its name. It was certainly not equipped with oars. Its name was likely a whimsical recollection of Scottish -English coasters capable of being rowed into shallow estuaries. Several rivers in England bear the name Ouse or Ouze.

British shipbuilding was stimulated by the demand for warships and privateers during the Revolutionary War and afterwards, when a merchant fleet had to be assembled to replace vessels lost to British registry and in action. The situation was repeated in 1812-13. In 1849, discovery of gold in California, long visited by American vessels, drew great rushes of immigrants. The merchantmen of the United States were insufficient for the demands of time-consuming voyages around Cape Horn and so British vessels, including many of colonial registry, joined in the trade.

The restrictive British Navigation Laws, already lax, were repealed at that time and Britain embraced free trade. Nevertheless, American vessels were so involved in internal trade that comparatively few could take advantage of the opportunity to join in British commerce. The U.S. Civil War and the subsequent thrust of energy into opening the midwest strained American shipping even further. Consequently the United States fell behind Britain in world trade. At the same time, Britain was advancing into steel hulls and steam power years ahead of other nations.

Throughout the 19th century Britain had a great need for vessels for purposes other than commerce. Wars and colonization required the transportation of huge quantities of materials and numbers of people around the world. From 1800-1815 Britain was at war with France, Spain and the United States. The clearances of the Highlands and settlement of Wellington's army followed. In 1839, the first of the Afghan Wars started and, about the same period, Ireland was ravaged by famines. A year later Britain was involved in the Opium War. Punjab became British in 1849. The Crimean War started in 1854 at a time when bellicose threats from America demanded troops in the British North American Colonies. The Indian Mutiny followed. Britain was uncomfortably close to the combatants in the American Civil War and later she was concerned with protecting Upper and Lower Canada against Fenian raiders.

The Franco-Prussian War of 1870 had Britain on a war alert, and within three years the Ashanti Wars started. The Transvaal was annexed in 1877 and Cairo occupied in 1882. South Africa was turbulent in 1896 and, before the century ended, was the scene of war. Meanwhile, New Zealand, Australia, Canada and even the United States were being populated with emigrants from the British Isles.

The situation through much of the century demanded wooden ships and timbers for more ships. Both were available in the British lands across the Western Ocean. Nothing so dramatic as an appeal for aid was heard nor was it necessary. Britain was at the height of its climb through the Industrial Revolution and free enterprise was in full flower. It was through

British businessmen, some of long standing and others newly opportunist, that the trade in ships and timber was conducted. Early in the century the free enterprise system crossed the ocean to the ports and forests of the British North American Colonies. No momentum could be built up, however, until the Napoleonic Wars had ended and vessels launched as privateers and others taken as prizes had seen their days afloat.

Quebec, the oldest and most stable of the mainland Provinces, had the largest population. The best of oak, birch, elm, pine, hackmatack and spruce grew within easy reach of the St. Lawrence River. Almost every workman was an artisan with axe and adze. One might reasonably expect Quebec to head the list of suppliers of vessels but that did not develop to be the case. The English-speaking component of the population was made up principally of U.E. Loyalist farmers, concentrated mainly in the Eastern Townships, away from the sea. Others, early in the century, were more interested in furs and inland trade. French-speaking Quebecois were concerned, for the first half of the century at least, largely with the business of subsistence farming and the fur trade. Neither race in Quebec produced shipwrights in proportion to their numbers, compared with those of the Maritimes.

Les Habitants undoubtedly possessed the necessary skills. Bateaux and goélettes had been launched along the St. Lawrence in greater numbers each summer for nearly two centuries. Ocean-going merchantmen and warships were built at Quebec years before the great battle on the Plains of Abraham. St. Lawrence ports are not as ice-free as those of the Atlantic Coast but such a factor merely demanded more winter construction and summer launchings as at Richibucto and Miramichi in New Brunswick. Most reasons for Quebec's failure to lead in shipbuilding are likely complex but two seem simple enough. The coasts of Acadia were longer and they were indented with the mouths of more timber rivers and creeks than were the St. Lawrence shores. At the same time, the settlers who came there from Britain and the American colonies to the south, already close to the sea in spirit, found the coasts and rivers generally more hospitable than the interior.

British newcomers to Quebec did construct vessels immediately on their arrival, for inland trade, for communication with the other colonies, for defence, for trade and even for sale to the old country. By 1820 some very substantial vessels had been launched on the St. Lawrence and many more were to originate there through the 19th century. Nevertheless, the industry was never to assume the proportions reached in Nova Scotia and New Brunswick.

Lumbering and shipbuilding were two faces of a glittering gold-plated coin minted in the Maritime Provinces early in the century. The twin industries were always stronger in New Brunswick than in Nova Scotia but the latter province led in retained ownership and utilization of vessels by an ample margin all through the period. New Brunswick's forests were far more extensive than Nova Scotia's but Nova Scotia had, proportionately, more arable land and of a nature more quickly developed. Nova Scotia was also closer to the best fishing grounds, had coal fields opened quite early and was somewhat better located for access to ocean trade, particularly in winter.

The two provinces developed in different directions. New Brunswick cut its forest and sold the produce in the forms of vessels and lumber almost exclusively to Britain. Nova Scotia grew into an independent trading "nation", host to the Royal Navy, purveyor of fish and groceries abroad, part-time salesman of ships and wood products to Britain and operator of vessels patrolling foreign ports in search of an honest dollar. Nova Scotia enjoyed much more versatility in commerce than New Brunswick did and savoured the sweet taste longer as well. Nova Scotia's economy was the better balanced and, accordingly, most of the astonishment due the shipbuilding industry falls to New Brunswick, the larger producer of vessels.

The period before 1825 was probably one of slow growth for both provinces with regard to shipbuilding although one cannot be sure owing to a paucity of adequate records. The picture is not at all clear for ports such as Halifax and Saint John and it is almost blank for others. Simon Graham's home port of Richibucto, New Brunswick, provides an example. Very little information about the town is available from records of any kind before publication of *The Gleaner*, a Miramichi newspaper covering the north Shore of New Brunswick from 1826 until it moved, late in the century, to Fredericton. Tradition, always suspect, is also scant in Richibucto.

Robert Cooney, in *A Compendious History of the Northern Part of New Brunswick and of the District of Gaspé in Lower Canada* published in 1832 but compiled years earlier, suggests a strong shipbuilding industry in Richibucto by about 1822. Marjorie Thompson, in a paper "Jardine Shipbuilders of Richibucto" adds support by finding that the Jardines, emigrant shipwrights from Scotland, were active there by 1816.[2] In the absence of other evidence one might suppose that shipbuilding followed the Jardines to Richibucto.

Only a small contradiction exists and that not yet published. A researcher of the family name *Mesheau* has uncovered the fact that the first bearer of the name in New Brunswick, Louis Anthony Mesheau, came to Richibucto as a boy, having been captured at sea in 1805 by Captain Jacob Powell, a privateer out of Richibucto and one of the earliest settlers of record there. Captain Powell adopted Mesheau and later had the lad bound to a trade. The articles of apprenticeship are said to be extant. Privateers demand quite a lot of building, rigging, arming, provisioning and manning, which suggests a fairly substantial base of operations in Richibucto much earlier than the Jardines. More evidence is found in a New Brunswick enactment, L Geo. III, Cap V, 1810, which undertook to see to the placing of beacons or buoys in Richibucto Harbour.

Hannay in *A History of New Brunswick* reports that in 1812-13 only one vessel, the sloop *General Smyth* out of Saint John, was granted a letter of marque, but this does not rule against Powell's vessel. Hannay does not mention any privateers of an earlier period of the Napoleonic War.[3] Many privateers were commissioned in Nova Scotia at the time, probably because the Province felt the onslaught of American sea raiders more acutely. In return at least 200 American vessels were taken as prizes into Halifax Harbour.

Nova Scotia and New Brunswick each had about 18 major shipbuilding ports but the fact is misleading because vessels were launched at almost every creek and cove around the coasts. The easy proximity of timber was not always a requirement, as shown by the construction of 165 vessels or more at Sackville, N.B., which is nearly surrounded by treeless marshland. The story of shipbuilding in the Maritimes is well told, although not completely by any means, by Wallace, Wright, Manny, Spicer, Parker and Armour and Lackey. Wright's *Saint John Ships and Their Builders* is particularly valuable for the graphs it contains. They pertain to Saint John but they reflect a picture for East Coast shipbuilding generally.

The peaks and valleys of Wright's graphs may readily be associated with the influence of events at home and abroad. The highest peak plotted is for 1865. It marks the close of the American Civil War but has more significance. About that time several factors began to combine in a manner that would end in the destruction of the Maritime Provinces' ocean-going enterprises. Within 20 years or so the timber trade, shipbuilding and seafaring were largely activities of the past regardless of the anomaly that saw more than half the world's ocean freight still carried under canvas.

By 1865 British shipyards had turned to iron (or low-grade steel) for the hulls of sailing vessels. Iron frames had ousted timber ribs earlier and this had been presaged long before, even in New Brunswick, when iron brackets began to supplant natural wooden knees. Iron-plate hulls were stronger[4], faster and more durable than wooden ones and, even more important for British shipowners, the use of a native product freed them from dependence on foreign timber.

Marine steam power was completely accepted by 1865. Thirteen years before, in 1852, following a disastrous and much-publicized fire that took many lives aboard the Royal Mail Ship *Amazon*, a side-wheel steamer, Britain decreed that all future vessels of the kind had to be steel-hulled and propelled by screw, not by paddles.

The year 1864 saw the British North American Provinces talking of union. Three years later Confederation came about. Ontario, the western part of the new country, had a much greater population than the Maritime Provinces and it was comparatively well industrialized; nevertheless the union of a seafaring economy with farmers and manufacturers was not as natural as it seemed to be. Politicians of the Dominion of Canada were committed to a westward expansion and businessmen were not looking towards Halifax and Saint John. The energy and funds that could have rehabilitated the Dominions' newly-acquired seafaring industries flowed away from the ocean that supported the eastern provinces. Thus, the Maritimes were crippled and growth of the new country was channelled inland.

Confederation of the four largest British North American Provinces came, then, just as the economic foundations of two of them, New Brunswick and Nova Scotia were threatened by an irresistible collapse. The situation may not have been recognized at the time yet the portents abounded everywhere. Not least among the signs were the complementing circumstances of a great waterway, the St. Lawrence River, already replete with canals, leading to the heart of the new country and, along with that, iron steamships which could cross the ocean and penetrate the river far more effectively than could sailing vessels. The iron steamers came from the river yards of Britain. Nova Scotia and New Brunswick could not supply them. It is ironical that one of the largest operators of iron steamers then was a company founded by a Nova Scotian, Samuel Cunard, and headed for years by a New Brunswicker, David Jardine.

Coal smoke lay on the North Atlantic not for the first time but now with serious intent, in 1838.[5] That year two steamers, *Sirius* and *Great Western*, crossed from Britain to the United States. Neither was a truly efficient design but *Sirius*, paddling along like a wing-clipped duck, passed by a brig, *Tyrian*, bound for Britain out of Nova Scotia but becalmed in mid-Atlantic. Aboard *Tyrian* was Samuel Cunard, already a shipowner of considerable stature and fortune. He had founded a packet-line in 1814, immediately on the cessation of war with the U.S.A., from St. John's to Halifax to Bermuda. Six years later he had packets crossing the Atlantic regularly between Liverpool and Halifax. Upon his arrival in Britain in 1838, Cunard straightway involved himself in the formation of a steam-packet service to carry the Royal Mail to Nova Scotia. It prospered under the popular name, The Cunard Line.

Other passengers who shared Cunard's chagrin as *Sirius* belched and puffed past *Tyrian* were Joseph Howe of Halifax, Judge T.C. Haliburton of Windsor, Nova Scotia, and Samuel Crane of Sackville, New Brunswick. Dr. W.C. Milner, in *A History of Sackville, N.B.*, quotes the *Times* of London as crediting Crane with urging Cunard to enter the steamship business.

At that time steamers, wooden-hulled, paddle operated, were employed at many locations around the shores of Nova Scotia and New Brunswick and so they were not a novelty on this side of the Atlantic. Indeed, the Province of new Brunswick had enacted legislation (L11 Geo III, Cap XXIV in 1812 to introduce steamers to the St. John River between Fredericton and Saint John. That was but two years after the start of organized steam transportation in the U.S.A., according to the *Book of Commerce*, Philadelphia, 1854.

Another factor which helped lay low the principal industry of the Maritime Provinces was an absence of readily mined iron in Atlantic Canada at a date early enough for its incorporation into shipbuilding. Iron and steel became available too late for retrieval of ocean trade because by then, the yards, the builders, the tradition were all but lost.

Even if the demand for wooden hulls had continued, New Brunswick had enjoyed, by 1867, all the prominence that could ever have come to the Province through seafaring. Her forests had been stripped of their fine timbers through the preceding half century. Lumber was still being shipped to Britain but the gold had worn away from that side of the coin, too. The brass that showed through was shiny enough to give the industry an illusion of value but, in fact, lumbermen — even New Brunswickers — had turned their attention to Quebec and to the Ontario forests of the Ottawa River Basin.

Nova Scotia, the trading "nation", had received a mortal blow to its seafaring at the same time but the industry was to bleed to death more slowly. It had a reserve of vitality accrued by the Province's diversification of business interests throughout the period of New Brunswick's unavoidable dependency on the selling of vessels. Since fishing and the mining of coal, gold and gypsum are well-known endeavours of the late nineteenth century in Nova Scotia, examples should be chosen from other areas of activity. The two that follow may serve to indicate the breadth of resourcefulness in the Province.

Henry A. Holder, in his memoirs, quoted by Marie Elwood in a paper *Father and Son, Two Halifax Cabinetmakers* (National Museum of Man, Mercury Series, 1976) said that his home was one of a number framed on the South Shore of Nova Scotia and designed to be shipped around the Horn to San Francisco to house the Forty-Niners; Holder's father had purchased one which was left over after the vessel on which it was to have been shipped had her full deck-load.

P. Pines, an expatriate American it appears, writing to the *New England Farmer* August, 1856, from Cornwallis, Nova Scotia, on July 14, 1856, said about Nova Scotia, "The business of the country has received a wonderful impetus from the high price which potatoes have demanded for the last few years." Later on he makes some revealing remarks to do with international stress, "The pending difficulty between the two countries is now a matter of great interest to the good people of the province. They feel much concern for the poor Yankees and compassionate their condition in case a war should take place. You cannot convince them but that Great Britain is almighty to destroy every seaboard town and city on the Atlantic Shores in an inconceivably short space of time and would carry devastation and death inland. This in their loving kindness they would regret — *for it would destroy the market for their potatoes.*"

A strange situation existed fifteen years after Confederation, when the days of shipbuilding in the Maritime Provinces were numbered. Home ownership of vessels stood at a peak. Nova Scotia ports had nearly 560,000 tons (registry tons) registered, more per head of population than any other country in the world had ever owned. This was the culmination of the Province's independent trading policies. The gross tonnage was made up of many fishing vessels, large and small, schooners trading to the West Indies and a number of large vessels vainly attempting to compete on the high seas with steel-hulled steamers. The average burden of all vessels was less than 185 tons, 7½% of the largest Nova Scotian vessel then registered, the *W.D. Lawrence* of 2458 tons.

New Brunswick had about 30% less tonnage registered. The Province that had been retailing vessels had not built itself a trading pattern similar to Nova Scotia's. Its timberlands were barren in comparison with the early days and lumbering had largely shifted to new forests in Quebec and Ontario.

Quebec, whose St. Lawrence steamship, *Accommodation*, had proudly voyaged from Quebec to Montreal in 1809 in 66 hours, had achieved even less. Its registered tonnage did not amount to 50% of the Nova Scotian fleet.

By the end of the century only shadows remained. There were few, if any, ships, barques, brigs, brigantines and barquentines in the harbours. Schooners, a few in trade but most employed at fishing, sailed seas comparatively empty of sails. Today, the shadows, even the memories have gone. Except for records being brought together at Memorial University of Newfoundland, little evidence of Atlantic Canada's great days of sail may be seen. Very few really old ships' logs have survived and when one such as Simon Graham's comes to hand, it must be regarded as invaluable for the rare glimpses of a hidden past which it provides.

## CHAPTER 2

## Simon Graham — Around the Horn

The helmsman overhead struck *Sybylla*'s bell just as Captain Simon Graham stepped through the hatch to his cabin. It was a robust clang, Simon noted approvingly, not a weak cheep like a country vicar ringing for more tea. The day was half an hour into the first watch and a slashing November wind blew from Symmes' Hole! The mate was welcome to the deck! He'll be busy, Simon chuckled, bending a new crew to the ship, only three days at sea; but that raw Nor'wester would keep the lubbers moving. It was shaping up for a half-reefed money-making gale which Simon favoured.

The captain set the ship's log-slate on his bunk and the two wood-framed leaves clanked a flat echo of the bell. He'd stop that noisy tendency tomorrow by having the carpenter fasten signal line around both frames, inside and out. That would also make them easier to grasp on a cold wet day and might save the slates if they were dropped.[2] He replaced his sextant in its lavishly decorated case with care. It was too precious to hang on the bulkhead, having once been the property of that rascally kinsman of his, John Paul, who styled himself John Paul Jones.

Off came his heavy wool jacket and shapeless cloth cap, onto their pegs by the door, and Simon sat down to demolish the fat mutton and boiled vegetables brought by his steward. With prosperous gales and no misfortune he might have time to call at Rio for enough vegetables to last him around the Horn. That reminded Simon: when he had finished writing up the log he should transcribe the notes he had copied from Captain Morrell's journal.

This American meat had a wooly flavour, Simon Graham remarked to himself. It was not nearly as tasty as mutton from his Scottish homeland. Given a few years ashore he could raise better sheep in Richibucto, New Brunswick, where he had become established. He shuddered as he recollected Richibucto's cold winters and smirked a little as he contemplated sailing over the Line, away from winter and into summer again. Now for his writing. He wiped his hands on his coarse shirt and bellowed for the steward.

His table cleared of dishes, Simon poured himself a noggin of brandy, then arrayed slate, foolscap, ruler, quills, ink and dusting-sand before him, and settled down to record the Day's Work, as the routine procedures of navigation were called.

He ruled ten narrow columns to the left of his page, leaving more than a third of the paper for "Remarks on Board". Briefly he considered another narrow column for longitude by chronometer but dismissed the idea from his mind. The chronometer was never reliable and so he'd use it only as a check against Dead Reckoning, hoping that somehow it would prove itself of value. Neatly he lined the page horizontally into quarter-inch divisions of which he would allow himself the use of one for each daily entry.

Across the page he wrote, "An Abstrack of Jurnal from New York to Valpariso and Lima in the Ship Sybylla³ Simon Graham, Master.

"Wednesday 20th Novr 1833 Sailed from New York — at 9h A.M. got underweigh from the East river in Tow by the Herculas Steemer.

"At noon the pilot left us at Sandy Hook light winds and varieable."

Simon paused here and then started down the page in the first column, setting the initial of each day of the week. He pondered briefly when he came to Sunday. How should he differentiate S for Sunday from S for Saturday? It pleased him to vary the Sunday designation. Often it was a Roman S with serifs, setting it apart from Saturday's flowing S in script. He decided upon D for Sunday in this log. Did it stand for Domini by which title he had known both his schoolmaster and the minister in his native Colvend, Scotland; or did it stand for Dimanche which the Frenchies used? Simon Graham's method appears to be a faulty variation of the Dominical letter system once used for the Ecclesiastical Calendar. The date of the first Sunday determined where the alphabetical notation started for the year. The 1st of January acquired an A; the 2nd a B; and so on.

Graham also headed up his columns ready for recording the components of course and position, and then:

"T21 at noon Reckoned in 40.33N 72.40W....at 4.30 PM Tacked close in with the East End of Long Island."

On Friday the 22nd, and Saturday the 23rd, he was still within sight of land and not ready to set a course seaward. Nevertheless, at noon on Saturday he sighted the Sun's altitude to determine latitude and, since by so doing he ascertained mid-day time precisely, he compared this with his chronometer to deduce longitude.

Something was amiss somewhere and Simon couldn't fathom the mystery, for he entered in his log, "At noon Obsd the Chnr only to Show 3.36 Greenwich time." That was a puzzler. From landfalls, Simon was carrying a longitude of 69° 54' West but at the rate of 15° for each hour of time difference, the chronometer was telling him that he was in longitude 54° West! What a curious situation that was, only three days out of the largest city and seaport in the western world, to find the chronometer defective.

One has to assume that longitude deduced from coastal features within eyesight, a few miles distant at most and marked on his charts, was fairly accurate. Nowhere later does Simon's daily work suggest a lack of mathematical competence to do with computing latitude and longitude. Nevertheless, here he was, setting out on a long and dangerous voyage without confidence in a most important piece of equipment. Had he not checked it before leaving New York? Was there no instrument mechanic there worth a seafarer's salt? Simon sounded surprised and disgusted but he should not have been; he'd had ample opportunity to service all instruments while in harbour.

The captain now turned his attention to the task which had been lurking at the back of his mind. He headed up a blank page left for the purpose: "The Cape Horn Gales and winds in General." Then, after judiciously testing the springiness of the quill's point on his thumbnail, he dipped into ink and began to transcribe from notes.

"The most Lasting are from S.S.W. to Sly E. they are most frequent in Summer months and often Last two or three days at a time. When the Southern horizon is filled with rising Clouds heavy and white in a Blue Sky it is a Sure indication of a Lasting Gale from the S. to S.W. whitch often Cums very Suddenly Scarcely allowing time to take in Sail. When the wind Sets in from the North and E. it Generally increases to a Smart Single reef Breeze at whitch it remains unless it hauls to S.E. from whitch quarter it will Blow at a moderate gale and then die away to a perfect calm. But if it haul to the N. you may depend on two or three days of pleasant weather untill it Hauls gently round to a N.W. where it will remain for 12 to 18 hrs. It will then Commence raising and finaly Shift gently to the S.W. when the weather will become Clear.

"North Gale Cums on gradually until it Blows a duble or close reeft Breeze and Last about 12 to 18 hours and then draws to the N.W. whitch Brings on rain and Shifts into the S.W. without relaxing its force and continues in that point 12 or 16 hours when it Dies away to a perfect calm.

"Such is the General Course of the wind weather in the vicinity of Cape Horn for the Season..., round about the first of November Northwardly winds Begin to prevail and with the exception of occasional changes Continues untill the furst of February. From this period until May the wind Generally Blows from the S.W. occasionally shifting to N.W.

"From the middle of May to the first of June Easterly winds and fine weather prevail and from July to October the wind varies from N. to W. and around to S.E. every four or five days."

As an afterthought Simon added, "from Capt. Benjamin Morrell Junr Jurnal."

Captain Morrell could spell far better than Captain Graham for, through twenty more years of logs the latter's spelling became more phonetic and less consistent. Lapses into his own inimitable style may be glimpsed in his copy of Benjamin Morrell's notes.

As Simon wiped off his quill and put away his scrivener's tools he contemplated the Cape gales. They did not sound at all formidable to a master thirty-seven years of age, twenty of them at sea.

For many days the voyage was uneventful. True, within a week Simon had recorded "Chronomater Stopt" but the total loss of an unreliable instrument meant little to him. Most of his years as a mariner had been spent without one anyway.

He bent a "new top main studding sail and rove new top Gallant studding sail gear." Occasionally he saw another vessel and once he remarked that he saw a dolphin, a curious observation for an experienced seaman. Once he found a ship following him "in company" and another "under our Lee standing to the South."

Simon marked "Christemous Day" without other comment. On December 27 at 9 p.m., "close in with St. Vincent, tryed to weather St. Antonio But Could Not and went through Betwixt St. Nicholas and Raza from whitch I take a Fresh departure." Simon's latitude and longitude by account from Dead Reckoning were fairly close to those on his chart and that must have been quite satisfying to him.

On January 1, 1834, Simon boldly marked the new year, "1824". He dropped a decade in that manner often through his career, not correcting the mistake until the next year came around.

On January 4, 1834, "2 Ships Standing together thy Both Showd English Cullers." Except in copying Capt. Morrell's notes, *they* was always *thy* to Simon.

Simon Graham crossed the Equator on January 8, 1834, but found the event too insignificant to record. He was more interested in the trade winds and a strong current in which he found himself. On January 14, "Water Changed Light Cullered tryed a Cast of the Lead but found no Bottom."

Two days later, having experienced some difficulty not worthy of mention, Simon observed "Carpinter Commenced to make a main yard."

On the 18th, Simon observed Sun and Moon together and deduced latitude and longitude. "Sight taken for Chr. at Same Time," and so Simon had been tinkering with the chronometer and had it working again!

On the 24th he *spock* the Brig *Elizabeth* of Cheapstowe bound from Rio to Falmouth and later a "round Starned Brig"[4] passed. Simon was greatly interested in the strength of the current he was stemming but on February 6 he was astounded to see a "Large ice Berg" which he noted in letters of proportionate size. Two days later he observed "grait quantaties of Sea weed."

On February 13, at 3 a.m., eagerly awaiting his first sight of the famous Cape, Simon made "Terra Del Fuego, Cape St. Innis E.S.E. 20 miles." The long-awaited adventure was at hand and Simon dropped the tedious business of dry entries in favour of a narrative of the rounding of Cape Horn.

"The Land on Terra Del fuego has a barren mountainous appearance, the peaks Stript with Snow, the valies is green and to appearance fertile. The Lower part of the high Land and part of the vailys is Covered with Low Brush wood But nothing Living to be Seen.

"F 14 at 4 A.M. Entered the Straits of Le Maine with a head wind and tide whitch Kept us all Day in the strait, Shooten at albotrosses and penguin we saw two of the Natifs huts one Canoe and a few of the Natifs about the hut and Shoar at 4 P.M. it Sprung up a fine Breeze from the N. and East whitch inabled us to Stear E.S.E. by Compas and get through the Strait.

"S 15 at 3.30 Spock the Ship MACKLELLAND from New York bound for Valpariso who Sailed a few Days Bifore us. At noon Cape Horn west 25 miles.

"D 16 at noon Cape Horn NEly N1/2N Ramarey Largest Island SW by S making us in Lat. 65.21 Long 68.06W...a fine clear Day the Snow Cled hils of tera Del Fuego is Showing ther Sharp Spicy tops to Grait advantage thy are Bleak and Barren now in the Midest of ther Sumer what must the poor meserable Savages indure who is Doomd to Spend ther winters amongest them.

"We have a Strong Easterly Current Seting against us we have Ben gowing at the rate of 5 miles an hour and has only Gained 6 miles these 4 hours. The MACKLELLAND is inshoar of us.

"M 17...the fore part of these 24 hours Strong SW Gails motherate the wind veering round to the N.ward a Ship under our lee Standing to the West ward I take hir to Be the MacKlelland...heavy westerly Swells.

"F 21...we was Boarded by his Britanic Magisties Ship PHILIDES, from Valpariso Bound to the river Plate.

"M 24...A brig Passed us to windward Showing American Collars.

"F 25...Sent up our royal mast and yards.

"M 3 (March)...Came to in 25 fathoms (45.64m) (in Valparaiso Harbour) All well after a passage of 103 days."

Simon found the harbour duties of a merchant mariner frustrating:

"After discharging a Small part of our Cargow and unstowing and Stowing the whole of it five or Six times for the Convenience of the marchants Geting a very Strict Overhaul from the officers of Customs having a Good Dale of trubel with the Seperation of my Seamen and the Chillean Ladies and ther intocksicating Drafts I Suckceeded in Geting ridy and Sailing March 17th 1834 — From Valparaiso Towards Arica."

Although sometimes chatty, Simon Graham saw the writing up of his log only as an obligation of his position, not as a bequest to posterity. His few words about Arica leave us quite disappointed.

"T 25...this morning we have a Beautiful vew of the Lofty Mountains of Pisagua who are Sending ther Lofty peeks abouve the Clouds. At 10 A.M. passed a Dead whail of a very Large Size and thousands of fouls around it at 10.30 hove to of Arica for Daylight to gow in.

"W 26 at 10 AM came to anchor in Arica in 6½ fathoms (11.87m) Soft Botom. Ships in the Bay are English man of war the Chalanger and 2 Brigs one American and the Cassiopia of Liverpool Capt. McGowan."

On the sixth of March Simon "hove up and made all Sail" towards Callao with never a word in his log about business conducted, "Leiving One Peruvian Ship of war, one French marchant Ship and the CASSIOPIA of Lpool." He passed St. Nicholas Harbour and some barren and dreary mountains: "The Only change of Senery is a snowtopt Mountain Showing Over or through Sum declivatie of the Lower hills or Deep Glen occasioned By vulcanic Eruptions of which the whol Coast is Greatly Marked.

"F 11...a Beautyful vew of the Amancaes Mts. who are Sending ther peakie tops far abouve the Clouds...at 4.30 Cum to in Callao in 6 fathoms and was Boarded by H.M.S. DUBLING and the American Schooner of war DOLPHEN. Delivered the Letters and papers to Mr. Barton, poart agent for the house....

"Sunday 27 Lord Jas. Tounsend Commanding H.M.S. DUBLING[5] took thre of my men out of the Jale of Callao which I had secured for Desertion. Demanded ther clothes and wages whitch I payed them took them on Board the DUBLING and had them Exemined By the Doctor who reported to Lord James that two of them was fit for Service but the third having the itch and other impediments he was returned to the Sybylla along with two Other Men from the DUBLING out of Confinement for Misconduck One of which is Lame and unfit for Dutie For whitch I have protested against his proceedings with the British Consul in Lima." (A fair copy of the Consul's report is held by the Provincial Archives in Frederiction, New Brunswick.)

"S May 3...at 11 AM hove up our anchor and made all Sail out of

Callao Bay after Lying 22 Days and discharging a littel and taking in Ballast at $1 per tun....officers hear is not very Strict and may be Bribed.

"M 5....on trial at Sea I find Jas. White unfit to take the helam[6] therefore is not intituled to Seaman's wages whitch makes Both the men from the DUBLING inferior one Lame and the other yousless.

"D 18....Mr. Samson Boarded us...and piloted us...and at 4 PM came to with our Small Bower in 10 fathoms (18.26m) of pt. Araines in the Gulf of Narcoia.

"T 23....hove up anchor and made all Sail....the Brig PORTER Capt. Gibson of Liverpool Came in hear. made a Seasure of on the Coast for Smugling....

"F 30...at 5.30 AM Boor up and at 7 came to with our Small Bower in 8 fathoms Sandy Botom (in Salina Voulana in the Gulf of Papagayo).

"D June 1 Mr. G.C. Samson arrived on Board and Left on June 3 for Nickerago.

"F 13 Cominced Loading Nickorago wood, Scorpions and Santapies (centipedes)."

On June 21, leaving behind the ship *General Smith* (Captain Taylor and Captain Meek)[8] Simon Graham happily made all sail for Liverpool, England. His passage to Cape Horn was uneventful except that, on Saturday August 30, "making a dale of water, Laid to to calk the huddens forward" and, on Tuesday, September 16th, John MacKie, a seaman, was buried[9] at sea in South latitude 51° 17', West longitude 78° 52' amid "hard gails".

"F Sept 19....almost Calm, heavy Sea.

"M Sept. 29....catching Cape pigons with hook and line."

On September 29, according to latitude recorded in his log, Simon Graham was at the southernmost point of his passage of Cape Horn. On October 2, he took the compass bearing of "Diego Ramariz", estimated the distance to the island and computed his position "from whitch I take a fresh Departure."

Simon passed the Falkland Islands on October 7 but, by Sunday, October 19, after twenty-four hours without wind and in strong currents, he was not at all sure of his position. His chronometer was obviously not operative for, having successfully determined latitude by observation, he was "Sounding on the Banks" and estimating longitude.

Monday, October 21: "Bending our Small Bower and puting the anchor on the rale with the Intencion of Caling at Rio Jueniro for another Crew and refreshments One Being Dead and Siven un abel to Cum on Deck with Scurvy and all hands more or less infected."

On Wednesday, October 22: "Hard gails making a Dale of water two more of our people Laid up.

"T 28 Hard Squals, rain and Lightning — only 5 men Can go on Deck two of them Boys one man yousless.

"F 3; This morning about 8AM Died peter Sawer, Swedish Seaman of Scurvy. He was long Cinfined a Chearful Good man and well respected.

"D (Sunday) November 2....at 9 AM run the Ship into Rio Janeuro was hailed at Sea a Crouse fort. Laid the Ship to. Thy continued to hail and fired two Blank Shot at us. We Brought the Ship to and Got on Board a Midshipman and 7 of H.M.S. SPASIAS Crew as I was Bed Sick as well as 10 of the Crew Leaving only 4 men to Bring the Ship in and work hir for a week. Before we was Qurantined four Days the 6 we Got our men on Shoar into the hospital the SPASIAS Crew was Qurantined along with them."

In those words a commonplace event was recorded, not mentioning the avoidance at the last moment of a great tragedy. Simon Graham proceeded in a matter-of-fact sort of manner to say that, on December 16, he sailed again with a fresh crew, leaving his sick men behind. The cause of profit-making had to be served, of course, and could not be slowed by an interest in human bodies. Of all necessities of commerce, men were most readily expendable.

*Sybylla* crossed the Equator on Sunday (marked E) December 14, 1834. Simon Graham's spirits were completely restored and, in high humour on December 25 he noted: "Fine pleasant weather and fair wind. All Stud Sails Set but No Goos for Cristinmiss."

On January 1, 1835, under his column "Remarks on Board," Simon noted "Smart Breezes NE by N To Begin the New Year" and, true to form, added: "1825".

Tuesday, January 27, saw *Sybylla* fast alongside Brunswick Dock in Liverpool. Simon closed his log with a note of fine nonchalance: "All well after a passage of Six months and 6 Days from Papagayos and Ten weeks and two Days from Rio Jeneiro."

Simon had earned a rest! He took passage with Capt. Watkins on the Barque "Bangiman Shaw" *(Benjamin Shaw)*[10] directly to Richibucto where he arrived on May 25, 1835, after a passage of 28 days from Liverpool. His voyage to the Pacific had been profitable, it would appear, for the next two pages of his journal are taken up with a description of a parcel of land previously purchased in Richibucto, New Brunswick, along with a plan and elevations of a house he then erected there.

His dwelling, modest, not more than a bungalow, perhaps 20' x 24' (6.1 x 7.3m) with four rooms and an entrance hall 6'x 4' (1.8 x 1.2m) had a loft which could only be reached by means of a ladder.

Years later Simon was to pen a note to his daughter: "I am now about to return to you, if not one of Richibucto's ritchest Settlers, one of its Quitest."

## CHAPTER 3

# Topheavy **Hercules**

After his voyage in *Sybylla* around Cape Horn, Simon Graham spent a year, until July, 1836, at home in Richibucto although, for three months of this time, he was mate of the barque *Richibucto*[1]. He may have been awaiting completion of his next command, the ship *Hercules*, under construction by John Jardine at his Richibucto yard. *Hercules*, 757 tons Old Measure, was the largest ship launched in colonial New Brunswick to that date. She was taken to Britain by Simon Graham on a Governor's Pass[2] and there sold.

Simon usually devoted the first few lines of each log to a narrative setting forth the procedure he followed clearing port to a point "from whitch I take my Departure." A line or two sufficed on leaving a harbour which was open to the ocean but several were necessary when departing an inland port. *Hercules* sailed from Buctouche, New Brunswick, and had to clear the Gulf of St. Lawrence and a last landfall there, St. Paul Island, before entering the North Atlantic. Simon's preliminary notes, before recording each Day's Work, would normally have been longer than the average. In this case they were much longer, taking up a full page.

In a bold hand he headed the page: "Ship Heriblas[3] Lanched July 16th. 1836." and then recounted, without any soliloquy or philosophizing, a course of events that is breathtaking.

"Sailed from the wharf Aug 3 and got over the Bar to Sea and arrived in Buctush on the 4th about 7 A.M.

"Tok in our full cargo and Sailed Wednesday 24th at 7 A.M. Passed the North Cape of Prince Edward Island at Midnight.

"Aug 25 at 6 P.M. passed the Magdalins and the N. Cape of Briton Island.

"Aug. 26 at 4 A.M. St. Pauls N.W. from whitch I take my departure. At 6 A.M. found 6 fot (1.83m) of water in the hold. Both pumps kept constantly working. Took in two reefs in topsails, 1st in foresail. Handed the Jib and Mizen and Mainsail. At noon reconed in 46.50N and 59.18W. At 6 P.M. finding the Leack to gain on the pumps we hove part of the deck Load overboard to Eas the Ship.

"Aug 27 at noon in 46.34 N 58.30 W. Leack still gaining. We Bore up for St. Peeters[4] — 8 foot (2.44m) water in the hold — at 7 P.M. threw overboard the remainder of our Deck Load to prevent the Ship turning top havy So mutch water Being in the hold..

"Aug 28 St. Peeters Nly W Dist 10 at 4 AM Braced the yards and stood in But the wind Being foul we thought it better to run for St. John's as Neccessaries for repairs might not Be had there. I Bore away and made all Sail along the Land. Both pumps kept constantly gowing.

"Aug 29 at noon Cape St. Marys N.E. Both pumps kept constantly gowing. Still 7 foot (2.13m) water in the hold.

"Aug 30 about noon Came to in the Narrows. Went on Shoar and got assistance to pump and warp[5] the Ship up the harbour of St. John's N.F.L."

Simon Graham unloaded his cargo and had *Hercules* repaired. On October 9, he sailed again for Liverpool, still making eight inches (0.2m) of water in 24 hours. The remainder of the log of *Hercules* is quite ordinary. Simon Graham "came to anchor with our Small Bower in Liverpool, all well" on Nov. 2, 1836, 70 days after leaving Buctouche.

*Hercules* survived as a merchantman for a number of years despite her inauspicious entry to seafaring. Actually she was typical of her time, a well-built, strong vessel although put to sea without any thought as to whether or not her caulking was as secure as it should have been. As with others of the period, however, *Hercules'* design incorporated a serious deficiency: she was topheavy.

By throwing his deckload overboard Simon Graham used the only means available to him to render *Hercules* more stable. It was a natural action under the circumstances, a recourse almost instinctive and one which must have occurred to any landlubber in the same situation. Simon Graham was making his vessel lighter, which he knew, and making it easier to recover from rolling, which he also understood. He may not have comprehended the mechanics of his action, however.

A vessel has a degree of buoyancy relative to the amount of water it displaces, which it loses, of course, if the hull fills with water. The centre of buoyancy is a point proportionately distant from all parts of the hull under water, the position of which takes into account the configuration of the immersed hull. The centre of buoyancy shifts as the hull of a vessel rolls and changes the shape of its immersed volume. In design and construction the centre of buoyancy should be located as high as possible.

The vessel also has a centre of gross weight or gravity which would be the centre of its mass if it were an homogeneous solid. The centre of gravity should be kept as low as possible. As a vessel rolls its centre of gravity changes relative to the centre of buoyancy.

Gravity tries to pull the vessel downward but buoyancy counteracts by pushing upward. If the centre of gravity is low and the centre of buoyancy is sufficiently higher, a hull cannot be overturned because the directions of the two forces are both working to right the vessel.

If the relative positions of the two centres are reversed they have an opposite action. As the vessel rolls, gravity tries to keep it rolling and buoyancy reinforces the action. Much more is involved — too much for discussion here — but a simple demonstration may be easily envisaged.

Imagine a model of *Hercules* balanced on a taut cable passing lengthways through its normally shallow keel. Since the cable supports the vessel, the centre of buoyancy may be assumed to lie along the keel. The centre of gravity must then be above. So long as the centre of gravity is directly above the centre of buoyancy *Hercules* will remain in balance; but the slightest movement of the centre of gravity will tumble the vessel and she will hang from the cable, bottom-up. The centre of gravity is seen then to have moved through 180º as the vessel rolled.

Imagine the same situation, but this time *Hercules* has a very deep and heavy keel and the cable passes lengthways through the keel where it meets the hull. The centre of buoyancy lies along the support, but this time the centre of gravity is below, toward the bottom of the keel. One may now push *Hercules* over onto her beam ends and each time she will return to an upright, stable position. The centre of gravity changed its position but could not overcome the centre of buoyancy except by becoming precisely balanced directly above.

Such an ideal keel design may be readily achieved with small pleasure craft with sails but it is not feasible for large merchantmen. Indeed, it is not practical for powered pleasure boats, which must plane over the surface; and such craft are, accordingly, less stable than sailboats.

The illustration provided is not realistic but it demonstrates the principle. It was not possible to set the centre of gravity below that of buoyancy in sailing vessels of the 19th century but the distance between the two could be kept short, relative to the shape of the vessel and within a permissible amount of roll. Simon Graham was actually trying to get *Hercules'* centre of gravity down within a safe limit because her centre of buoyancy had been lowered.

Simon Graham's years of intensive seafaring between 1830 and 1855 saw pronounced redesigning of oceangoing vessels. Valuable improvements were made. They are now easily recognized and picked out of the period but the agents of change are not so apparent. Hulls became longer, slimmer and less deep with regard to width or beam. Bows were trimmed of excess timbers and sterns lost their lofty, square, chunky appearance. The topsides of hulls (the freeboard)[6] were brought closer to the waterline, tumble-home practically disappeared and overall lines assumed more graceful proportions. The large angle between bowsprit and hull was greatly decreased.

It might be supposed that all modifications grew out of improved design principles and the development of better construction materials. Some did, of course; but the most important influence was a change of legislation which, in effect, removed the most important reason for launching patently defective hulls. Knowledgeable shipwrights and master mariners had long known precisely where the main weakness of design lay but its inclusion in construction had to be condoned in the interests of profit. Its eradication resulted in a new hull shape which offered improved prospects of safety.

The width of a vessel before about 1854 was always much greater at or close to the waterline than at deck level. This inward lean of the hull, a mark of early design, is called tumble-home. Although other reasons for tumble-home have been suggested, it is clear that this feature in a merchantman was intended in part to offset top-heaviness and to limit the amount of rolling of the hull. As well, the resultant curved shape is stronger against pressure and blows than a straight wall would have been. The heavy ballast of guns and shot permitted even more tumble-home in a warship and this was also a valuable aid against being boarded easily.

Simon Graham was a colonial New Brunswicker, even if only by adoption, and his vessels were nearly all products of his home province. Nevertheless, except for comparatively minor colonial legislation, both mariner and craft were subject to the laws and customs of the United Kingdom. Also, the vessels — their building, loading and sailing — were absolutely controlled by the times. That is, they could not deviate from going practice without great danger of proving uncompetitive. Going practice, for a very long time, was to take advantage of a flaw in legislation to do with determining tonnage of a vessel.

For hundreds of years the laws of Britain had required registration of new British vessels before putting to sea, if they were to enjoy the benefits of restrictive trade legislation. Registration merely established nationality of a vessel and no great cost was entailed. However, for purposes of identification and for determining fees for harbour use and wharfage at home and abroad, the load-carrying capacity had to be determined and recorded on the vessels' registry certificates.

The method of computation was as follows. Length of keel, main beam width[7] and depth were multiplied to obtain a theoretical volume. The result was then divided by a calculated allowance (before 1835) of 94 cubic feet (2.66 cu.m.) per ton. The method yielded a standard for relating the sizes of vessels and cargo capacity.

The flaw in that simple device lay in an arbitrary assumption that the vessel's depth was one half its beam. Unscrupulous shipowners accordingly had their hulls built with depths as much greater than half-beam as the vessels could bear without being unsailably topheavy. Thus their holds carried part of their cargoes free of port fees. More honest merchants had to follow the same procedure if they were to remain competitive. *Rees Cyclopaedia*, 1819, in a major article on shipbuilding expressed the situation in this way: "...for as the depth is out of the question, the contractor finds a saving in less breadth and great depth, which make against stability and...both are exceeding injurious to the construction of vessels."

So little attention was paid to actual depth that, until about 1835, often length and breadth were the only dimensions recorded when a vessel was registered. Thereafter, all dimensions are usually found. In 1855, implementaton of legislation enacted a year earlier in Britain saw the actual depth of a vessel taken into account. Significant changes in the depths of British and British colonial hulls were effected almost immediately. Examination of the dimensions of vessels registered before and after that date reveals a striking decrease in the ratio of depth over beam.

Two vessels, both ships, may be compared, the common criteria being near-similar registered tonnages. *Marco Polo,* Saint John, New Brunswick, 1851, 1625 tons, was 36.3' (11.06m) wide and 29.4' (8.96m) deep, 0.81 being the ratio of interest. *The Forest King*, Hantsport, Nova Scotia, 1877, 1602 tons, was 41' (12.5m) wide and 24.4' (7.44m) deep, 0.595 being the pertinent ratio.

*Marco Polo* was unusually deep at 29.4' Nevertheless, before 1855, the depths of New Brunswick and Nova Scotia hulls were generally above 0.7 and subsequently, about 0.6 of beam width. After 1855 few vessels built in eastern British North America exceeded 24' (7.3m) gross depth. Some of the larger clippers built in Britain and America were deeper but the ratio remained lower. Since *Marco Polo* was an unusually fast sailer a comparison should be sought with another.

*Red Jacket*, Rockland, Massachusetts, 1853, 2006 tons, 44' (13.4m) wide, 26' (7.9m) deep, (ratio = 0.589) crossed the Atlantic from Boston to Liverpool in only 12 days. Until the ratios of depth and beam of the two vessels are compared it is tempting to attribute *Marco Polo*'s speed to her unusual depth. In fact, early American Clippers, of which *Red Jacket* was representative, set the standard of shallower hulls followed later by British

32

and British colonial vessels. Circumstances astonishing to those convinced of the supremacy of early British marine architecture are exposed by the situation.

Simon Graham's vessels were topheavy and prone to dangerous rolling in cross seas. Simon aggravated the tendency, as did all masters of his time, by carrying high deck-cargoes of timber. His craft were often unsafe. They could put to sea only because men who had to jeopardize their lives to earn a living, were prepared to sail them. Simon and his crews knew full well that the risks they took could have been greatly decreased.

To understand and accept the fact of top-heaviness in early vessels it is useful to consider the terminology and peculiarities of nineteenth century measurements. These often mislead researchers, especially those who fail to employ a measure of skepticism. For example, *Running Far In* by John Edward Belliveau reports that "as early as 1811 some 75,000 *shiploads* of timber had left the province (N.B.) in a single season." This is impossible, of course. Surely someone, somewhere, read shiploads for loads. In *New Brunswick, A History: 1784-1867*, W.S. MacNutt defines a load as 50 cubic feet when quoting quantities of loads exported.

A load of timber in those days was 50 cubic feet (1.4 cu.m) if round, 40 cubic feet (1.13 cu.m) if squared. The 40 cubic feet for squared timber (which stows without waste space) is actually the standard American shipping ton, still in use. The British shipping ton is 42 cubic feet (1.19 cu.m) although timber still goes by a variation of load measure. Squared balks run at 40 cubic feet while sawn lumber (requiring spacers) is measured at 50 cubic feet per shipping ton. Lt.-Col. Jos Gubbins observed, in his 1811-13 diary[8] that settlers sold timber at Saint John for 20 shillings ton of 40 "square" feet.

A shipping ton is thus a measure of space occupied. The actual weight of cargo, provided that ores and coal are shipped on the proper vessels, is relatively unimportant. Ton seems to have come to us from tun, a wine measure of 252 (old) gallons (209 Imp. gals or 950 litres). It was a cask equal to two pipes and a volume of 40-50 cu.ft. seems reasonable for the "squared-up" cask.

Use of a standard shipping ton demanded a standardized measuring of vessels which had to take into account that more volume of hull than actual cargo space was necessary. Three official methods were employed at different times for sailing vessels and a fourth may have run informally with the others. They have proved a source of confusion because sometimes the method used was designated along with tonnage and sometimes it was not mentioned.

The three official methods were: Builders' Old Measure (OM or BOM) from 1773 until 1835; New Measure (NM), used subsequently until 1855; Moorsom's, adopted in 1854 in Britain and 1864 in the United States. The informal method, Carpenters' Measure, had no official status in British North American colonies although the term was employed quite often.[9] References to it seem to stem from the United States Act Section 8, December 1792, which required the master carpenter to describe a vessel and measure its tonnage and obtain a certificate before moving the vessel to a port where it might be officially surveyed and registered. The term is not recognized as being meaningful in Great Britain.

Old Measure multiplied length by beam by depth and divided the result by an allowance of 94 cubic feet (2.66 cu.m) per ton. Length applied was that of the keel by measurement less three-fifths of the beam (greatest width) measured at deck level. Depth was assumed to be one half of the beam for the purposes of determining tonnage, depth in that sense meaning that of the hold (inside), not the vessel's draught from loadwaterline to bottom of false keel. New Measure, by enactment in 1835, differed mainly in that the ton allowance was reduced to 92.4 cubic feet (2.62 cu.m). Measurement in the United States was similar except that the ton allowance was 95 cubic feet (2.69 cu.m).

Moorsom's Measure (17 and 18 Vict., cap 104) superseded all others in that the actual volume of a vessel was determined from many internal measurements, with no assumptions, this being divided by an allowance of 100 cubic feet (2.83 cu.m) to obtain tonnage.[10]. The Moorsom method is the basis of modern rules which, for steamers, are complicated somewhat by definitions of what spaces shall be included and how they should be measured.

After 1855, one finds numerous instances of Moorsom's method referred to as New Measurement. The *Oxford Companion to Ships and the Sea*, for example, makes no reference to the 1835 law under "Tonnage" and so implies that Moorsom's is the "new" measurement. De La Quille in *Dictionaire de Marine* fails to notice the 1835 law and actually calls Moorsom's 1854 method "New Measurement." *Chambers Encyclopaedia* of 1877 ignores Moorsom, at the same time setting forth New Measurement of 1835 with a complex system of internal measuring and a factor of 3500 cubic feet, sometimes used after 1835, it seems, although the method was never accepted in law.

Variations of Builders' Old Measurement, mainly to do with measuring length, existed for half a century before the 1835 law. Warships under sail were measured by the same rules as merchantmen until Moorsom's revisions. The method used thereafter computes the volume of water displaced and divides by 35 cubic feet, the approximate volume of a long ton (2240 lbs.) of seawater. Until the introduction of the Plimsoll line in 1876, a fully laden merchantman sank to the level which Simon Graham referred to as the loadwaterline. This line was required to be marked on vessels as early as 1694.

Tonnages of record, that is, those used for registration purposes appear, at this date, to be hopelessly confused. At the very least, the need is indicated for an intensive study to bring order to the situation. For example, to approximate the registered tonnages of vessels registered at Saint John, N.B. between about 1825 and 1865, all the laws and their variations must be employed, to find which yields the tonnage of record, without regard to which law applied officially at the time. The changing shapes of the vessels can readily be educed from the data, nevertheless.

Shipping records of the early 19th century are scant and poorly organized in Canada except at Memorial University in St. John's where much valuable collation is being performed. Data there is being analyzed by computers programmed for answers to questions of long standing. The first of these appears in *Ships and Shipbuilding in the North Atlantic Region, Proceedings of the Conference of the Atlantic Canada Shipping Project, March 31 — April 2, 1977,* published by the duplicating centre of Memorial University.

Some mistakes are bound to be made, of course, and one is to be found in the *Proceedings.* It is a faulty conclusion that has to be noticed because it is part of a scholarly work and because it contradicts views expressed here.

In a paper "Measuring British Dominance of Shipbuilding in the 'Maritimes', 1787-1890," included with the *Proceedings*, Richard Rice finds no validity to arguments which, as he put it, "roundly damned (tonnage rules before 1855) for nefarious effects on naval architecture."

Rice's arguments are so extensive that more space would be required to examine them than can be allowed here. Accordingly, the postulation of a few pertinent points able of ready proof must serve instead.

1) The accuracy of tonnage rules set forth in connection with *Hercules'* topheaviness may be ascertained through reference to texts noted in this book and, of course, the pertinent laws.
2) Examination of Rice's contentions, i.e., the basis of his work as well as conclusions, suggests that Rice may not have realized the extent of the confusion that exists with regard to tonnage laws and registry.
3) Examples given in this book show clearly that British vessels were often deeper than half the beam width and that an offsetting change

occurred immediately after 1854. The more precise view,[11] to which there may be some exceptions, of course, is obtained by comparing the beams and depths noted on registry certificates granted between 1835 and 1854 and later.

The results of Rice's computer analyses must, unfortunately, be suspect. It is not possible at arm's length to know the cause but it may concern dates and application of the tonnage laws. Thus, if registry data after 1855 are used, the actual depth of a vessel having been taken into the computation of tonnage, and this compared with Moorsom's rule, differences are found to be negligible. If registered tonnages for the preceding half century were used along with either Builders' Old Measure or New Measure, differences remain small and related to the variance of 1.6% plus or minus between ton allowances (92.4 c.f. and 94 c.f.). On the other hand, if registered tonnages between 1835 and 1854 are compared with the rule of 1835 *but substituting the actual depth for the arbitrary half-beam*, substantial disagreements appear.

In passing, the ratios that apply to the Biblical vessel (Noah's Ark may be of interest. The ratio of beam to length was 1:6) and that of depth over beam, 0.6; both ratios being in accord with those developed after about 1855.

## CHAPTER 4

# *Devonport* — *She Missed Stays!*

*Hercules* must have been a sound vessel because she sold after docking at Liverpool. Simon, too, was in fine fettle for, soon after Christmas, he put to sea once more. In an unusually bold hand he headed up a new page: "Abstract of a Jurnal from Liverpool to Philidelpha In the Barque Devonport, S. Graham, Master." *Devonport*[1] did not complete the voyage, so it may be ironical that this was one of the few occasions when Simon Graham used the positive preposition "to." Usually he was wary enough to say "towards."

Simon cleared port on December 28, 1836, dropped the pilot at the Light Ship, passed "hollowhead" (Holyhead) and Tusker on the 29th, the Old Head of Kinsail and Cape Clear (both on the south coast of Ireland) on December 31. Cape Clear was his last landfall and on Sunday (S) January 1, 1837, Simon began to enter the Day's Work.

*Devonport* was plagued with troubles to do with her rigging. On the second day out: "Sprung our main topmast head, Sent down top gallant yards and mast."

On January 5: "Sent down fore topgallant mast and yards, unbent chains.[2]" The next day was so calm that "all Sails Lowered down to Save Chafe." At the same time Simon ruefully noted a difference of 30 minutes between longitude by account and by chronometer.

By Monday, January 16, the difference had increased to 56 minutes. It is not possible to know now if longitude computed from dead reckoning was inaccurate, if the chronometer was defective or if both were faulty; but it is certain that Simon's failure to know his position played a part in *Devonport*'s misfortune later.

On the same day Simon recorded strong gales S.W. and, "At 4.30 Seaman Wm. Smith fell from the rigging and was cilled." On the seventeenth: "At 10.20 Burried him in the Sea." That was probably the only obituary written for William Smith and one may wonder when and how his family learned of his death.

On Thursday, January 19: "At 5.30 Carried away our main yard in a Squal and Split the fore Sail top mast." On the twentieth strong gales from the South and West split the fore topsail and forced *Devonport* to "ly to" for two days. Then, "the Close reef eyelot holes of the main topsail

Burst out. Brock the main Spencer Gaff and Started of the Starboard[3] Bumkin and Split the Covering Board. Split the Close Reeft main topsail, unbent it and Bent[4] another." On the 24th, Simon replaced spars and yards and bent new sails.

On Wednesday, January 25, longitude disagreement amounted to $3°10'$, a substantial difference. On that day: "Got our fore topsail Bent and the Larboard Main and Fore rigging Set up."

The crew worked at setting up the rigging on the starboard side of the vessel on January 27. The following day, "the ruder Brock Lose from the Stock. Bent our fore yard again but not Brock." The rudder must have been replaced easily since it was not mentioned again. On February 12, *Devonport* lost her "traymast."[5] The weather then improved and on the 15th, "the people" were painting the cabin, "putting on top Bulworks" and setting up rigging. The weather stayed generally fair and presumably Simon kept his crew hard at work so as to have *Devonport* in as presentable condition as possible when he made harbour.

The reassuring picture painted by all this good housekeeping is deceiving. Simon Graham did not know precisely where he was and he was more than a little worried. His Remarks Column shows him plotting course and distance for Cape May, New Jersey, $38°55'$ N. Lat. $74°55'$ W. Long. approximately. By February 26, Simon had begun to realize that he was much too far south although in the vicinity of Cape May's longitude. He changed course and began to tack north, alternating $15°$ East and West, seeking the Delaware River.

On February 28, Simon decided, after consulting his chronometer, that he was not as far West as indicated by Dead Reckoning. He cut a full degree and thirty minutes from his longitude and rationalized it in this manner: "By Chr. My D Reck Being Out." That is, he considered that longitude deduced by plotting course and distance placed him farther west than he actually was and that his chronometer was right. It was a grave error of judgment. Nevertheless, he thought *Devonport* to be perilously close to the shore for he "Bent Cabel" — attached a stout rope to his anchor — to be ready to club-haul[6] in an emergency.

Friday, March 3, blew "Strong Gales and now very thick." Simon made his position $38°\ 59'$ N. Lat. $74°33'$ W. Long. — a little North and East of Cape May. He had to rely on his chronometer now until he made a landfall he could recognize. This is his last entry in his log: "Sat. 4 at 4.30 made the Land about 15 miles South of Cape Henlope(n). Tryed to Stay the Ship but She Missed Stays and struck the Ground and Drove in on the Beatch. All hands got on shoar Safe." Cape Henlopen is well South and

West of Cape May, being approximately 38°40' N. Latitude and 75°10' W. Longitude. Simon must have driven *Devonport* hard and unwisely through the night and parallel to the shore without knowing how close he was. When dawn broke he found himself with land ahead and on his larboard beam and was unable to tack his vessel.

Under a steady blow from the stern or quarters, a square-rigged vessel achieves more efficiency than one rigged fore and aft. Both can adjust their sails to accommodate the direction of wind but the square-rigger can trap a lot more pressure in its high, wide spread of canvas.

A ship's performance, in contrast to a schooner's, drops off under a wind shifting quickly and often, because its numerous sails require appreciably more time to trim. More men are required for the task also but that is a matter of economy. A schooner can slam its spanker booms from side to side very quickly without real loss of speed.

No vessel can sail directly into even the lightest breeze, but it is possible to make good headway fairly close to the wind, as the mariners' expression goes. The angle of approach depends largely upon the rig and skill in managing the sails. The closest that brigs and ships can come is about 5½ points or 62 degrees. (32 points separated by 11¼ degrees make up the compass card of 360 degrees.) A schooner can reach about four points. Barques can do little better than ships but barquentines and brigantines can come a full point closer. Ability to sail close to the wind was a valuable property in a sailing vessel.

A vessel standing close to the wind can never make a position on its windward side (the side the wind strikes) if it stays on one course. Indeed, it is driven farther and farther away at a steadily widening angle. To reach a point due north against a north wind, that is, in the eye of the wind, a ship must sail in zigzag fashion, first about 62° east (or west) of north (and the wind) and, when that course becomes unprofitable, it must swing through 124 degrees and sail 62 degrees west (or east) of north. Such alternating courses must be held if the ship is to maintain its general direction of voyage. That method of travel is known as tacking. A ship is on the port tack when the wind strikes its port (left) side. When swung through 124 degrees to the left, the wind will strike on the starboard (right) side and the vessel is on a starboard tack. When sailing as close to the wind as possible the vessel is said to be close hauled. A vessel drives under a stern wind, reaches under a wind on its beam and beats against a headwind.

Tacking can be accomplished by either of two methods, both of which have variations. They are always difficult, even potentially dangerous in high seas, and under any circumstances tacking calls for the highest order of seamanship. Both actions are easier and more quickly completed by schooner-rigged vessels. Accordingly they are safer for such craft unless size in rough water becomes a factor.

A vessel can tack by swinging its bow to port or starboard directly through the eye of the wind. A schooner must traverse about 90 degrees in so doing but a ship must continue until it has swept through another 35 degrees. The manoeuver is so comparatively simple for schooners that it goes under no other name than tacking. The far more complicated and time-consuming sequence of actions for a ship is known as *coming* or *going about*, sometimes as *staying the ship.*

A schooner tacks on one sharp command by the skipper who has been watching for the right combination of wind, sea and sail conditions. The helm and spankers are then thrown over together, the vessel shivers and shakes as she comes through the direct force of the wind but, when tacked with sufficient headway, the schooner is almost immediately on her new course.

Sailing vessels tack also when running before a stern wind. The expression is, more properly, tacking to leeward. The vessel travels with the wind first on one quarter and then on the other, the purpose being to keep all sails drawing better than they would if directly before the wind. As the vessel changes direction its stern rather than its bow swings through the eye of the wind. The procedure is also called gybing or jibing.

A ship must prepare to stay — Simon Graham's term — or go about. The deck watch must be augmented, certain braces and halyards manned, the best seamen stationed at critical belaying points, the master and mate properly positioned. The sails must be well trimmed and the vessel held not too far off its wind and not too close. All that done the mate sings out, "All ready to go about, Sir!"

The master's usual reply to any such advice was a terse "Very good," followed by an order; but, when staying ship, the first order might well be delayed. Let us take the sequence from *The Practical Navigator* (Bowditch), 1851: "To tack in a dangerous rough sea when her staying is doubtful."

> ...Take advantage of the smoothest time when the ship has the most headway...to haul down the jib if set and not to put the helm a-lee all at once but to luff the ship up by degrees, to shake her sails.
>
> When they shake give these orders: *The helm hard a-lee! Let go the lee sheets forward!* but not the lee braces and foretop bowline as that practice backs the headsails too soon and stops the ship's headway which ought to give power to the helm, till the wind is brought ahead, or the ship will not stay.

*Raise tacks and sheets; and mainsail haul!* when the wind is a point on the weather bow; this swings the yards round sharp that the main tack may be got close down, whilst the headsails becalm the fore-leech of the main and main topsails; while the wind blowing aslant on the after-leech of these sails acts jointly with the rudder to turn the ship's stern, so as to bring her about the right way. When she has fallen off five or six points, *Let go and haul!*

*The Practical Navigator* goes on at some length to deal with hazards attending those actions but its dry account does not convey any of the tenseness and excitement of this ordinary and oft-repeated manoeuver.

Would she fly up to the eye of the wind? If she didn't, she *missed stays* and remained on her old course. That's what happened when Simon Graham drove *Devonport* ashore! He could not tack and get his vessel away from danger.

At the moment — a long moment indeed — when the ship was seized by the direct force of the wind, her sails were taken aback. They had been shivering and uncertain of action but now they were shaken violently and the hull shuddered in sympathy. The ship lost headway. Now! If she took sternway she might never go about the remaining six points of her tack. Nor would she fall back on her old course. She was *in irons*, no longer under control and in a most dangerous situation until her head fell off one way or another. Even then she was in great difficulties: she lay broadside to heavy seas and in jeopardy of capsizing.

The other method of tacking, far more common to large ships than to schooners, was *to wear* or *wear ship*. In this manoeuver a ship turned her bow from the wind and described an incomplete figure-eight. Thus, on a port tack, to make a starboard tack, the vessel turned to starboard until she had her stern to the wind. A few tense minutes followed as the ship gained headway: she had to cross the wave troughs and chance being pooped by a following sea. A mariner would far rather take heavy water over the bow of his vessel than over its stern. The danger was less.

Then, with enough headway to complete her manoeuver, the ship ran as briefly as possible broadside to the wind (and seas) and then came to starboard again on her new course. At the moment of least headway, before the new set of sails were in order, the ship was once more crossing the troughs but this time bow-on to the seas.

Wearing ship required at least as much work at the sails as going about and much more time was consumed. Certain advantages offset the time and work, however. Less hurry was entailed and so, fewer chances of mistakes arose at critical moments. More important, the ship gathered headway, sufficient almost to ensure that she would not miss stays or end in irons.

Merchant mariners envied warships their large crews when wearing or going about, because merchantmen were almost always short-handed.

A glimpse of what was entailed in the master's operation of a ship may be taken from the chapter "Evolutions at Sea," in the *The Practical Navigator*. Its date, 1851, clearly accords with Simon Graham's career and it is interesting to consider that within a decade, advice to mariners under sail was removed from the Bowditch publications. Procedures for the following requirements were outlined, amongst many others, in the 1851 edition.

"To anchor with a spring, in order to present the vessel's side to a place or ship you wish to cannonade" (One of 24 notes to do with anchors).

"To tack a ship in getting to windward as much as possible" (A variation of staying).

"To tack a ship without endeavouring to get to windward" (i.e. in an emergency).

"To veer a ship without losing the wind out of her sails."

"To veer a ship that has lost her foremast."

"To veer under bare poles." (This advised that a number of seamen sent aloft into the weather shrouds, those on the weather side, will help by catching some wind.)

"To box-haul a ship; or the second method of veering." (This was done when great swells prevented tacking or when a ship missed stays. It was a procedure of handling sails and rudder akin to that of wearing ship within a smaller area.)

"To club-haul a ship." (Another method, entailing use of the anchor, when the ship is expected to miss stays.)

"To bend a course in fair weather."

"To bend a topsail in fair weather."

"To set a mainsail...foresail...topsail."

"To take in a course...a topsail."

"To take in the foresail in the time of veering."

"To haul in a lower studdingsail."

"To haul down a topmast-studdingsail."

"To brail up a mizzen."

"To take in a topgallant sail."

"To unbend a course...a topsail."

"Of a ship overset on her side." (Cut away her masts!)

"To steer a ship when her rudder is lost." (This suggested making a rudder attached to a spar lashed into position, the latter serving in lieu of the sternpost, the rudder being served by tackles.)

The mark of a sound master mariner was not his ability to command in fair weather but his judgment in times of emergency. Mature judgment is gained only from years of experience which suggests that writers who have extolled the skills of youthful masters may have been mistaken. The astounding numbers of sailing vessels lost at sea,[7] year in and year out, speak clearly of demands for seamanship not fully met.

## CHAPTER 5

# Caledonia, The Poets' Barque

Simon Graham's reputation as a trustworthy mariner does not seem to have been tarnished by *Devonport*'s undignified arrival in America. Within five months he commanded a spanking new vessel and was again daring the North Atlantic Ocean.

In the meantime he must have visited his family in Richibucto[1] while awaiting orders from his owners .He does not tell us where or how he spent the spring and early summer months but his log-book provides two tantalizing hints.

The master mariner may have been in the company of a master shipbuilder for, after the log of *Devonport*, he devoted a page and one-third to writing up the rules for masting vessels. Two-thirds of the second page were then given over to a tedious computation in chains and links entitled "Misurement of a Peice of Land" which is indisputably his Richibucto lot.

*Caledonia*'s log begins with these words: "Abstrack of a Jurnal from St. John N.B. towards Hull in England in the Barque Caledonia of St. John Built and Lanched at Black River in New Brunswick July 8th, 1837."

Captain Graham sailed from Saint John on Friday, August 11, dropped his pilot on "Satterday" and arrived in Hull safely on Friday, September 15, after a passage of 36 days. *Caledonia*[2] overtook another vessel from the Bay of Fundy that must have encountered rough weather. Her master recorded: "Tuesday September 12...at 8 P.M. backed our main yards and was Boarded By the Rolla or Arora of Hull and Suplyed them a Barrel of Beef Being entirely out 45 days from St. Andrews N.B."

Simon Graham left Hull on October 13, and made Saint John again on November 28, 1837. It is possible that he spent Christmas in Richibucto but, if he did, he made a hard and fast ride back to Saint John, for he left port, bound for Liverpool, England, on December 27. The new log shows that *Caledonia* ran through heavy weather much of her voyage. It does not recount any problems but they appear to have been substantial, as this comment shows: "Monday February 5....Came in at passage Waterford very Leaky and our pump Lether all don."

*Caledonia* stopped at Belfast from February 17, to March 7, and then made Liverpool in one day. The time spent in Belfast may have been enforced, because Simon Graham closed his log with the words: "Thursday March 8th Got into Liverpool All Well after the Longest passage Ever I had." It was of 71 days' duration.

*Caledonia* left Liverpool on "Aprile 1st" and after an ordinary sort of crossing came to anchor "of partrage Island" (Partridge Is., Saint John, N.B.) on the 7th of May, 1838. On this voyage Simon Graham marked Sunday with "G"; in the previous log he used "A".

*Caledonia* left then for London, sailing from Saint John on June 9, 1838. On Saturday, June 16, her master "Spock the Comat of St. John from London."

On June 25, at noon, longitude problems arose again. A week earlier Graham had taken a lunar observation which indicated "1$^0$ 10' West of Dead Reckoning." Now he had a number of longitude positions from which to choose. The column in his log for June 25, shows 40$^0$28' but, above it and agreeing with an earlier calculation, 45$^0$16'. He had taken a sun shot at noon and noted "41.38 time per watch 43.08." Early that evening, "I had a Set of Lunars Betwixt the 0 & )$^3$ whitch Gave us in 42.39W from whitch I take a fresh Departure." Can it be only a coincidence that the mean of the four dubious figures is almost exactly 42$^0$39'?

Notwithstanding, Simon Graham made London soon after July 9, when he took on a Thames pilot off Ramsgate Light. *Caledonia* departed London for Saint John on August 9, and on Wednesday, September 19, "Came to of Partrage Island all well after a passadge of 42 Days from the Douns. Thursday got along Side of the Ballast Wharf." *Caledonia* had returned to Saint John lightly loaded and heavy with ballast.

The barque sailed from Saint John on Sunday, October 7, 1838, bound for Newry, Ireland, where she "came to with the Best Bower" after 27 days. That was a fast crossing and it is amusing that, midway through the voyage, her master recorded that he had been in very bad health for a week and unable to "keep the Ship's way."

*Caledonia* was sold in Liverpool on January 3, 1839. Her master took passage to Cork, Ireland, by "Steem Boat" and to Saint John on the Barque *Brothers*.[4] He arrived in Saint John on March 14, and "went home to Richibucto...arrived on the 16th through Deep Snows and Cold Weather."

The seadog fancied himself a rhymster. His logs are full of poems which are revealing and significant with regard to his life and the period in which he sailed. On the barque *Caledonia*, he found a companion poet in his first mate who wrote the following, handsomely recorded by his superior officer.

## On Leaving St. John Oct 1838

The winter winds are Keen and Cold
and Brooks are all frose o'er
the fields are clad in raments white
all dazling with hore

the very people in the Street
all Seem as Struck with woo
I wish Our Ship was Load Complete
its time for us to gow.

And if you take a Looke above
to vew the Shades of Night
the aurora borealis race, Bewilder quite your Sight
a traditional omen of strong winds
So prevalant we Know
We will begin for to unmore
its Time for us to gow.

To all the friends we Love So well
We now must bid adew
a Sigh in all we Can Bestow
to those we Love so trew
Bound to Britanias peacefull Isle
the Seamen cry aho
then run the anchor to the Bow
its time for us to Gow.

When sailing out we Cast a wish
to those we Leave Behind
Some thinking on his wife and Child
And others on ther friend
But One and all must trust to him
Who Makes the Winds to Blow
then spread the canvas to the gale
Its time for us to gow.

E. Halladay
Barque CALEDONIA

Simon Graham and his mate shared a dashing style, one that paid only token service to such attributes as spelling, punctuation, and metre. None of the verses has the polish that could quite easily have been applied regardless of the fact that all were read over and over again. Sometimes a line was changed to bring out a different thought, occasionally alternate endings were supplied and quite often a stanza that met with special approbation was incorporated into other poems. It does not seem to have mattered much if themes proved incongruous so long as the whole limped along in brave style. Concept, not finesse, counted with these poets.

Generally, Simon Graham's poems are poorly structured single-rhyme couplets but now and then one sees in them inspiration of a kind that touches a chord. Consider this example in which spelling has been improved.:

> Call us not weeds, we are flowers of the Sea,
> For Lovely and Bright and gay-tinged are we
> And quite independent of Sunshine or Showers,
> Then call us not weeds: we are Ocean's gay Flowers.
>
> Not nursed like the plants of a summer pasture
> Where gales are but sighs of an Evening air
> Our exquisite, fragile and delicate forms
> Are nursed by the Ocean and rocked by the Storms.

J. Banes, evidently the cook on one of Simon Graham's vessels, had his name written into posterity when he applied for a letter of reference. We don't know the tenor of the evaluation Simon set down for others but we have his private assessment of the unfortunate man:

### J. Banes Carracture

> A Caricture our Cook dos want
> and I dare not dispute it,
> But if its to obtain a Birth
> He'd do as well without it.
>
> To Long a Cobler he has Been
> Ever to gow to Sea
> For Telling Leys he'll wear a Crown
> I am shoar of Kingdoms three
>
> He drinks he's Idol and profain
> unto a grait degree
> and happy happy Shall I Be
> the day that we are free.

Simon Graham was a fatalist, as men who constantly face danger often are; and he didn't ask for much out of life. Give him wind to fill his sails and he'd do the rest!

### To January the 1st 1843 at Sea

> Thanks to the all imperieal power
> for all his goodness past
> I hope this year will prove to me
> More prosperous than the Last

And though I take the Liberty
the infant yiar to haill
I hope that it will favour me
with many a prosperous gaill

Untill that fate has me asigned
unto Sum happier Shoar
where Stormy winds and Swelling Seas
Shall trubal me no moar.

There in Sum Sollatery Calm retreat
I fain would Setteled Bee
then I with Joy would ever mind
that happy forty-three

Simon Graham

Graham had a son, James, who died at sea aged 2 years 7 months, about 1827. The father never forgot the child and one suspects that, before he died 51 years later, Simon Graham arranged for his tombstone to record James' death also. Only to the father could such an act have been important. One sees a hint of it in these agonized lines written about 1850:

Deep in the wild Abyss he lies,
Far from the cherished Scene of home
Far, Far from hir whose faithful sight
A husbands trackless course persued.
Whose tender fancy loves to roam,
With him o'er Lands and Oceans new
And gild with hopes deluding foam
The gloomy pathway of the Storm.

Several verses exhibit a great love for children. That which follows, a little better organized than most and, therefore, possibly not his own composition, reveals a belief in kindly discipline.

### The Laird O'Cockpen

If ye'll no tak your Brekfast just let it alone
The porridge can wait till ye're hungry again.
Though Saucy e'en now ye'll be glad of them soon
Sae tak ye the pit now an lay down the Spoon.

Ye'll weary for them ere thy weary for you
And when thy grow cule thy'll no blister your mou'
A two, three hours fast might be guid for ye
An help ye to drive the ill humours awa.

48

Now fat littel doggie that toddles alang
Sae pampered an picken he Scarcely Can gang
At daintiest dishes he turns up his nose
But scrimp him a wee he'll by blythe at his Brose.

There's none Kens the guid o' a thing till its gone
Yon barefooted laddie ye met wi'yest un
Had he such a Coggie head no let it cule-
No Just let them Stan till ye come home frae the Schule.

The Best Cure for Bairnies when nice wi' ther meat
Is the frish air a morning wi' nothing to Eat
Sae tak your ain time like the Cattle out Bye
Just eat when your hungry and drink when your dry.

A strong distaste for landlubbers is apparent in this rueful advice, composed 21 April 1850:

Shoals of Land Sharks Standing ridy,
Eatch poor Sailor to Devour.
Within ther grasp thy'll try to have you
Ere that you Can reatch the Shoar.

But ther Caress I pray you mind not,
Your Gold is the God that they adores.
Gold. But once Safe in ther pocket
Soon thy'll turn you out of doors.

All your tears, all your intreaties,
Friendless Stranger though you Bee,
Unless some Money's in your pocket
Ther house no more your home can Bee.

Occasionally, far less often than one might expect, notwithstanding many references to the Almighty, Simon Graham implored aid from a Supreme Power. Two stanzas from four written at sea 3 December 1849 are typical:

God be our pilot and our guide
While steering o'er Life's dangerous Side.
From rocks and Sands pray Keep us free
So thickly set in Life's dark sea.

....

....

Therefore keep Caution on your Side
And Pray to God to be your Guide,
To Stear you Safe that Heavenly way
To realms of Everlasting Day.

A shrewd insight into human nature came with seafaring, as evidenced in this chauvanistic musing on the frailties of womanhood.

> But wives Like dogs thy may forget
> And only bark when at the gait
> But when you Cum more near
> May Cindly clasp you in ther arms, and Shade a Joyfull tear.
> And if a while with them you Stay,
> Might former Joys renew
> And youthful pleasures fill Hir mind
> And Still to other may prove Cind
> And Loving feelings too.

The dour old mariner could laugh at his own plight, too. In 1843, when he was 47 and doubtless well aware of the fact, Susan and Mary Patterson sang him a song which he found amusing. Simon recorded it with his logs but, before applauding his honesty, it is necessary to be assured that he did not find it flattering.

> So See, So See how well he wears
> his age Since Last we met him
> I think dull time with all his Care
> has managed to forget him.
>
> His age But no, we that forget
> for dates we do not hunger
> He mearly is and who is not
> the man who has Ben younger.
>
> The man, the man, the man, the man,
> the man that has Ben younger
> He mearly is and who is not
> the man that has Ben younger.
>
> His hair has never betrayed a fall
> it still is dark and Curly
> be sure if you wear wigs at all
> Like him adopt one airly.
>
> He still retains his taunting air
> his limbs is Ever stronger
> and yet he is, do what you will
> the man that has Ben younger.
>
> When furst I met him in the park
> with Joy unfeigned and real
> I paused five minutes to remark
> the highest beau ideal.
>
> Thats five and forty years agow
> indead it might be longer

and yet he is, do what We will
The man that has Ben younger.

And Still his glass is raised to Scan
the fairest nymph that passes
and Still the figure of the man
attracks all other glasses.

For femal adoration Still
his Spirit seems to wander
and yet he is, we all know well
the man that has been younger.

The man, the man, etc.

Sung by Susan and Mary Patterson,<br>1843.

The master mariner liked a thoughtful poem and it did not have to be one of his own. E. Halladay, mate of the barque *Caledonia* left this somber reflection which his captain thought worthy of safeguarding.

### Jany 27th 1839

A Severe Gale in Whitch a grait Many
Lives and Ships Were Lost.

A Gloomy Morning how awful the Storm
What Dreadful account will we hear
of Sum ill fated Ships By this Hurricane borne
Where no hand of releif can Come near
Me thinks that I now hear the Crys of distress
As Lonely I walk on the Shore
of Some that perhaps in a minute or less
will Ne'er in this worald Cry More
Oh what dreadfull news is this that I hear
of Some Stately Ships that I've Seen
Whitch had only Left port about 12 hours before
with numbers of Emigrants in,
Beside all ther Crews whether British or Not
Humanity kindels a flame
in Each feeling Breast when we think of ther fate
half frozen then Dashd in the Main
But its not only those on the Sea that hase Suffered
from this Storm nere equald Before
But Numbers that went to ther Beds in good health
But Ne'ere in this Worald wake more
for where in ther Dwellings and Citys Secure
by the force of this terrable Storm
ther houses unroofd and ther Mordred before
Ever daylight had gilded the Morne

So then let you not think your lives quit Secure
Althou that you live on the Shore
As we Every day See that we can't tell the hour
that in this worald we must be no more

E. Halladay

Simon Graham summed up his philosophy very tidily in one brief verse with the words:

And if at a party I Should Bee
With Ladys of a High Degree
My Self to Custom would Conform
And Stay at Night till three nixt Morn.

The old seadog worked hard and played hard!

## CHAPTER 6

# Amy and the Day's Work

On May 3, 1839, Simon Graham left Saint John, N.B., in command of the Barque *Amy*,[1] not a new vessel by any means, but a perfect lady at sea. He made the port of Hull in Yorkshire, England, on "Tuseday July 8" without difficulty.

This must have been Captain Graham's first voyage around the north of Scotland because he carefully described his landfalls as he did on his first passage of Cape Horn. He appears to have been intrigued with this view of his native land, for it is clear in his log that he tacked close to the shore just to observe the landscape.

On this voyage, as on the last two on *Caledonia*, he carried a column in his log for Longitude by Chronometer. Its records are seldom in agreement with Longitude by Account and it is strange that, although faithful in observing for latitude each noon, the start of the sailor's day, the Captain did not always record Longitude by Chronometer.

*Amy* got "underweigh"[2] from Hull on the 28th of July, and came to with the small bower in Saint John on the 10th of September.

On October 5, Captain Graham left Saint John and, after spending a day in Belfast, made fast at the dock in Dublin on November 20th, 1839. He took *Amy* back to Saint John, sailing from Dublin on December 9. The voyage was slow in the teeth of westerly winds but uneventful. Simon marked Christmas Day with only the note, "Strong Gails[3] W.S.W., Dubel reefd Top Sails." He came to "of partarug Island — Snowing very thick — after a passage of 58 days," on February 5, 1840.

Simon Graham had time for a quick visit to Richibucto but he made no mention of where he spent a full month before sailing again for Hull on March 15, 1840. He came into the dock at Hull on May 27, and "discharged 2 Lighters."[4]

*Amy* was sold to a London firm and "I took passage with Capt. Hinnell of the Ship Calcutta[5] of and for St. John N.B. and Sailed Satterday May 23...and Arived in St. John Tuesday July 7th....And Left for Londonderry Satterday 11th July and arrived Monday 13th and Joined the Barque Cambridge[6] on the Stocks – Lanched Aug 27 – 1840, Loaded and Sailed Satterday 17th, 1840."

Simon Graham's logs, kept with meticulous and unvarying care for more than 30 years, clearly show the devoted attention that had to be paid to the demands of navigation. Day by day, year in and out, Graham and ten thousand master mariners of his ilk scrupulously noted every significant detail of their journeyings. This assumed two forms on the same page of Simon Graham's log-book, both important but entirely different in nature. One reveals a simple and easy chore: the maintaining of a succinct diary of weather conditions and important happenings. The other presents the nagging, never-ending task of recording position at sea along with progress towards destination.

Before starting upon his daily entries Simon Graham always set forth the circumstances of leaving port, as shown in the example which follows: "Abstract of a Jurnal from St. John N.B. towards Lpool In the Ship Swan, S. Graham Master. Sailed 17th Sept. 1844, 18th at 8 a.m., Bryre Island[7] N. Ely. E. Dis. 6 miles from whitch I take my departure."

The style of this introduction, for that is what it was, varied with Graham's whims. Sometimes it was an "Abstract of a Voyage from Liverpool to New Orleans" and, when merely indicating a continuation of a voyage, it became simply, "From New Orleans to London." In the latter case, having previously set down the circumstances of starting his voyage, Graham sometimes gave scant attention to observing those to do with his return or continuation toward another port. The length of his first formal entry, always in larger and more elaborate script, varied with the complexities of leaving harbour. More was entailed in departing London, a busy inland port, than sailing from Saint John, and this required the recording of pilot, towing and other steps in getting under way.

This necessity fulfilled, Simon Graham always drew a double line under the paragraph and across the page. Then he ruled vertical columns under twelve headings. Always abbreviated, they read from left to right:

> Day of the Week
> Day of the Month
> Course
> Distance
> Difference of Latitude
> Departure
> Latitude by Account
> Latitude by Observation
> Difference of Longitude
> Longitude In....(i.e. by account)
> Longitude by Chronometer
> Remarks on Board

The widest column accommodated his Remarks on Board which were, in fact, his diary. On uneventful days the space proved sufficient for terse notations regarding wind and weather. When anything else of significance had to be recorded Graham began in the Remarks column and then went to the left of the page and, filling in only the two date columns, he continued his notes across the page in as many lines as necessary.

Each column received a daily entry without fail with but one recurring exception. Longitude by Chronometer was often not recorded. This should have been the most simple of all the data ascertained and so the omissions, perhaps one a week on average, assume some significance. That aspect will be explored in due course.

The determination of position and progress each day made up what was known as *The Day's Work*. The term implies that the procedure involved in obtaining data constituted the master's foremost responsibility. Before examining what was entailed it is necessary to establish one principle. Ordinary pictorial maps do not permit the selection of a bearing from one point to another by means of a protractor unless, perhaps, the points are quite close to one another and are also near the earth's equator.

The reason behind that inadequacy lies with the fact that it is impossible to render the surface of a sphere upon flat paper, filling it fully and doing so with accuracy. A precise representation of the earth's surface on flat paper can only take one of the forms of the detached peel of an orange. Any other cartography must distort areas proportionately to distance from the equator. Several mapmaking methods are employed to minimize distortion but none overcomes it completely.

Nevertheless, a map may be prepared so that all points on it relate to a grid of North-South and East-West lines, in effect, establishing a system from which co-ordinates may be scaled. Then, employing trigonometry, the navigator may compute accurate bearings and distances between points. Simon Graham had no trigonometry, it appears. At least, all his computations were by simple arithmetic, and this greatly limited the means of navigation open to him.

The North-South lines are called Meridians of Longitude. Since the earth rotates in (nearly) twenty-four hours it is convenient to relate longitude to the earth's circumference. Thus, the earth rotates through $15^0$ every hour, completing the turn through $360^0$ in a day. This day, actually the Sidereal Day, is approximately four minutes short of our twenty-four hour day. In ordinary life the discrepancy is adjusted every fourth or Leap Year. When computing time from longitude which, it is obvious, is quite simple, the discrepancy must be taken into account immediately.

For purposes of practical use, one Meridian of Longitude must be designated the zero or start line. That which passes through Greenwich, England, is most commonly accepted as *the* Meridian and from it may be measured degrees (up to 180°), minutes (60 to a degree) and even seconds (60 to a minute) if great precision is required, East or West of the Greenwich or zero Meridian. Thus one of the two necessary co-ordinates may be established.

The intersecting lines that, with longitude, yield co-ordinates are called Parallels of Latitude. They are the angles that may be theoretically measured from the centre of the earth, using the Equator as the zero or start line, North or South to any point on any Meridian of Longitude.

From charts marked with meridians of longitude and parallels of latitude, a navigator may determine latitude and longitude for recognizable points quite readily, or he may plot his position as the intersection of longitude by chronometer and latitude by observation of a star. By subtraction (or addition) of one longitude from the other, the base of a right-angled triangle is determined. The base lies along a parallel of latitude and its length is expressed in degrees and minutes of longitude. It lies always on an East-West line. The lengths of minutes of longitude along parallels of latitude vary because the meridians of longitude converge. A navigation triangle must be computed for each change of course and daily for a continuing course. The base, expressed in nautical miles, is termed the Departure of the course. Simon Graham entered it daily in his sixth column.

Subtraction or addition of latitudes yields another side of the triangle referred to earlier. It is also an angular distance but this time it lies along a meridian of longitude although it is, in fact, difference of latitude. Graham entered Difference of Latitude in his fifth column.

Minutes of latitude vary in length because the earth is not truly spherical. They measure approximately 1.145 miles (1842.7 m) at the Equator and increase to about 1.157 miles (1862m) at the Poles. At a latitude of 40° North or South of the Equator a minute measures 1.150 miles or 6072 feet (1850.75 m). From such an averaging, the British Nautical or Admiralty Mile of 6080 feet (1853.18 m) was determined. It was Simon Graham's unit of measurement. By solving the spherical triangle just described, a mariner could assign both a direction, by true bearing from North, and a distance in nautical miles. The true bearing had to be converted to a compass bearing for practical purposes. The mariner could also scale — measure directly — his course and distance from a map properly prepared with a grid, and that is what Simon Graham did very often.

The course taken from a chart or computed from co-ordinates of latitude and longitude is an angle turned clockwise from the meridian. It is called an azimuth and is usually confined, for convenience, to $180^0$ or less. Thus, to $180^0$ it is a North Azimuth and between $180^0$ and $360^0$ it is a South Azimuth. Mariners, however, broke the azimuth into quadrants, referring courses to the points of the compass. Midway between North and East is a direction Northeast; on either side lie directions such as North-Northeast and East Northeast and so on. Continuing behind the observer, a Northeast bearing becomes Southwest.

True north is a projection into the heavens of the axis about which the earth spins once a day. The earth rotates from West to East and so the heavenly bodies appear to revolve around either the North or South Pole projections. The position of stars relative to one another are apparently fixed, being so far distant from Earth, and that fact makes possible their use to determine latitude, longitude and time of day. In Simon Graham's day and, in fact, for many years before, the British Admiralty published tables of positions of stars at various times. From such data mariners could calculate their positions as will be seen later.

Valuable as the stars are, indeed, absolutely necessary for precise navigation, they do not offer a practicable, simple manner of use. Excepting the Sun, they cannot easily be seen through daylight hours. The compass takes their place for directing a course. Its needle does not point to Astronomical North but to a shifting magnetic lode near Earth's North Pole. It is affected also by nearby magnetic ore bodies, by weather, by iron in a vessel's hull and sometimes by the cargo. A mariner's first responsibility was to know the conditions affecting his compass and to maintain its relative accuracy. This he could do by reference to the stars, Sun and Moon.

The day-to-day steering of the vessel was done by compass. The vessel's course was entered each day in Graham's case, in the third column of his log, immediately following Day of Week and Day of Month. In the fourth column, Distance, was entered the number of nautical miles travelled that day. The vessel's courses by compass and distance could then be plotted to show, day after day, the Traverse of the voyage. That method of navigation is known as Dead Reckoning. Latitude and longitude accumulated by Dead Reckoning were entered in Graham's seventh and tenth columns respectively.

Dead Reckoning is quite accurate under ideal conditions but, if a storm drove the vessel off course, even backwards on its last leg, Dead Reckoning provided no means of starting afresh. A competent mariner could allow for drift or leeway caused by wind and even for drift occasioned by currents. He could not, however, determine where he was after a week of adverse wind that interrupted his traverse. Thereafter, navigation was by guess and by God! Reference to the stars was necessary to establish latitude and longitude unless he was within sight of a feature of land whose co-ordinates were provided by his chart. We saw that, when leaving Saint John, Graham sighted Brier Island, distant 6 miles — "From whitch I take my departure"[8] He used the plotted co-ordinate of latitude and longitude for that point.

Distance travelled daily was determined for purposes of Dead Reckoning by means of the log-line by which the vessel's speed through the water was measured. It was an ingenious scheme employing simple equipment.

Waves and swells present an impression of the ocean's water changing position with regard to points on the seafloor but this is misleading. True, there are ocean currents but, generally, although its surface roils and heaves, an ocean is not a flowing body of water. The vessel is driven through it by wind action and so, if a buoyant object is cast off the vessel it falls astern at a rate proportionate to the vessel's speed.

To measure a vessel's speed the following contrivance was necessary: a float that could be cast overboard and which would drag sufficiently to draw out a line; the line itself marked into certain uniform divisions; a reel to wind the line upon and a watch or sand-glass. Far more elaborate arrangements were in use later but, throughout Graham's career, that was all that most mariners had to determine rate of progress.

The float was a quadrant of oiled wood about one half of an inch thick taken from a circle of about a foot in diameter. Its circular edge was judiciously weighted so that it would float vertically, point upwards. A bridle of light strong cord about two feet long attached firmly to one extremity of the quadrant's arc and to the other by means of a peg fitted into a hole. The quadrant-float was called a chip or ship.

From the bridle a light strong line ran back to the winding reel which Graham once referred to as a *swifter*, the same name used for the capstan and by spinners and spinsters for their yarn-winding device.

The rope had a stray line, a lead length, determined according to the vessel's height above water, or freeboard, which permitted the chip to be thrown clear of the wake. The stray line was separated from the long line proper by a piece of bunting woven into it. The log line was then divided by knots of cord spliced into it at uniform locations, 47' 3" apart, the first being of leather. Other divisions were marked by two, three, four knots and so on. Midway in each length was a simple knot as a half-way telltale.

The spacing of 47'3" bears the same relationship to a nautical mile as an interval of 28 seconds of time does to one hour. Thus 6080 feet divided by 3600 and multiplied by 28 produced 47.286 feet or a negligible amount less than 47'3". It follows that if six intervals (six knots!) were drawn out in 28 seconds of time, the vessel was travelling at a rate of six knots or six nautical miles per hour.

The vessel's speed was measured every hour, night and day, by the mate of the watch. Unless already wet from use, the log-line was soaked and stretched. Then, all being prepared, the chip was thrown over the stern and into the wind which blew it into the water directly astern. Thrown to leeward, the chip would have settled at an angle to the vessel so causing a defective measurement. One man threw the chip and another turned the glass on the mate's command "Now!"

When the sand had emptied the upper glass 28 seconds later, the cry "Now!" caused the man tending the line running through his hand, to cut short its paying out. He and the mate read the knot-marker nearest and the speed was noted. The sudden arrest of the chip proving too much for its peg to hold, the peg came loose and so the chip swung free to be easily hauled back on board the vessel.

The mate recorded each hourly measurement on slates framed in wood, two of which were hinged together to open as a book. This was called the Deck Log. At the end of the day's run the hourly log was totaled to show the distance travelled. The master then entered the total, in Simon Graham's case, under Distance, the fourth column. Earlier he had entered, in the third column, the bearing of the course.

The following diary entry in his log-book reveals Simon Graham's attention to detail. On September 26, 1844, nine days out of Saint John, N.B., towards Liverpool, England, he wrote: "Sounded off the Grand Bank at 6 P.M. from whitch I take a fresh departure, the Log Line being Marked Shoart."

The vessel, the ship *Swan*, was new to Graham. The log-line was apparently new and wrongly divided. By scanning previous entries in Graham's twelve columns several pertinent aspects may be deduced.

Graham's longitudes computed by Dead Reckoning were falling short of those taken from his chronometer and it may be supposed that Graham suspected something was going awry. He assuredly knew enough about log-lines to ascertain if the divisions were correct (he must have had a measure of some kind aboard) but he was not confident of his chronometer.

Graham had found the error in his log-line early in his voyage and this permitted him to take some remedial action before it was too late to be worth while. He had not crossed the Grand Bank and he knew that longitude could be taken from his charts when he came upon the Bank. He sounded with a lead and line until shallows of the right depth showed where he was. Then he scaled the longitude of the point from his chart and "took a fresh departure." To that entry all subsequent computations were referred. At the same time he checked his chronometer and found it acceptable, perhaps with a constant or controllable increasing error.

Graham almost certainly prepared a new log-line although, since he had a chronometer, he could have checked his sand-glass and have computed a constant to apply to the line.

## CHAPTER 7

# Cambridge and the Stars

Simon Graham first took *Cambridge* to Saint John for a crew and then, on October 19, 1840, he set sail towards Cork, Ireland. The voyage began on an ominous note. Within a week he had noted tersely: "Fine. Making a Dale of water." Notwithstanding, by Nov. 10, Graham had visited Cork looking for orders and, finding none, had "anchored abrist of Coave with Small Bower and 30 fathoms (54.79m) of chain."[1]

Graham was given his orders. They were for points more distant than he may have anticipated. They took him first to Glasgow on the Clyde River, where *Cambridge* took on cargo. Then, on March 11, 1841, Simon Graham headed a new page, "An abstract of a Jurnal from Glasgo towards Monte Video And Buenos Ayres in the river Laplata in the Barque Cambridge."

*Cambridge* cleared Greenock, Port of Glasgow, and stopped below Gourock to take on water. Her master did not say whether he docked his vessel or had water brought out in casks by lighter but it seems that he went ashore. Let him tell his story in his own way: "Shot at and Lamed a hair and was Taken and Severely thretened By a Cloun But Laughed Hertily at him and Came on Board and got underweigh with the furst of the tide." It appears more likely that, having been taken, that is, arrested, Simon was released with a reprimand. *Cambridge* left Gourock safely but almost foundered in the wild Irish Sea. On Saturday, March 20, Simon Graham recorded this flat account of high drama.

"At 4 p.m. a Sea Struck the Ship and Carried away Reals, Bulwarks, Stancions & Covering Board and Cabin, Capston and a Grait deal More Damage in Ships Stoar and Cargo.

"At 4.30 Boar up for Cork and on tuseday March 23 we Got Safe into Cove thanks Be to God for all his mercies."

*Cambridge* was under way again on May 11, but the experience had shaken her master. At least, it had jarred his already shaky spelling. He wrote in a subdued hand, "From Cove towards Monto Veydios and Boynos Ayros."

Two notes on this uneventful voyage indicate that Simon Graham was not all work and no play. On June 5, at 8 a.m., "Spock the Maia of Liverpool 24 days from the Downs Bound to port Philop. At Noon Capt. Sproul

Came On Board with two Gentelmen passangers. I went and Dined on Board the Maia." On July 13, "Put out the Boat to chace a turtel But did not get it."

*Cambridge* made Buenos Ayres on Friday, July 23, 1841, where: "got into the rhoads[2] and went on Shoar with the Pilot and Saw Mr. Galt Smith our Consignee and reported the Ship in the Custom house. John Daily was our pilot up."

On December 2, 1841, *Cambridge* set sail for "Cork or Falmouth." Her captain was not sure of his final destination. He marked Christmas Day with a large "CD" and New Year's Day, 1842, which he noted as 1841, with a fine poem:

> Cind providence again is pleased
> in mercy unto mee
> My days to Bless with another year
> and forty-two to see
> Oh may he Cause his guiding arm
> My Guid and Guard to Bee
> And Safely Lead me on through Life
> in peace to forty three.

On February 2, "had a visit from the Capt. of the Ship Julian of Briman, Whailar, and I gave him a Littel Coffee, he being Short and 98 days from New Zealand Bound to Briman with Sperm Oil." On that day latitudes and longitudes all agreed in the ways they should. Nevertheless, the next day at noon found a substantial correction necessary: "By the Bearince of Fyal and Lat Obsd I make our place 38.53N and 29.07W from whitch I take a new departure."

On February 12, *Cambridge* made Cork, Ireland, and on February 18, came to in Liverpool. "All well So Ends Our Voyage" were the words Simon Graham used to close the log.

Fyal (Fayal) is one of the Azores Islands. Capt. Graham's computations placed his vessel North and West of the island and clearly within view of it. The location is obviously correct but some questions are raised because it is substantially different from a position derived from traverse data recorded earlier. Simon Graham said that he used the new position to start his traverse afresh. How was it, then, that Dead Reckoning and position by star observations agreed only the day before? The answer is twofold. Earlier, Graham had been (consciously or otherwise) meaning his positions by Dead Reckoning and by observation, being confident of neither. (As Smythe says, in *The Sailors Word-Book*, " 'mean,' as a general term implies the medium, but a mean of bad observations can never make a good one.") Later, notwithstanding an observation, he scaled his vessel's position, based on intersecting compass bearings, from a chart showing the latitude and longitude of Fayal.

One star, the Sun, is most suitable for the marine navigator's purpose. It is easily identified, observation is simple and calculations are no more complex than those necessary for other stars. One observation indicates the meridian and permits computation of latitude, time and longitude. Clouds may obscure the sun and preclude its use but no more often than they shut out stars at night.

The observation of a star is merely the act of measuring the vertical angle between the star and a horizontal plane and the horizontal angle between the star and a reference line while simultaneously recording the time of observation. The star's position for the time of day and day of the year may be found in tables that make up an ephemeris or nautical almanac. Such tables were prepared and distributed by the British Admiralty and the United States Navy for general use. By simple and algebraic addition or subtraction, after certain corrections have been made, the required information may be deduced.

The theory is complex, resting as it does on astronomy and spherical trigonometry but the application may be learned by rote. Moreover, the regularity of the sun's daily course simplifies its use.

At the moment the sun reaches the peak of its climb it is noon, although subject to minor corrections, and the observer is looking due North or South, depending upon whether he is in the Northern or Southern Hemisphere. If at that moment an alidade[3] on the vessel's compass is turned to the sun, the deviation of the needle may be determined. The compass may thus be kept under control. If a chronometer showing Greenwich time is then compared with the local time, noon, shown by the sun, longitude may be deduced by factoring the time difference by $15^0$ for each hour.

Determination of latitude from an observation on the sun at noon is only a little more involved. The sun ranges north of the equator, in the northern hemisphere, between March 21 and September 21, and south of the equator through the rest of the year. The angular distance from the equator to the sun is the sun's declination of the moment. It is positive (plus) if north of the equator and negative (minus) if south. The declination may be taken from tables. If subtracted *algebraically* from the sun's altitude (measured vertical angle) and the result subtracted from $90^0$, the latitude of the point of observation is obtained.

The relationships of triangles in the celestial sphere may be obtained in a few minutes from any standard surveyors' text but some brief comments may be in order. The sun apears to move, owing to the earth's rotation, in a plane parallel to the equator. It marks out a great celestial sphere enclosing the earth whose north-south axis, at $90^0$, will pierce the celestial sphere at a point common to all observers in that hemisphere of the earth. The sun's altitude is measured from a plane tangent to the earth at the observer's station but latitude, the angle sought, is measured between the equator and the observer from the earth's centre.

Any star of record in the ephemeris and even the moon, whose travels are equally regular, may be observed at any time it can be seen. The procedure is no more difficult than observing the sun but, having to be performed at night on a heaving and rolling deck towards a small faint point of light, star observations were less popular.

Graham occasionally took lunar readings and, when both were in the sky at the same time, he measured the angular distance between the sun and moon. The first instances of his using this measurement are recorded in the log of the Barque *Grampian*, New Orleans to Liverpool, in 1845. It may be that he had just learned the method.

Early in his career, possibly only for the experience to be gained, Graham observed "Aldebaran, Spica East and Regulus West" but thereafter he ignored night stars. He was in the South Pacific Ocean at that time and could not see Polaris, the star most easily identified and observed in the North Atlantic. It may be found in the Northern Hemisphere at an elevation roughly equal to the observer's latitude and in line with two stars of the Big Dipper (Ursa Major) which was known as King Charles' Wain to Graham.

Polaris lies very near to earth's axis produced northerly into the sky, a convenient arrangement made by the Big Bang that distributed the universe. The stars are so far distant that they do not appear to change position relative to one another. Nevertheless, because Earth rotates, the whole pattern of stars seems to swing around its axis daily. Polaris, brightest of the stars close to earth's north polar axis, travels around a tight little circle never more distant than about $1^0$ 15' measured as an angle from an observer from the star to the axis or true meridian.

If a very ordinary telescope were set up in a suitably dark room an observer might watch Polaris make its round trip unfailingly every sidereal day. As it crosses the meridian at its highest and lowest points as observed it is said to be at Upper and Lower Culmination respectively. When most distant from the meridian horizontally, Polaris is at Eastern or Western Elongation.

The best time to observe for latitude is at culmination, for then the star moves sideways without greatly changing altitude. This gives the observer a little more time to make an accurate observation. Elongation suits the observer better for determining the meridian, for the star drops or rises at elongation without much lateral shift of position.

The observer may refer to his ephemeris and determine when the star will be in the required position. Then, with a surveyor's theodolite or mariner's sextant, timepiece and notebook, he must be ready and watching the star's movement until he records his angle at the proper moment. Tables in the ephemeris advise what to add or subtract from altitude and horizontal angle, at various times for each day of the year, to obtain latitude or the position of the Meridian. Conversely, if the observer is patient and waits for culmination or elongation, he may calculate the time and determine the accuracy of his watch.

The procedure really centres on the observer having the correct time or ascertaining it. If he is sure of the accuracy of his timekeeper he can observe at any position of the star provided that he is competent to make quick readings of his instrument when movement is most pronounced.

Graham observed the angular difference between the sun and the moon, the one serving as a reference for the other, and calculated longitude from information in his Nautical Tables. Such an observation is not always practicable even when both sun and moon can be seen because refraction makes early morning and late afternoon readings quite inaccurate. The period between 1000 hours and 1400 hours is best.

Here then is Simon Graham's method of navigation in a nutshell or, perhaps, a cockleshell. He ignored the complexities of navigation arising from the earth's spherical shape. If he understood that the shortest distance *could* be the arc of a circle (great circle sailing), he was unable to employ the knowledge owing to dependency upon the whims of the wind and the lack of a reliable chronometer. Instead, he sailed the meridians and parallels of latitude whenever possible. Failing that, he set a simple compass bearing from his point of departure. In either case, his aim was to strike a recognizable landmark from which he could set a final course.

He computed triangles of latitude and longitude on the basis that the area to be crossed was a plane surface; and so, from *plane* sailing we have, today, *plain* sailing.

## CHAPTER 8

# *Hannibal* Wrecked!

Simon Graham left *Cambridge* in Liverpool and assumed command of the Ship *Hannibal*[1] "of Miramichi" out of Liverpool, bound for New York, on April 28, 1842.

The voyage was uneventful, if bad weather is put to one side, it always besetting the mariner, until May 17, when the first of three unusual happenings occurred. On that day Simon spoke a vessel whose name, as best it can be determined, was *Similion* of Portsmouth. She was 26 days out of London and had lost her fore and mizzen masts. *Similion* had on board the crew of the *Colward* (?) of London "taken from the reck of do."

On May 21, a "stearige passanger" whose name is obliterated by water stain, died of dysentry and was buried at sea.

Nature compensated for the loss for, a few days later (date uncertain), "Lillee Fitzpatrick was Brought to Bed of a daughter."

*Hannibal* made New York after a passage of 49 days and "passangers — all got on Shoar." Her master sounded surprised at the feat.

A week later Simon Graham exultantly noted that he "Sailed airlie on Tuseday morning for Richibucto." He made his home port in 12 days, one of which was wasted in air too calm for progress. It required exactly 24 hours from "Cape torminton"[2] to Richibucto where he arrived on July 3, 1842.

A full month was required to load *Hannibal*, doubtless with lumber, and it may be that Graham did not hurry the work. He sailed for Cork, Ireland, on August 20, "for orders." It is clear that the owners did not have a customer for the cargo.

On Sunday (marked B) September 11, *Hannibal* passed an American ship standing to the westward with her foreyard carried away.

*Hannibal* was redirected to Dublin from Cork and she arrived there, sound, after a passage of 35 days. On "B" (Sunday) 27th of November, 1842, the master headed a new log, "An Abstract of a Jurnal Kept on Board the Ship Hannibal from Dublin towards Savanah."

The voyage was uneventful and the weather fine. In whimsical spirit Captain Graham recorded this thought on Christmas Day: "Wishing the good folks on Shoar Mutch Joy of ther Roast Goos I am at Sea."

On Sunday (a) January 1, 1843, he printed: "Fine New Years Day" which brought on an urge to poetical expression, for he then took up two lines with a business-like wish: "Now though I take the Liberty the Infant Year to haill, I Hope that it will favour me with Many a prosperous Gaill. 1843."

On Sunday, January 27, 1843, Graham and his ship were in Savannah, Georgia, and Simon "requested the Nathanial Hooper of Marblehead to report us She Being outward Bound for Liverpoool."

Simon Graham was back in Liverpool (on May 3, he passed "Hollow" head) on May 4, 1843. He "engaidged 2 Steemboats and towed up and got into Yunion Dock after a passage of 29 days and all Well." He left Liverpool on May 8 (had he sailed in ballast from Savannah?) and made Richibucto, N.B., without problems on Sunday, June 11. He loaded at "Buctush" (Buctouche, N.B., near Richibucto), left for Cork for orders on July 21, and began to offload his cargo in Dublin 36 days later.

Graham was in luck; he was ordered back to Richibucto and *Hannibal* sailed on September 6, 1843, from Kingston Harbour, Ireland. On the 23rd, he "passed one of the Halifax Steem Packets" — an omen of things to come. With fine disdain he neglected to record her name.

A day later he "spock the Brig Integratee of North Shields for Miramichi. Likewise the Brig Matilda of and from St. John Bound for Cork with crew in a Mutenous State."

On the 27th, "Capt. Lewis of the Brig Ostrea of Weymouth and a gentelman passanger Mr. Craford came on Board Being short of Lamp Oil and we Supplied him. He was from Weymouth Bound to Quebec for flower and Timber." On October 11, Simon was safe in Richibucto with no more damage to his vessel than a few split sails.

*Hannibal* cleared Richibucto on November 22, 1843, and got into Brunswick Dock, Liverpool, on December 15. This time she passed Holyhead; previously he had passed "Hollyhead" and "Hollow Head." The Captain had some spare time in Liverpool and devoted it to filling the rest of his log book with original poems. Some are dated 1843 and some earlier. One reveals something of Simon's puritanical character and is of historical significance in that it shows a merchant's sign for a house of easy virtue, earlier than the more recent red light.

### To An Old Friend With a New Face

Your Self and your famely I wonce did respect
But I am Sory your Conduck is now gon to wreck
Your pride is unbounded in Every Ones Eyes
whitch may Cause you a fall from whence you'll not rise

But from whence dos the welth cum that causes this pride
From the prostitutes Earnings that along the Streats glide

to the Baisest of Carractures your house it is free
and I trust o'er its threshold you ne'er Shall See me

For your Self and your ritches I Both do dispise
and Shunned you Should Be By the good and the wise
only those that is Squandering a fortune away
is welcom Companions for You J. McKay

In ruins Broad path if your Children should stray
and a while from your home Should absent them away
Just inquire at the Grean Man the Landloard will Know
for through that Broad Channel thy are Sure for to Gow.

J. McKay has lately bought a house and put the Sine of a Grean Man[3] Over the Door."

On April 14, 1844, Simon Graham left Liverpool for New York. He made the great port with only the normal damage of broken spars. *Hannibal*'s water casks must have been of poorly seasoned lumber for several leaked and lost 1050 gallons (3½ casks).

The infant child of Mr. and Mrs. Clark, passengers, died at noon on May 31, and was buried at sea three hours later. Despite that, when the master got into harbour on June 1, he noted "all well."

On June 25,1844, *Hannibal* began her final voyage. She left New York for Saint John, N.B., in fine weather and "the people" spent two days painting ship. On the third day she was driving through "Thick Fogg and Small rain." Then, on Friday, 28 June, 1844: "at 9.40 hard a Surf under our Lee put the helm a Starboard to Bring the Ship to the wind But Being So near the ground She would not Stear But fell Bow By and Struck Bilged and Filled with water. About 11 PM it Cleared that we Could See the Land only about 20 Yards from us. Went on Shoar...and found we were at the mouth of Beaver River, 14 miles from Yarmouth N.S."

Graham's chronometer showed his position farther east than that indicated by Dead Reckoning. The mistrusted instrument was right but its owner ignored its warning. Even a few hundred yards to the west, *Hannibal* would have been safe.

Mariners before Christopher Columbus had no pressing need for a system of precise navigation. They were coastal travellers and rarely out of sight of land. The more venturesome who dared crossings of open water were guided well enough by stars and the crude magnetic needles of the day, but that situation changed quickly upon the news of rich worlds beyond the horizon. The shortcomings of navigation by Dead Reckoning then proved a tremendous handicap on the long wandering voyages that became ordinary.

The common log device of measuring speed and distance must have been well established by Columbus' time because it is so simple and obvious a scheme. Nevertheless, it is unlikely to have been the earliest method used. "Walking the log" must be older. A chip was thrown into the sea from the bow of the vessel and its progress towards the stern matched by the mariner who noted the time required for the chip to travel the known length of his deck or his pacing. "Walking the log" is a technique well understood by fishermen, even today, in Newfoundland.

Astronomers of Caesar's Rome computed time, latitude and the true meridian by observation of stars. The instrument employed, the astrolabe, was crude but functional. In its simplest form it was not much more than a rudimentary device for measuring angles but in its most sophisticated guise it embraced a self-reading emphemeris. When designed by a skilled craftsman the astrolabe yielded adequate data to observers possessing only a small knowledge of mathematics.

In essence an astrolabe was an inscribed metal ring bearing a bar across to support a rotating alidade. When the astrolabe was held at eye level by a free-swinging swivel which permitted the device to hang plumb, a star could be sighted through the alidade. The act of rotating the sighting arrangement moved a calibrated pointer around the suitably engraved ring, so indicating the information sought. The addition or substitution of discs marked to resolve the movements of particular stars made the instrument a versatile and valuable navigation aid. The astrolabes owned by Columbus, Cabot, Cartier and Champlain are seen to be virtually unchanged from those of Roman times, specimens of all periods being available in museums for comparison.

The astrolabe was doubtless developed for terrestrial surveying. At least it was employed almost exclusively for such purposes until mariners began to venture the oceans of the world. The astrolabe was small, light and simple but those features limited results to coarse approximations. Nevertheless, it became a popular navigation instrument because there was none other to challenge it.

Towards the end of the 17th century the orrery made its appearance. It was named after the fourth Earl of Orrery for whom one of the very first was built. The orrery was a co-ordinated arrangement of rings by means of which the movements and positions of the sun and its planets were illustrated. It was actually a solar ephemeris and practical to a limited extent. The orrery seems to have pointed up the need for an instrument more suited to observation but less a ready-reckoner than the astrolabe and, in 1731, John Hadley invented the sextant.[4]

Hadley's instrument, designed solely for measuring vertical and horizontal angles, was also intended for the land surveyor. Its arc was actually an octant, $45^0$ or an eighth part of a circle. That proving not quite sufficient for marine purposes, a Captain Campbell, R.N., increased its arc length in 1737 to $60^0$, a sixth part of a circle, which prompted the name *sextant*. Land surveyors eventually found an arc of $45^0$ too little and enlarged it to $90^0$ (with horizontal measurements in mind) and they naturally called the larger instrument a quadrant. Not long afterwards, fully circular contrivances with handles and longer sighting tubes were developed, Mendoza's instrument of about 1800 being typical.

The more elaborate instruments were more versatile than the sextant but their refinements were not necessary at sea and, for land use, hand-held instruments were less accurate than tripod-mounted theodolites and circumferentors (compasses with alidades) developed about the same time. The sextant proved ideal for marine use owing to its compact size and a convenience of operation not foreseen by Hadley.

The sextant was an arrangement of mirrors which enabled the observer to sight two objects at the same time. When the sighting was achieved, by rotating a mirror at the pivot of an arm, so moving the arm along the limb or sextant arc, the angle subtended was measured. Owing to mirror reflection, the angle indicated was double the true angle and so the limb was graduated to correct the reading.

The two objects sighted by a navigator could have been stars if their angular difference was required but usually the sighting was between a star and the horizon. The latter, being somewhat more than seven miles distant at sea, served as a reference for roughly levelling the sextant. The navigator later corrected for height above sea level by subtracting a figure found in his Nautical Tables. He also allowed for refraction, always subtraction, again from tables.

A rigid instrument such as a surveyor's theodolite could not be operated quickly enough to obtain a reading at sea. The vessel's heaving and rolling made it impossible to fix on a star and a level plane of reference was of course impossible. The unforeseen convenience of the hand-held sextant is that it made the observer part of the instrument. As the observer's mind concentrated on the simultaneous sightings of two points, the brain directed his body, legs and arms to flex and accommodate the vessel's unpredictable motions. A hand-held instrument had many deficiencies but the body's ability to compensate for erratic influences made the combination perfect.

Many observers found the sighting tube (three of which were provided; open, low and high magnification, interchangeable) an unnecessary nuisance and dispensed with its use. They merely sighted through the ring intended to hold the tube. Vision traveled to an object glass, the lower half of which was a reflecting mirror and the upper half transparent. Through that little window (for vertical angles) the horizon was kept in view. At the same time a mirror (the index glass) at the pivot of the rotating arm was adjusted to reflect the star into the lower half of the object glass. Deliberate, considered actions were not often possible. The observer had to dexterously flip the mirror back and forth in harmony with the pitching of the vessel's deck.

It was most difficult to find and hold to a pinpoint of light in such a manner. As well, on a dark night when a star gleams most brightly, the horizon might not be visible. That accounts for the unpopularity of night observations; it was far easier to observe the sun. A dark glass was interposed to cut glare and the observer sighted the lower edge of the disc. A variable correction of about 16 minutes, taken from tables, brought the angular measurement to the sun's centre.

It was a valueless effort for a seaman, unless also an explorer, to determine his latitude in harbour, particularly from stars, as Graham once did, and so such exercises must have been mainly for the benefit of the experience. Nighttime and daylight observations in harbour and almost anywhere ashore had to be performed without benefit of a natural horizon. To overcome the problem explorers employed a trough of mercury into which they reflected the image of the star. The mercury always presented a level surface and, in fact, offered a better reference plane than the horizon. Mariners, at least those less dignified than naval officers, merely poured a film of molasses deep enough to accommodate the vessel's roll at anchor, onto the head of a cask.[5] That made a splendid dark mirror. Navigation problems can be sticky, indeed!

Hadley's invention provided a means of obtaining accurate measurements, no more, no less. The navigator had to be an accomplished astronomer-mathematician because tables of data were not available. There was little point in printing them since determination of latitude, local time and the meridian, however useful, did not permit precise navigation. The element of longitude was lacking.

Everyone knew what was needed to correct the situation — a timekeeper which would be reliable at sea. As early as 1530 a Dutch scientist, Gemma Frisius, had proposed that if a dependable clock were carried aboard, a mariner could determine longitude by methods we have already discussed. The obstacle to implementation of Frisius' suggestion lay with the construction of clockwork mechanisms at the time. This obstacle would not be resolved for a full two hundred years.

Pendulum clocks worked well enough ashore. If they gained or lost time it was a comparatively simple matter to adjust their hands (most employed only an hour marker) from a sun dial at noon. Adjustment could not be permitted if a clock were to be used to compute longitude, but that was an academic aside in any case; pendulum clocks just would not function under adverse conditions at sea.

The need for a trouble-free clock mechanism grew increasingly urgent as European mariners wandered farther and farther from their home ports. The cause of profit could not be served unless seamen could follow the most direct routes to their destinations. One after another the seafaring nations of Europe offered magnificient rewards for a clock that would solve navigation problems.

In 1714 the British Admiralty advertised a prize of ten thousand pounds sterling for a clock that would remain accurate to four minutes of time, one degree of longitude, after crossing the Atlantic to the British West Indies. Twenty thousand pounds, the cost of building a man-of-war, was the tempting bait for an improvement over the minimum standard of one degree. After years of hard work and several successively better models, John Harrison, a Yorkshireman, claimed the British reward. On H.M.S. *Deptford*, travelling to Jamaica and back, Harrison's timepiece varied less than three seconds per day over six weeks at sea. Even better chronometers were to be built, but Harrison's had at last made precise navigation possible.

In 1767 the British Admiralty published Nautical Tables for seamen and the tedium of finding positions at sea was greatly reduced. Nevertheless, the high cost of hand-crafted clockworks kept good chronometers out of reach of most mariners for many years. The following excerpt from R.H. Dana, *Two Years Before the Mast*, Sunday, October 5, 1834, makes the point:

> ...We immediately took in our studding-sails and hauled our wind (i.e. the Brig *Pilgrim* running in for the land. This was done to determine our longitude; for by the captain's chronometer we were in 25°W., but by his observations we were much farther, and he had been for some time in doubt whether it was his chronometer or his sextant which was out of order. This landfall settled the matter, and the former instrument was condemned, and, becoming still worse, was never afterwards used.

Dana was not at all clear about longitude "by observation" and by chronometer but it may be accepted that the ship's timepiece was defective. The captain, of course, determined the longitude of the land-fall by reference to topography and his charts. Dana, on his first voyage, fifty days out of Boston for Valparaiso by way of Cape Horn, did not note the latitude of the land-fall because he had not yet learned such niceties of seamanship.

Months later he recorded latitude and longitude quite regularly in his diary.

It may be of interest that Simon Graham, returning to New York from Valparaiso, Chile, in the Ship *Sybylla*, was not far distant that day. His sextant was old but sound. It had been the property of Admiral John Paul Jones, U.S.N., 1747-1792, and it had served on many a hazardous voyage.[6] (In 1938 the sextant, which had pictures of incidents of Jones' career painted on its case, was given to President Franklin D. Roosevelt, who collected documents and souvenirs of the Admiral. It was presented by D.L. MacLaren, Mayor of Saint John, later Lieutenant Governor of New Brunswick, and accepted by President Roosevelt in the name of the people of the United States. The sextant had come into Mr. MacLaren's possession from his father, a resident of Richibucto, who had bought it from Simon Graham. The sextant and its case are now in the United States' Naval Museum at Annapolis, Maryland.)

## CHAPTER 9

# Grampian *and the De'el*

A fine new vessel awaited Simon Graham in Saint John. She was the *Swan,*[1] a ship just completed by James Smith, master shipbuilder. Her master took her to Liverpool, for sale there.

She sailed on September 17, 1844, and the first log entry on September 19, contained this blythe comment: "Light winds from N.E. Standing down the Bay Crew Mostly Drunk." What a way to put to sea! The men were tractable, however, and the next day saw "the people clearing decks and all Sail Set." Then, after strong gales and a hurricane, *Swan* made "Hollow Head" and, on the 14th of October, Liverpool. The passage was only 26 days.

The owners had a Barque, *Grampian,*[2] ready to put to sea after Simon Graham had spent a couple of months ashore in Britain. *Grampian* sailed on January 1, 1845, for New Orleans where, upon being towed in by the Steam Tug *Shark*, she came alongside the levy on February 23.

The *Persian* towed her back to sea on April 17th. Graham "spock" many vessels and on May 20, he "Exchanged Signals with H.M.S. Appollow with troops. Thy Reconed in 49⁰ 10" West." Simon underlined the longitude as if doubtful of its value. His own reckoning showed 47⁰15' by account and 44⁰51' by chronometer. He showed his lack of confidence in the Royal Navy's ability to navigate by continuing with his own figures. They served him well enough and he "came to at the Magazen all well" on June 6, and the next day "Docked Ship in the Cowburg."

*Grampian* sailed from Cobourg Dock, Liverpool, on July 3, 1845, bound for "the River St. Laurance."

On the 16th, he showed his number to the Ship *Sybella*. Was this his old love, *Sybylla,* wedded to another master?

On the 22nd, he laconically recorded a vessel's dying moments with these words. "45..32N. 37..57W. Saw the Brig Mary of what port not marked. Sent the Bot on Board to Se if any person was there But found non. She was lying on her Beam Ends all the Sails washed of the yards Bot(h) top Gallt posts on End. We sounded in 55 fathoms close to hir."

Simon Graham obtained "Pilot Alex. Chamberland from the Brig *Ann Emma* bound to "Swanse in Wails G.B." and on August 2, came to at Rimouski, Canada East where, upon delivering his "instrucksions", he was ordered to Grand Bay in the River Saguenay.

On August 3 (Sunday, "D"), the crew "refused Duty Saying ther allowance of Bread was not Suficiant and thy would not work Ship unless thy got more. I gave them 1 lb Eatch and promised one and a quarter per man per day untill our return Being ¼ above the allowance Signed for. On these terms thy have turned too. Ther names is Thos. Underwood, Jno Irvin, Becham Waldon, Joseph Hopkins (and) John Brown."

August 8, found *Grampian* moored with the two bowers, one in 18 and the other, 15 fathoms, in Grand Bay. She had spent five days tacking, becalmed and under tow in the St. Lawrence before reaching the Saguenay. She sailed for London on August 30, clearing the "Sagany" that "Satterday", the Customhouse the day following and "Cape Gaspy on Tuseday when made the port light of Anticostia." Except for the normal misfortunes of losing part of her topgallant bulwarks, the barque made Commercial Docks in Port of London without trouble in 25 days.

She left London October 15, 1845, and made Savannah, Georgia, without difficulty 48 days later. The weather was generally fine and Simon Graham had his people painting inside the barque. *Grampian* returned to Liverpool, February 15 — March 12, 1846, having encountered "Havy gaills" which "Stove in Bulwarks and Brock Stanchions on the Larboard waist" but otherwise all went well. Off the coast of England "a grait many Schooners in Sight."

In Liverpool, *Grampian* was re-rigged as a ship and she left Waterloo Dock for New York on April 15, 1846, square-rigged on the mizzen mast.

On the evening of the 29th, "an Old Woman Wife of a Welsh man died and at 9 A.M. this morning Aprile 30th. We Comited hir Body to the Sea."

"Thursday, May 21, at 7 P.M. Came to at the Qurantine anchorage Steton Island."

From New York *Grampian* sailed to the St. Lawrence River again. Her master sounded cautiously off Sable Island, known then as now as the graveyard of the Atlantic and "Kept the Lead gowing Every 2 hours." Memories of *Devonport* and *Hannibal* must have inspired caution.

Rather than round Cape Breton the ship made for the Straits of Canso which were passed after lying in Chedabucto Bay for a day owing to fog. She had "a grait many Small Schooners in Company."

The weather was fine but the crew were not allowed to loaf and enjoy it. They were set to painting inside the ship.

*Grampian* showed her number as she passed Buctouche but Simon

Graham didn't put in to Richibucto. Instead, he put a letter and three parcels on board "Mr. Jno Jardine's New Ship the Atalintic,[3] to be forewarded into Richibucto." On the 25th of June, *Grampian* made Metis, Canada East, 22 days from New York.

She sailed from there with a cargo of lumber and up-to-date with the latest innovations for speaking to other vessels on August 14, 1846, bound for London. Signals and "tilligraffs" were sent and received many times before *Grampian* cleared the Gulf of St. Lawrence. She made London on September 12, 1846.

From London, *Grampian* journeyed to Saint John, making port under the pilot, Scott, on November 3, thirty-nine days out of London.

On December 10, the vessel departed for Cardiff, Wales, and was in difficulties immediately: "All hands Nearly Drunk." A week later, labouring in heavy cross-seas, she was making considerable water and the pumps were manned steadily. "The Crew Came aft in a Body to Request that I would put in to Sum port as thy considered the Ship not Seaworthy in hir present State." The course of events reveals the master's decision with regard to the request.

Two days later *Grampian* lost her foresail and fore topsail. Simon Graham had no stomach for quips on Christmas Day and his records for December 26-29 show why that was so.

"Still making a grait dale of water. One of the pumps won't throw no water.

"Very havy gale of S.W. Wind. Weegie[4] Brock and one of our pumps won't pump and making a dale of water.

"Moderate. Out all reefs. Took the Starboard pump on deck. Top gallant Bulwarks tore away amidships."

On January 1: "Hoisted our Larboard pump to percil[5] it as it won't pump any."

January 4: "Split our fore topmast Staysail and both topsails main lift brock."

On January 6, her captain had *Grampian* lying to. He had a new fore topsail and staysail "ridy" for bending but could not get the job done until the next day when he also got a new main topgallant sail bent.

The weather abated and the ship made Cardiff on the 31st of January, 47 days from Saint John.

From Cardiff *Grampian* made for Valparaiso, sailing on March 29, 1847. A month of fine weather kept the people busy at tarring the "riggins" and painting the ship. All went well until May 5, when the crew were making a mainsail for the longboat. On the next day the master noted a difficult situation and characteristically neglected to record the outcome. "The people," he said, "refuse to take in Sail on account of a Differance with the 2nd mait. Split our fore topsail."

Simon Graham was not acquainted with either Samuel Coleridge or the superstition of mariners that assigns the souls of lost seamen to albatross' bodies. Perhaps Coleridge was not Simon's kind of poet. At least, the albatross fable was not one of Graham's superstitions for on May 12, he shot one of the birds.

Graham rounded Cape Horn without undue difficulty and, being an old hand at this, his third passage, he didn't bother with recording the topography. Perhaps he had more serious matters pressing him for, on Sunday, 7 of June, he noted: "at 5 PM the crew refused duty and would not cum on deck on account of puting two men in irons that was fighting — Wm. Clamonts and Wm. Baker Scott."

On the 7th, at noon, "the people Still off duty. At 3 P.M. people turned to work. I then Let one man out of irons and 6 P.M. Let Wm. Baker out." And so we are provided with a glimpse of the master's character. He was what Scots call *determined*: what others term stubborn.

On the 8th, both pumps were blowing. The crew lifted the larboard pump, found a large hole in its chamber and repaired it by filling with "boiling" lead. That day their captain flirted with fate again and caught an albatross. On the following day the starboard pump had to be repaired.

On June 19, *Grampian* came to in 30 fathoms in Valparaiso with the small bower after a passage of 83 days. "All Well thank God for all his Mercies."

In Callao the old seadog met the challenge of his crew head on again and the sterling worth of the Royal Navy was illustrated. These entries cover July 7, 8, and 9, 1847.

"Five of our Crew was taken on Shoar by the Capt. of the Port's Boat and put in confinement for Being drunk and fighting — and fined $5.00 Each.

"I had them brought on Board. Thy refused to assist in getting the Ship under weigh for whitch we were detained that night.

"I went on Board H.M. Ship Collinwood and got the assistance of a Boats Crew to get the Ship under weigh and the officer of the Boat took on Board with him who Still refusing to work and was the ring Leader. After that the other four turned out to work."

The Royal Navy, it may be recalled, was renowned for its ability to break the toughest men. The man who wouldn't work made a bad bargain by opting for the man-of-war. He must have known the foul reputations of the King's Ships.

The ship came to the famed "Chinco Middel Island" and commenced loading the infamous fertilizer, guano. Ten days later, partly loaded, she was ready to cross to Piscos. First, a leak that developed had to be stopped. The master noted that it was only "a seem missed in caulking." The vessel was now watertight but her loading could not be continued. "All holy days. No work can be don," was the disgruntled comment taken into the log.

By September 29, the ship was in south latitude 40⁰ and well on her way back to the Horn; but her leak had not been stopped. She was still making "a good dale of water." Notwithstanding, *Grampian* drove for Cape Horn and successfully navigated the angry waters. Her master must have learned from his passage in *Sybylla*, because the crew had no trouble with scurvy.

*Grampian* crossed the Equator on November 26 in fine weather and in due time came to anchor with her small bower in Cork. From Cork she travelled to London and made the West India Docks on February 5, in a passage lasting 26 days. From London the ship beat up the English Channel and the Irish Sea to arrive in Belfast on May 3, after a voyage of ten days.

*Grampian* sailed from Belfast on May 17, 1848, bound for New York where she came to inside Sandy Hook on June 23. The weather was fine and the "brezes motherate" throughout the 38 days of travel. The vessel came in close to the shore of "noviscotia" and there "spock the Comodore of and bound to St. John 35 days from Lpool."

In this log the master provided a rare glimpse of his cargo and the size of his vessel. On June 14, after anchoring inside Sandy Hook he wrote: "Got underweigh and Bate up to Staten Island. R hands all Well. I went up to N. York and had to return to take the names and ages and ocupations of all our passangers. Reported and Landed passangers on Monday 26 June 1848. 7 passangers two many By Room Rite By Tonage, 274 Souls misuremint."[6]

The witless run up to New York without the information concerning the passengers suggests that this was Graham's first voyage carrying human cargo. He had transported people before but they had been cabin passengers, perhaps 8-16 each voyage. The 274 souls (had Simon been navy-trained he would have called them *live bodies* were clearly those unfortunate travellers known as steerage class who were herded 'tween decks like cattle and there left to fend for themselves. It is worth recalling that the ship's last cargo had been that foul (fowl?) smelling guano.

From New York *Grampian* sailed to Dalhousie, N.B., and made the run between July 1, and July 13. The weather held fair and the people were painting, of course. Graham passed his home port of Richibucto once more without being able to stop there: "Spock Ben Robishaw a Richibucto pilot and set a case and Sum Letters on Shoar."

The captain's visit to Dalhousie was his first and he was not at all impressed by either the town or its citizens. Outward bound from Dalhousie for Cork, for orders, he composed this masterpiece in gall-heavy ink, one of two variations on the theme.

### Dalhousie No More

If you gow to Dalhousie the folks there you'll find
will appear very friendly and Seem very Cind
if you chance to deal with them your heart will feel Sore
and you'll wish to return to Dalhousie no more

The men thy will flatter the Ladies seem Cind
You would take them for angels thy dress up so fine
But Look well to your Self when you pay off your Scoar
or you'll wish to return to Dalhousie no more

For if the Deels out of Dublin its there him you'll find
his name is Ingraven on every Sign
his sons are well scoold and one in Eatch Stoar
and I hope I return to Dalhousie no more

Its aspect is Barren its Bleek and its Cold
his children wants home ere thy grow very old
and I hope thy'll be gon ere I visit that Shoar
Should fate Send me Back to Dalhousie once more

Should fate Send me Back, but I hope it not will
to those Imps of peridition I would gave a pill
a Bundle of Bibles I would Leive in Eatch Stoar
and a deel in Dalhousie you'll never See more.

One Sermon is only preatched there in three weeks
and then thy are busy amang timber creeks
for the Sight of a person (parson) thy mortaly abhore
So I hope to Dalhousie I'll never gow more

Of grace thy are voide and thy consciense have none
a church thy would rub if the person was gon
Like Tigars alls prey that Cums into ther power
and I hope to Dalhousie I'll never gow more.

The sea had been kind to *Grampian* until her master taunted the devil's Dalhousie minions. Her voyage from Dalhousie to Cork, in the words

Wellington used to describe Waterloo, was then a close run thing.

She sailed on August 14, 1848, and all went well until September when, as is seen from the date appended to one of his poems, Simon Graham lashed out at Dalhousie. Then, in the words of the log, some data being omitted in the interests of brevity, this is what the ship had to endure.

"Sept. 1: Havy Gails. Brock the main royal backstays. Split fore topsail and mainsail. Lying too part of the times.

"Havy Gails. Handed all Sail only the Close reefd main top and Laid too. Very havy Seas.

"At 1 P.M. the ruther[7] stock Brock and the ruther unshiped and Sunk. Commenced to get a Spar over the Stern to Steer with But the Sea ran So high that we durst not venture it.

"About 5:30 P.M. Shipped a Sea that stove one of our Boats, Sweeped away all our Stud Sails, Spair Spars and a grait many things of the deck. Deck load on the Lee Side mostly on float.

"Larboard topgallant Bulwarks and rails all Sweept away.

"Set a small bit of our main Spencor to keep hir head to the Sea But it Split and we had to hand it again.

"Ship making a grait dale of water and has a grait List to port.

"More moderate But Still Blowing very hard. Lying too with Close reefd main and mizin topsails and fore topmast Staysail for a Storm Trysail. People imployed in geting a ruther fixed and assisting the Carpinter.

"Kept no reckoning. Still Lying too. Drifting.

"Got the Spars and fixings over. Set Jib and Staysail But the Ship would not Kip away nor Stear So we took it in and Condemned it as yousless.

"Evening more moderate.

"Still Lying too. All hands imployed mending Sails and assisting the carpinter to get a ruther made.

"Carpinter imployed about the ruther. Sent down fore and mizen royal yards.

"Moderate.[8] Carpinter Still imployed making the ruther. People[9] Shifting and Sending up our Best topsails.

"Blowing strong. Ruther made and all ridy to Ship as Soon as the weather is Suiteable. A Ship and Brig passed us Close Bound But did not Speek us.

"Moderate but too havy a Sea for Shiping the ruther. About 6 p.m. the Chiftian of and from Belfast to Quebec with passangers 15 days out, passed us and offered us assistance if wanted.

"Moderate but (too) Mutch Sea to do anything with Shiping the ruther.

"Sept. 12: Havy Sea. At 3 P.M. the Sea more Smouth. Put overboard the ruther and got it Shipt. Made Sail East."

The log doesn't say *Grampian* was close to foundering but without headway and lacking the means of steering she was at the mercy of an ocean that had taken many a better vessel.

On the 15th, the master spoke the Brig "times" of Prince Edward Island, Capt. Davis, 6 weeks out of London and gave her 215 lbs. of bread. The brig, too, must have had a rough handling in the storm.

On September 28, 45 days after leaving the Devil in Dalhousie, *Grampian* made Liverpool, "All well."

From Liverpool she sailed for Mobile, Alabama, and after 59 uneventful days put into port there. The log does not reveal how the people spent "Crismass" Day but on January 1, 1849, they were painting, tarring, rigging and cleaning up! The return voyage lasting 40 days was equally unremarkable. Liverpool held no outgoing cargo for *Grampian*, it seems, and so she shifted anchorage to "London Derry", four days distant.

From Derry *Grampian* made her way to Philadelphia, safely navigating Cape Henlopen of sad memory. *Devonport's* unhappy plight, a result of passing too far south of Cape Henlopen, must have come to mind because a similar disaster was precluded by staying well north, then cruising southerly along the New Jersey coast until the cape could be rounded in a dignified manner. The ship made Philadelphia on July 11, 1849, after 36 days at sea.

# *Grampian* and the Medicine Chest

On July 22, 1849, *Grampian* sailed for Quebec leaving three of her people behind in Philadelphia. The mate, Wm. Kinnell, and seaman George Thompson became ill just as the vessel got under way on the 21st. Soon after, a near-tragedy occurred: "In the act of Lousing the main topsail, Robt Mitchell, apprentice, fell and had his Left arm Brock in two places Betwixt the Shoulder and the Elbo. Both under Jawbones Brock and the right eye Socket fractured. I went on Shoar and Brought off a Surgen who Set the Bones and Bandaged the wounds."

The master must have contemplated continuing the voyage even with Mitchell in such a desperate plight. How could the apprentice have eaten or been fed at sea? Better judgment prevailed or else Mitchell's moaning proved unnerving as the shock wore off. He was sent ashore in the ship's boat to be cared for in hospital.

*Grampian* was delayed briefly by an adverse current as she tried to enter "the Gut of Canco" and so encountered a situation that seems to have been hidden from historians. Nova Scotia harboured a lair of pirates in the Straits! The ship's log recorded: "Two Boats with armed Crews Came off to Board and Size the Ship for the Gut Light mony. I would not admit them. Thy attempted to Board By force presenting two duble Barrled Guns, Several pairs of pistols making havy thrates that thy would fire. But I had heard of ther rubing and dismantling vessels Cuming through the Gut and would not allow them on Board."

Bravo for Simon Graham! It is not difficult to imagine him with arms crossed and cradling a pistol as he defied those Bluenose pirates. It is quite possible that he carried other firearms locked in his cabin but if the crew were determined to defend *Grampian*, most of them likely had only belaying pins and marlin spikes as weapons. The cook and carpenter had recourse to some fearsome tools, of course.

Again the demands of trade and commerce denied the master mariner the privilege of visiting Richibucto. Instead, as he paused off the harbour entrance: "Mr. Irvin[1] and Son, Richibucto pilots Came on Board and Brought Capt. Hannah Jnr. of Ship Albion[2] and my Son who Stopt 15 minutes."

*Grampian* came into the Port of Quebec on August 11, 1849, 18 days out of Philadelphia.

From Quebec she made London's West India Docks on October 7, 1849, "all well" after a passage of only 29 days.

Back across the Atlantic came the redoubtable old vessel. She left London on October 9, and came to in Savannah, Georgia, on January 1st, 1850, docked at the "Lower Cotton Priss" and began to discharge ballast. She had, apparently, brought some weighty material to trim the hull, worth putting ashore, with the intention of loading with baled cotton.

Two comments in the log are of interest. Early in the voyage the master, "Tryed the Chrometer and found hir correct." Midway across the Atlantic: "Threw the dog overboard on acount of him taken fits."

Simon Graham departed Savannah on 27 March 1840, careless on this and the two following voyages to the extent that he did not bother to note, as was his custom, his port of departure, his destination, his vessel and its master's name. He was fifty-four years old and, though he had shore leave between voyages, he hadn't been home to Richibucto for many years. It might be suspected that Simon was getting tired but for contradictory evidence proffered by several romantic poems, alluding it would seem, to personal experience and written about this time.

The ship sailed for Liverpool and got into Brunswick Dock on April 26, 1850, 28 days from Savannah and then departed on May 30, 1850, for parts unknown, at least, not indicated. As usual, *Grampian*'s master was chary about revealing his cargo but he was also inconsistent with regard to the kind of comment entered in his log. On this voyage, on the second day out, he provided a clue. "Serving out provisions to passangers," he said. These were steerage folk; cabin passengers ate at a table.

On June 24, Mrs. Clark died of "old aidge" and was buried at sea. All others survived the passage, it seems, and on July 13, *Grampian* was "at the Quirantine Ground, had the passangers Examined by the Dr. and Inspector," in Boston, Massachusetts.

On August 2, 1850, she put out for Chicoutimi, Canada East. On the eleventh day the ship lost another seaman: "At 4.30 A.M., C. Robertson Died from the affects of drink taken at Boston Before he came on Board. He had Ben Delierious Since the 4th and had to Be put in Irons 3 days But was taken off a few days Before he died. At 8.30 his Body was Burried in the Sea." The only treatment for an intractable man at sea in those days, however sick he might be, was to place him in irons. His liberty menaced every man-jack aboard.

*Grampian* lay at anchor at Chicoutimi "below the mills" on August 19, 17 days from Boston and then travelled from Chicoutimi to London's West India Docks in 29 days, arriving on November 2, 1850. Towing up the Thames by the *Black Eagle* cost £25-11-0.

Again Simon passed Richibucto without visiting his home.

A few pages of jumbled accounts listing some of Simon Graham's early receipts and disbursements have survived. On one of them, headed up "1833, Ship SYBYLLA in London," is this tantalizing expenditure: "Medecen Chist £1-10-0." The ship was preparing to sail for New York with a crew of 15 and 9 passengers and a medicine chest valued at $6.00 American currency, the cost of a boy's wages for one month!

Elsewhere in the same record occurs the payment of £1-4-6: "Bread and Milk for 7 weeks at 6 p. day" which suggests that she was prepared for 49 days at sea. The budget for medical expenses appears then to have been half a cent per head per day. No matter how one interprets the figures it is clear that the master intended little recourse to the medical department.

Dixon's *Law of Shipping*, New York, 1859, advises that by general maritime law a seaman hurt or ill not by his own fault was entitled to be cured "at the expense of the vessel." The medical treatment was to include the services of a physician brought on board when necessary. Dixon also pointed to laws of the United States that required all but the smallest of vessels to be provided with a chest of medicines accompanied by directions for their use, put up by an apothecary of known reputation. The law did not specify that the apothecary's reputation be a good one and Dixon did not go much further in his discussion of the rights of sick and injured seamen.

It is fair to suppose that the contents of medicine chests of the period varied with the fancies of the apothecary and the master and it is likely that few of the medicines included had any real value.

Assuredly, either in the chest or in the master's cabin were an assortment of medical texts. High on the list of worries that nagged at a conscientious mariner was the problem of how to play the doctor when a valued seaman needed help. Simon Graham was not an exception. His library included at least two medical handbooks, both of which have survived: *The Modern Practice of Physic*, Robert Thomas, M.D., London, 1825, and *Modern Domestic Medicine*, Thomas Graham, London, 1832, which bears the following flyleaf note: "Simon Graham's Book, London, May, 1833; July 4th, 1834, Lying in the Gulf of Popuguyon Loading Nickarago Wood; Port Bow Bova; Lower Hold full."

A few examples taken from *The Modern Practice of Physic* will indicate, even to the layman, the limited value of such works.

> Synochus or Simple Continued Fever...synochus and typhus blended together...(caused by) debility...induced by great fatigue or violent exertions; by long fasting; by want of natural rest; by severe evacuations;

by preceding disease; by errors in diet; by intemperance in drinking; by great sensuality; by too close an application to study; by giving way to grief, fear or great anxiety; by depriving the body of a part of its accustomed clothing; by exposing one particular part of it while the rest is kept of its usual warmth;...marsh miasma from moist earth, slime, mire or mud.

Opthalmia or inflammation of the eye...when found not to yield to bleeding, both general and topical, duly repeated, purgatives, emetics, fomentations, and other means which have been pointed out, it will be proper to put a blister at the back of the neck or behind the ear on the side with the eye which is affected....

Hypochondriasis or hypochondriac affection...known likewise as low spirits or the vapours, is a certain state of mind along with dispepsia, wherein the greatest evils are apprehended on the slightest grounds and the worst consequences imagined from any unusual feeling...seems to depend on a loss of energy in the brain or a torpid state of the nervous system induced by...close and intense study, long and serious attention to abstruse subjects, the constant remembrance of some material loss or disappointment...great anxiety of mind, leading an inactive, indolent or sedentary life, immoderate venery, or the use of a crude, flatulent or unwholesome food, being guilty of great irregularity and intemperance, and by continued evacuations.

Sardonic laugh...a fit of laughing arising from no evident cause which continues often in a violent degree for three or four nights...large doses of opium might probably afford some relief.

It is apparent that a seaman's ordinary life, regardless of unusual behaviour (excessive venery, for instance) and habits (long continued evacuations) could cause almost any ailment of record. The remedies offered were just as quaint. Consider, for example, "parcusis or deafness: Tobacco smoke is a remedy which has been employed in some cases of severe and long continued deafness...with great success and efficacy. The mode of using it is to fill the mouth with the smoke of the strongest tobacco, instantly to close the mouth and nose...to make all possible effort...to force the smoke through the nose...; this forces the smoke through the Eustachian tube into the ear;...repeated until both ears give a seeming crack, immediately on which the hearing returns."

Bleeding (cupping) was a standby in nearly all cures for inflammation, accepted by all physicians. Only the time of employment was disputed. Some insisted upon immediate bleeding; others thought it should follow certain preliminary measures. The rule was to bleed every few hours until inflammation became subdued, — up to 30 oz. at first from a robust man and then 10 oz. every 6 to 8 hours.

Most of the prescriptions compounded by apothecaries appear innocent enough but since they have lost favour to more sophisticated drugs, their worth may be judged to have been small. Some remedies for internal use were dangerous, nevertheless, in that they contained such poisons as arsenic, mercury and sugar of lead. Often their deadly qualities were recognized to the extent that the physician was warned to halt the treatment when evidence of poisoning presented itself.

Surgery had reached a higher level than internal medicine and some competent techniques and instruments had been developed by the middle of the 19th century. Two circumstances hampered progress of surgery as a corrective art; the lack of an anesthetic that would immobilize the patient so the surgeon could work slowly, with confidence; and the absence of any knowledge whatsoever of germs, the need for cleanliness and the value of antiseptics.

Chloroform and, shortly afterwards, ether, came into general use midway through the period but, understandably, they were never part of the ordinary medicine chest. The germ theory, so called, was developed about the close of Simon Graham's career and, after a hard struggle put up by recalcitrant sawbones, it was accepted. Only then did doctors wash their hands before and after treating each patient and use an antiseptic, if only carbolic soap, to inhibit infection.

Before antiseptics, the risk of infection as a result of surgery was so great that patients would have nothing to do with the knife while they were conscious and strong enough to resist. Wise surgeons, although they could hardly refuse to amputate mangled limbs, hesitated long before exploring the abdominal cavity. Thus, the likelihood of successful surgery being so meagre, many people preferred to take their chances with a natural recovery rather than endure the agony of surgical attention followed by, say, gangrene.

In the absence of an anesthetic, speed was the surgeon's most valued skill. Guinness *Book of Records* gives credit to Robert Liston of Edinburgh, 1794-1847, for the fastest saw in the surgery business. He once removed a patient's leg at the thigh in only 33 seconds taking, at the same time, three fingers from his assistant's hand.[3] We see that Graham lasted longer at seafaring, for all its perils, than Liston did at surgery.

The procedure for removal of a mangled arm below the elbow, at sea, was as follows. The patient was stupified by means of laudanum, morphine or even strong rum, gagged and then securely held by two stout seamen. A tourniquet was applied to the upper arm and then the surgeon, he with the strongest stomach and who fancied the task or, perhaps, a surgical team made up of the cook, the carpenter and the sailmaker, set to work.

At a point below that where the bone was to be sawed, a cut was made through the flesh and the skin along with some fat and muscle was rolled back above the actual amputation point. This was in preparation for the fashioning of a pad over the stump, later.

Part of the flesh around and between the two bones that make up the arm was then cleaned away and the central strip of a three-tailed strip of old cloth was passed between the bones. By means of that simple device the material for the pad was pulled back away from the amputation area. The bone was then sawed through as quickly as possible after veins and arteries had been tied off.

The pad and flap material was then drawn down and sewed into shape. All the ligatures holding well after testing by relieving the tourniquet and their tails hanging out for later removal, the stump was coated in ointment and then wrapped.

The cook had earlier made the salve of mercury from the medicine chest blended with rendered suet and lard. He had also prepared an adhesive plaster of litharge and resin mixed, melted and poured onto a piece of linen.

None of the items used was sterilized, of course, or even washed. The surgeon wiped his knives on his pant-legs as he progressed through the different stages. A week later the wound could be examined and, if infection had not set in, the bandages came off in another week.

The entire operation was done on a couple of boxes covered with old canvas. The operating room was in the ship's hold. The light was from a lantern held by a steady old seadog who'd seen many such endeavours. The only applaudable aspect was that all costs were borne by the vessel!

One aspect appears strange. Simon Graham was a studious man, one who constantly sought knowledge. His library, quite extensive and wide-ranging, suggests this and his writings support the picture of a person anxious to educate himself. It may be wondered then, how Simon at the age of 39, a widely travelled mariner, could not have learned how to control scurvy before his first voyage around the Horn. The cause and cure had been known for a full half-century or more. Even such terms as "anti-scorbutic" were in use by naval surgeons. Medical texts of the day were vague and uncertain regarding cause but most described the disease and set forth the remedy for it quite adequately.

It will have been noticed that when Simon put into Rio with nearly all his men disabled, the port authorities immediately quarantined the ship along with the unfortunate middie and boat's crew from H.M.S. *Spasias*. That was fair enough: no one knew what disease *Sybylla* was bringing into port. A few days later, however, the doctor had identified scurvy and had lifted the quarantine. All that was required was a diet of fruit and vegetables.

Speculation regarding the contents of the ideal medicine chest of the day may now be in order. It probably held an assortment of sharp, slender knives, some forceps, a few clamps, lancets and bistouries, a couple of fine saws, several needles, all wrapped in greasy rags to prevent rusting. In numerous compartments there may have been small bottles of laudanum, opium, camphor, ammonia, tincture of belladonna, sulphuric acid, mercuric oxide, submuriate of mercury, various lead oxides and sulphates along with a few other assorted drugs and chemical compounds such as tartarized antimony, all of dubious worth. There may also have been a treasured brace of eyestones hidden in a safe corner of the chest.[4]

Certainly there were large bottles of julep, emetics, cathartics, prepared cough syrups and potions for specific ailments, all villainous in appearance, taste and odour. Boxes of basic materials for infusions, such as Jesuits' (Peruvian or Cinchona) Bark and a few herbs were stuffed here and there.

Notwithstanding the desirability of such a well-stocked chest, nothing like it could have been bought for $6.00 and that suggests that *Sybylla's* medical stores contained only a few basic remedies. The master may have kept his instruments separately in his own chest.

The pliers for pulling teeth were held by the carpenter who, unless a blacksmith was aboard, also assumed the position of dentist. His responsibilities were generally not demanding owing to the assistance provided by scurvy in the removal of teeth.

## CHAPTER 11

# *Grampian* and *Laurel*

*Grampian* "hauled out of the Blackwall Beson" on January 10, 1851, bound for the west coast of South America for guano. It required 23 days to make the Lizard, from whence the master took his departure seaward.

Thirty-three days from the Blackwall Basin this note entered the log: "Found a Cat that was Brought on Board the night Before we Left London and had not Ben Seen Since. A Near Skaliton and Could not Stand alone."

On February 20, "the Carpinter finished a new Poup Lather."[1]

The people were kept busy painting masts, other parts of the ship and cleaning up generally. When the carpenter had finished his new ladder to the poop deck he was put to work "dubing the waterways squire with the decks." The weather stayed fine and *Grampian* benefited from a thorough sprucing up.

On March 3, Simon Graham spoke (for the first time: always before, he "spock") a barque bound round the Horn for San Francisco "with chronomoter Stopt and had passangers on Board." He knew full well the significance of such a situation!

The weather continued fair and that was just as well for, on "Aprile 16 our ruther head Brock and the Iron tiller Came off. Ruther Stock too rotten. Got it put right again." The usual litany of broken spars and ripped sails is recorded, of course, but the ship rounded the Horn and made Coquimbo, Chile, without great problems.

Graham listed a dozen vessels he found there along with their masters' names, among them, the *Lady Blaney*[2] of Saint John, Capt. Wiseman, Master.

From Coquimbo, *Grampian* travelled to Callao, Peru, and then to the Chinco Islands for guano. The vessel loaded and washed down, the boats (used for loading) taken aboard, she returned to Callao and from there made all sail for Cork, Ireland.

Again, blessed with fine weather, the people were kept busy at small chores and the carpenter caulked the cabin. Their master still had not read *The Rhyme of The Ancient Mariner* and so he continued to shoot albatrosses. One of them measured 9 feet 7 inches across the wings! It comes as no surprise that, after flouting time-honoured superstitions, *Grampian* got into trouble!

She lost her fore and mizzen topsails in a gale so strong that all sails were handed except two left close reefed. The vessel began to labour and make water, at the same time taking heavy seas. One smashed over her beam and took away stanchions, rails, and bulwarks. The poorly-named Pacific Ocean relented, however, and a few days later permitted the ship to round Cape Horn.

The albatrosses were left alone and the vessel enjoyed fair weather and good breezes until December 1, in south latitude 38⁰, when she started to make water again, or more quickly, it may be assumed; and the pumps were manned steadily. Each stroke brought up stinking liquid guano; but it would have been far worse had the pumps not worked at all! Simon Graham was not one to dwell on the problems that beset him but on January 14, 1852, he noted that *Grampian* was labouring greatly, leaking and shipping water. Notwithstanding, his vessel, redirected from Cork, was unloading in Liverpool on February 7, 1852, thirteen months after leaving that port.

The old mariner usually sought no respite from his ocean travels, but this year, unless a log has been lost, he took a long rest. Graham was not at sea again until September 18, when he was bound from Liverpool to Charleston, South Carolina. Some correspondence suggests that Simon operated a rooming house, one large enough to sell spirits, in Liverpool, with his wife in charge while he was away.

On October 4, tragedy struck. "About midnight...fell from the mizen stay assisting to take in the Spencor[3] and is mutch hurt." The incident seems to have taken place while the master slept and, although he left space for the man's name, he never got around to filling it in. That day another unknown was found dead. He was a boy who had stowed away in Liverpool amongst bags of salt that made up the ship's cargo. Several bags burst under the ship's heaving and rolling and the boy smothered. He was buried at sea, along with his dream of a life in the sunny southern states.

*Grampian* came to in Charleston on October 30, 1852, and that was the end of her so far as Simon was concerned. He took a different vessel, by no means a new one, back to Britain.

The first three lines of the log, Charleston to Liverpool in the Ship *Laurel*[4] provide a rare insight into one of the little problems that constantly thwarted a shipmaster's intentions. On Friday, December 10, 1852: "At 7 AM dropt the Ship from the Wharf into the Rhoades to get the crew on Board Satterday night. Eleven men was put on Board and one about 1.30 Sunday morning But he Lept on Board the Steemboat and Could not Be found. At 4AM the pilot Mr. Aldrit Came on Board. We hove up and So had to Leave him." In this incident the offsetting wiliness of an experienced master is revealed.

Simon Graham planned to sail on Sunday and so, on Friday, earlier than otherwise necessary, he moved his vessel from dockside out into the roads where, once aboard, his men could not readily escape the ship. Then, with a boat's crew of sober sailors, he or the mate marched on the taverns and rounded up the carousers, none too steady on their pins, and took them out to *Laurel*. A sock full of sand, deftly laid alongside an objecting seaman's head with just the right amount of nicety rendered him amenable, leaving no mark for the morning. The unfortunate sailor was due for a big headache in any event.

Most abducted seamen accepted this high-handed treatment with fair grace. They realized that it was, in fact, for their own good. One of the men, however, found the captain's game an unfair one and, when the tug came to tow *Laurel* out of the harbour, he seized the opportunity to desert. It is a mystery where he could have hidden when a search was made for him aboard the small tug.

On December 29: "Lying too under a Close Reeft main topsail. The wheel chain Stanchions drew out of the Stair Caused by the Brecking of one of the Reliving table Straps." Nevertheless, *Laurel* was safe alongside Albert Dock in Liverpool on January 8, 1853, and was "clear the 18th."

Graham commenced his next log without noting the name of his vessel, its destination or even the month of departure. Nor did he note the new month's name later. It seems he left on January 25, 1853, sailed through February and came to in Charleston, South Carolina, on March 8, 42 days at sea.

Two days out of Liverpool the master found he had three more hands than had signed on as crew. William Rafferty, Peter Hanlen, and John Laury had stowed away, bound for the home of the free but, inadvertently, into an area where freedom was not yet universal. The log does not tell what fortune befell the three adventurers but soon after they were discovered the people were tarring rigging and painting ship; and it is likely the three free hands were put to work also.

*Laurel* headed for Liverpool on June 6. Two days later: "A Cullard Stowaway made his appearance and Stated that he was a native of North Carolina and free and that he deserted from the Surveying Cutter and Swam on board the *Laurel* and hid himself for the intencion of Leaving the Cutter." *Laurel*, it seems, was a lucky ship so far as free hands went.

Simon Graham often noted ships at sea lacking spars and this voyage was no exception. "A Ship passed with no main topsail yard nor main royal yard."

The steamer *John Bull* towed *Laurel* into Liverpool for ten pounds on the 13th of July.

From Liverpool Graham took *Laurel*, in ballast it seems, for he had the people scraping the hold, to Maranham on the East coast of South America in a passage of 50 days. The voyage was uneventful although the log contained this rueful note of old acquaintanceship: "I think the Chr. has Stopt...$3^0$ 1" by the watch timing."

Back to Liverpool Simon drove the vessel, leaving Maranham on October 18, 1853, and passing through the usual bag of mixed weather. On October 31, the foremast head was sprung.[5] "Sent up a Spair Spar and Secured the mast head the best manner we could." Later on the people were employed at setting up the rigging for the new spar.

She made Liverpool on November 17, and then set sail for Maranham once more. *Laurel* was soon in trouble with heavy gales of wind. "Brock our main topsail Sheet and all the foot from the reef blew away. Mizen topgallant sail blew from the yard, handed. The gail is terefic with Havy Sea....Bore up to the North Channel to repair damages. Strong gails while handing the reefd foresail.

"John McKeachie fell from the Lee or Starboard yardarm into the Sea and was not missed until next morning, the night being very dark with a fall of Sleet and rain and our main topsail had the close reef blown away in the act of clewing it up a few minutes before.

"Unbent our fore topsail and repairing the foot that was Blown Luce when handed and the Bolt roups shook off it and bent it aft for main."

All that happened while the ship was beating around the Irish Sea trying to get out to the Atlantic. Ireland was passed to the north, instead of to the south as intended, on March 6, sixteen days after leaving Liverpool. The weather was so foul that the master got 30 days into the month of February and, deciding upon a clean slate, started again on March 4. On the 13th, "a Sea Brock our Whiskar Crances[6] and filled the house on deck."

On the 18th of March, the ship had "the furst fair or leading wind since we Left Liverpool January 16." Just as might be expected subsequent log entries had much to say about repairing, painting, tarring rigging and such necessary chores.

*Laurel* had seen enough of Maranham on her earlier voyage; that is apparent. Before reaching the harbour on this occasion she grounded. Her master had a boat out sounding and setting anchors so that the ship could be twisted around. This was likely accomplished by means of a spring on the anchor cable. Finally the sails were backed and she came free. Simon Graham took her around the shoal. He had found deeper water inshore but would not try the shallows again.

She "boar" for Maranham and took a pilot on board but *Laurel* gave him a rough time also. The pilot took the harbour bar too early on the tide and the vessel grounded again. The anchor was let go ("gow") to prevent the vessel being driven ashore. "She shivered and twisted a good dale in the Strong tide and at high water dropt (off) and got into our proper morings on Tuesday 18. Commenced to Discharge."

On June 9, 1854, the vessel sailed for Liverpool and arrived at its home port after a passage of 39 days. Her master spoke the Schooner *Wave*, of and from Halifax, 18 days out, bound for Barbados, as well as a ship 110 days from Sidney, Australia.

Thursday, September 7, 1854, must have given even our phlegmatic master mariner a thrill. On that day he "Sailed passanger in the Highland Cheef'...Capt. McMillan — from Liverpool for Richibucto by Miramichi." He paid no attention to Capt. McMillan's navigation until close to Newfoundland where, with proper caution, he too kept a log.

The reason for interest in the *Highland Chief*'s position seems to have stemmed from several days' failure to observe the sun owing to clouds. Sure enough, the chronometer played a part although Simon does not say whether it was his or Capt. McMillan's instrument. "At 3 P.M. chr. showed in 60.50 with 1$\frac{5}{10}$ Lousing dayly."

On October 1: "Came too at the Horce Shoe."

October 2: "Came too at the Curantine Ground."

October 3: "Got up to New Castle all well after a passage of 45 days."

Richibucto would have been easily reached from Newcastle by means of stage coach or by water and, within a couple of days, the old wanderer had his feet propped up by a fire on his own hearth. He stayed at home a full ten months and bought hardwood, new clothes, rum and other sundries, built a chimney and installed three large windows in his home.

## CHAPTER 12

# *Perekop* — *Pack Up!*

It is difficult to decipher the name of the last vessel in Simon Graham's logs. For a long time it was thought to be *Packup*, an eminently suitable sobriquet, but diligent search proved it to be *Perekop*[1] She was a potential killer but fate did not intend Simon Graham to die in the ocean's billows. Here is the essence of experience aboard *Perekop*, taken from one and a half pages of foolscap that make up the log.

"July 31, 1855: Left Chattam in tow with Mr. Thos. Holderness steem boat[2] from Richibucto...anchored...on August 2 got over the bar and to Sea.

"August 3: Dead Man's Island and came through the passage between Bryar Island and the Magdalens. Set up main rigin and back stays.[3]

"August 4: Came to Blow. The Ship Lay over and made a grate dale of water, gaining on the pumps 18 inches to 3 feet.

"Took in Spanker and close reeft the mizen topsail. The main and fore topsail yards joined with the perals (parrals)[4] and would not cum down to reef. We hauled up the mainsail and to righten the ship hove a part of hir deck load over board."

The *crew* (no longer Simon's *people*)had seen enough of the vessel in those few days between July 31 and August 4. Graham recorded: "Ship's crew in a very mutunas Condition, paying very Little attention to the orders of the officers and yousing very abusive and profane Language. Carpinter making a weigher."[5]

Mutiny is an ugly word but the seamen were not in an attractive situation. Their master was determined to make for the open sea. On August 5, he had set the main top gallant sail while the ship was still "making a dale of water." Notwithstanding the conditions of ship and crew the log noted: "I take my departure from the bearance of St. Paul's in 46.57N and 59.39W." Later on, "mainsail being bent and fiting riging." Then, "People refuse to set up bowsprit shrouds[6] or do any ships duty but pump hir and sail hir."

*Perekop*, a leaky vessel with some of her fixed rigging not yet in place, was passing over the Grand Bank of Newfoundland. One's mind leaps back to *Caledonia*'s passage in January, February, and March 1838, which required 71 days at sea. For all the crew knew, *Perekop* could require even longer if, indeed, she was ever to make port.

On August 9, the crew, some of them at least, set up a top mast and its lower rigging but their anger at the master was not abated. Two days later, with 6 feet of water in the hold and the pumps manned steadily to keep the ship afloat, a wind carried away the bolt of the parrals of the fore topsail yard and the bolt that the fore brails[7] hook into on the rails. "Crew in a muntunas State, disobeying orders and will only make or take in Sail when it pleases themselves or to Do anything Else."

Perhaps it was that the crew *could* not obey orders. Pumping is killing work that cannot be relaxed no matter how weary men become. Slackening as fatigue overcomes the crew sends a vessel straight to the bottom. The men knew they had to pump but did not see that unless sail were made and progress maintained, the ship would founder when they tired. "Allax" Rodgers, a seaman, was either bone-weary or bone-headed for, as Simon put it, he "refused Both the Mait and me to assist to Bend the foresail that had brock from the yard."

"August 13: Still making a large quantatie of water. Crew Still very disorderly.

"August 15: Shifted a Tear of the deck load and wanted to Shift another but Mr. McCulloch refused to do it and all hands nocked off as thy will only do what thy pleases and when thy pleases.

"August 16: The Steward reports to me that he has opened the last bbl of Beef and Pork that is on board and that we have Ben yousing 53 lbs. dayly and 33 lbs. is the full allowance @ 1½ lbs. per man and that we have only 12 lbs. of coffee on board, the Crew forcing him to gave duble allowance. They are firing pistols ocationaly to intimidate and force ther demands."

The near mutiny of *Perekop*'s crew drove all thoughts of the ship's condition from the master's mind as he wrote up his daily log but it is unlikely that the leaky hull had healed itself. She was afloat only because of hard work at the hated pump handles, the summer weather staying fair.

"August 18: Crew viry disorderly taking from the Gelly all the Bread for the Cabin Breakfast and part of the Coffee. Headed by Sheperd. Smith[8] obladged to leave the forecastle and sleep and eat aft being thratened by Crew.

"August 19: Crew thrown a Quantatie of Beef overboard[9] that was served out for the day.

"August 20: Pump Sucking.

"August 22: Spock 2 Cork pilot Boats and one fishing Boat from whitch the Crew Bought Sum fish and potatoes. About an hour after another fishing hooker Came but as the Crew had Ben Supplyed I ordered not to Cum along side but the crew got roops to heave hir in defyance of my orders and calling me all the abominable names they could think of, yelling and making a grait noise and disorder in the ship."

So the fishermen were treated to a spectacle which must have been later recounted with hearty guffaws in the public houses when the hooker made its home port.

On August 25, *Perekop* came to in the Mersey River. In a masterful understatement her captain recorded, "All well after a passage of 23 days." Ship, master and crew were most fortunate to have had such a speedy crossing.

Simon Graham went ashore with the ship's papers and remarked that the crew had "All Run and Left the Ship" by the time of his return. His men were not fools. They were under no misapprehension of their position. Doubtless a platoon of marines or the Liverpool constabulary was pacing Prince's Dock, eagerly anticipating the arrival of the unruly crew. They were cheated of that pleasure and, without doubt, the seamen lost their wages. They may have deserved worse but one is glad that the North Atlantic was also cheated of another prize.

*Perekop*'s log is not long nor does it provide more than hints of answers to questions that come to mind. Nevertheless, the hints, coupled with scraps of information obtained by research, and blended with some general knowledge, permit a little more to be added to the picture of the desperate crossing.

*Perekop* was a brand new vessel and, obviously, her caulking was not completely sound. She was built through the winter and launched in the early summer, as most Maritime vessels were. To that extent, including the resulting leakage, her early career was paralleled by *Hercules*. The two ships were, however, built in different yards some forty miles apart and so the faulty caulking cannot be attributed to the same careless builder. Without more revealing logs such as Simon Graham's it is not possible to say that all vessels leaked on first putting out but, upon considering all aspects of shipbuilding, that contention urges itself.

*Cambridge*, built at another location, made "a dale of water" on her first crossing. *Swan*, alone of the new vessels taken to sea by Simon Graham, built at a fourth site, did not leak. At least, no problem was recorded in her log.

It is apparent that *Perekop*'s master was not greatly concerned by the circumstances, which may suggest that they were commonplace. As well, experience had doubtless taught him that small leaks low on the hull introduced water at an alarming rate owing to differential head of pressure. He would have known, then, that the rapid filling of the hold soon levelled off as the difference in head became less.

## Chapter 1

*"A First Rate Ship of War With Rigging, Etc., At Anchor" and "The Section of a First-Rate Ship of War."*

*These copperplate engravings, published in 1812, show the largest type of warship of the day and indicate the huge quantities of timber required in construction.*

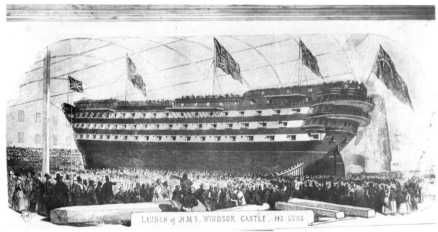

Windsor Castle *was one of Britain's largest men-of-war. Launched in 1849, she had been constructed for 120 guns. The hull was then cut in two and 23' inserted to allow for steam engines (propellor drive) and another 20 guns. A forest of select trees was required in the building of this monstrous vessel.*

Marco Polo, Saint John, N.B., a portrait by John Johnson, reproduced by courtesy of The New Brunswick Museum, Saint John, N.B.

This vessel, launched in 1851, was sold to the Black Ball Line of Liverpool, England, and became famous on the run around the Cape of Good Hope to Australia. She ended her days in 1882, driven aground near Cavendish Beach, Prince Edward Island.

*The barque* Richibucto *of which Simon Graham was briefly first mate. The hull and sails of this vessel would have attracted no attention in the late 1700s.*

*This old unsigned, unidentified portrait shows a ship typical of the 1830s-1849s with barque and brigantine in the background. Ship and barque are likely typical of all Simon Graham's early vessels.*

Ship Hercules Lanched July 16th 18_

Saild from the Wharf Augt 24th and got over the Bar to Sea
And arived in Buctush on the 2th about 7. A.M.

Took in our fuel Cargo and Sailed Wednesday 24 at 5 A.M.
passed the N Cape of prince Edwards island at Midnight

25 at 6 P.M. passed the Magdalins at Mid Night the N Cape of Bird isld

26 at 4 A.M. St pauls N.W from 12 Miles which I take My Departure —

" at 6 A.M. found Six foot Water in the hold Both pumps Kept
Constantly working took in 2 Refs in topsails 1st in fore Sail
Handed the jib and Mizen and Mainsail
At Noon Reconed in 45.50 N 59.18 W. at 6 P.M. finding the Leak
to gain on the pumps we hove part of the Deck Load over the
to Ease the Ship

27 At Noon in 46.34 & 58.30 W Leak Still gaining we Bore up
for St peeters — 8 foot water in the hold — at 4 P.M. threw
Overboard the Remainder of our Deck Load to prevent the Ship
turning top heavy So Mutch Water Being in the hold

28 St peters N by W 10 Dist 10 at 4 A.M. Braced the Yoads and Stood in for
But the wind Being foul we thought it Better to Run for
St Johns as Necessaries for Repairs Might Not Be had there
Bore away and Made all Sail along the Land wind N.N.W.
Both pumps Kept Constantly gowing

29 At Noon Cape St Marys N.E Cope Race Ely N.N. Light winds
and Variable Both pumps Kept Constantly gowing Stell about
7 foot water in the hold

30th About Noon Came to in the Narrows went in Shore and got
Assistence to pump and warp the Ship up the harbour of St
Johns N.f.L

Oct 7th Sailed from St Johns 3.30 P.M. the pilot left us
Made all Sail for Liverpool England after unladen most
of our Cargow and Loading it again Now Making about
8 inches of water in 24 hours

*First page of the log of the ship* Hercules.

*Having the tiller bar on deck saved valuable space below, especially on small vessels. This example comes from a model, Britain's Queen, constructed c 1839 by James Lawton of the shipbuilding firm, William and James Lawton, Saint John, N.B., from lines provided by a Mr. Richey of Lloyds' London Office. Two other models in New Brunswick Museum have a similar arrangement.*

*Crank-operated pump of the last half of the 19th century. (Model in The New Brunswick Museum)*

## Chapter 8

*Night: tracing the vessel's progress. (*London Illustrated News, *January 20, 1849)*

*"She...Struck, Bilged and Filled with Water." (*London Illustrated News, *Sept. 4, 1852)*

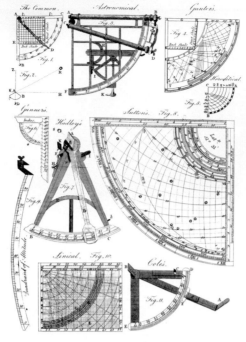

Quadrants. Hadley's sextant in the centre. (c 1812)

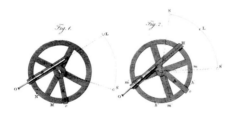

Mendoza's circular instrument.

MASTER'S CERTIFICATE OF SERVICE.

(Issued pursuant to the Act 13th and 14th Vict., cap. 93.)

Nº 39.7__

Number Thirty-Nine Thousand Seven Hundred and _Twenty seven_

*Simon Graham*

Born at _Kirkcudbright_ County of _Kirkcudbright_ on the _26th Feby 1796_
Has been employed in the Capacities of _App Mate & Master_ _38_ years in the
British Merchant Service principally in _the Foreign_ Trade.

Bearer's Signature _Simon Graham_

Granted by the REGISTRAR GENERAL OF SEAMEN, LONDON. By order of the BOARD OF TRADE.

_M Brown_ Registrar.

Issued at _London_

this _10th_ day of _February 51_

*.* Any Person Forging, Altering, or Fraudulently using this Certificate, will be subject to a penalty of FIFTY POUNDS, or THREE
MONTHS' Imprisonment with or without HARD LABOUR; and any other than the Person it belongs to becoming possessed of this Certificate,
is required to transmit it forthwith to the REGISTRAR GENERAL OF SEAMEN, LONDON.

Nº. OF REGISTER TICKET.

*Simon Graham's ticket*

*Graham's seal with the philosophical motto: "Such is Life." He also used a
signet ring bearing the arms of Graham of Montrose to which, likely, he
was not entitled.*

*The side cover of a small wooden box owned by Simon Graham. It bears the note "SIMON GRAHAM, SCHOONER DERWENT" and the date 1823 which appears to have been wrongly retouched to 1828, too late for the* Derwent.

*John Paul Jones' sextant, later Simon Graham*

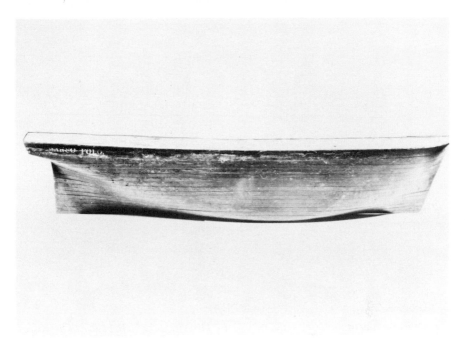

*The half-model from which* Marco Polo *was constructed.*

*Some details of rigging after about 1850. The location is the foremast top. Below are the shrouds and above are the topmast shrouds. Immediately below the top may be seen the futtock shrouds. The iron bracket and chains which hold the foresail yard are more sophisticated than early arrangements.*

*The barque* Thomas Cochrane, *627 tons, Dorchester, N.B., 1867. The vessel was small for the period yet it was almost 70% larger than* Sybylla. *She had a true clipper bow and stern. Her construction site sloped so as to obviate the need for blocking at the bow. Notice the riggers on the foremast.*

*The barque,* Queen of the Fleet, *941 tons, Dorchester, N.B., 1876, a fully evolved clipper shown on the port tack. The artist was W.H. Yorke, 1892.*

*The forecastle deck of an old model in The New Brunswick Museum portraying a vessel of about 1860 with clipper lines not extending, however, to the bow at the forecastle. The handles behind the twin Samson posts were the means of operating a steel jeers winch below. The little roundhouse was likely for spare sails which mildew quickly below deck.*

*The forecastle deck of **Marco Polo**, not greatly different from those of vessels 20 years earlier and lacking the sharpness of a clipper prow.*

Edna M. Smith, *736 tons, the last barque built in New Brunswick, newly launched at Harvey Bank, N.B., in November 1903. The vessel's masts are ashore where she was built. The barque* Thomas Cochrane, *Dorchester, N.B., 1867, was launched fully rigged.*

*Laying the deck and caulking seams of* Edna M. Smith. *The view forward the poop shows the vessel was launched stern-to.*

*The interior of Edna M. Smith on the stocks*

*Pit-sawing or whip-sawing for the Edna M. Smith. The guyed winch may have been a usual accessory but photographs of such an arrangement are rare.*

*The framed bow-opening is typical of those intended to facilitate the loading and unloading of long timbers and deals in timber droghers which had two or more similar ports in the stern as well. Notwithstanding other photographs of* Edna M. Smith *afloat show no bow-ports.*

*The bow of* Edna M. Smith *"in frame."*

*The modern clipper bow of* Edna M. Smith *still sported a pronounced cutwater and residual beak.*

*Two views of* Huntley, *a tern schooner of 1918, Grand Manan, N.B., courtesy of* Grand Manan Museum.

*Partridge Island, Saint John harbour: early 19th century, courtesy of* Public Archives of Canada.

*Bluff-bowed vessels, sketched c 1765 by F.J.W. Desbarres for a detail of* The American Neptune, *charts of the Atlantic coastline.*

*Saint John from the rock, Sandpoint, 1834, by General N. Smith, courtesy of* The New Brunswick Museum.

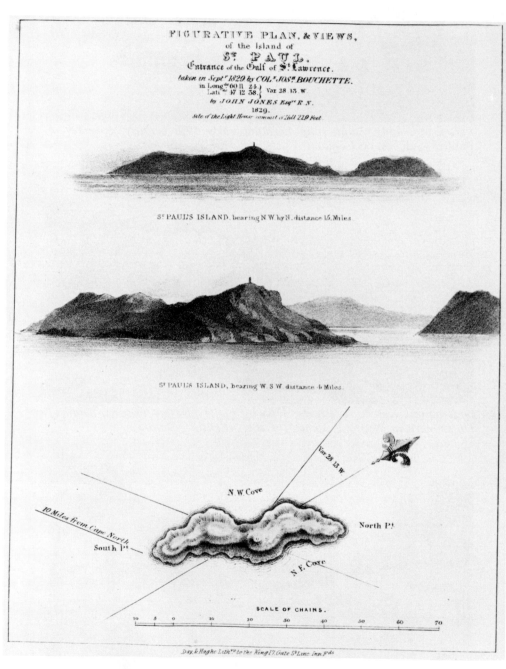

*St. Paul Island in the Gulf of St. Lawrence, "from which I take my departure."*

An abstract of a Voyage from Lpool
To Ruchibucto in the Ship Hannibal S. Graham
Master at 4 PM. May 8th 1843 Sailed from the Cowburg
Dock. Wind S.E at 7 pm the pilot Left us out Side the Wanks
9th at 6 Am passed below NW a Large fleet in companie

| | | | | | | | | | | | |
|---|---|---|---|---|---|---|---|---|---|---|---|
| | | | | | | | | | | | Departure from Saltees Lat 52 |
| W | 10 | SbyW | 51 | 33-3 | 38-2 | 51-33 | 57-33 | 1-2 | 7-36 | 7-38 | Fine wind at South |
| th | 11 | SebyW | 133 | 55-4 | 121-1 | 50-38 | " | 2-56 | 10-48 | | Strong gales & rain SW |
| F | 12 | NebW | 98 | 42-3 | 85-5 | 57-20 | | 2-22 | 13-11 | | Do weather and Showing Weat |
| S | 13 | SmW | 106 | 104-0 | 20-0 | 53-5 | 53-05 | 32 | 13-43 | 13-31 | More Moderate and Clear W |
| S | 14 | SSW | 109 | 16-3 | 107-2 | 52-48 | 52-47 | 2-58 | 16-41 | | Hazy wind at SE with haze |
| M | 15 | SSW | 96 | 23-3 | 93-1 | 52-24 | 52-35 | 2-33 | 19-14 | 18-55 | Moderate with a havy Westerly Swell |
| T | 16 | SbW | 157 | 46-7 | 154-1 | 51-39 | 51-42 | 4-11 | 23-24 | | Smart Breeze & hazy SE |
| W | 17 | SebW | 102 | 38-3 | 92-4 | 51-4 | 51-01 | 2-27 | 25-51 | | Light airs from SE Changing NW |
| Th | 18 | SbW | 191 | 46-4 | 185-3 | 50-14 | 50-14 | 14-53 | 30-45 | | Strong Breezes at E.N.E |
| F | 19 | SbW | 150 | 43-5 | 143-5 | 49-31 | 49-31 | 3-43 | 34-28 | 33-57 | Light and Variable from |
| S | 20 | SbW | 103 | 10-9 | 112-5 | 49-20 | 49-20 | 2-53 | 37-21 | | Strong Breezes at Nw |
| S | 21 | SW | 109 | 107-2 | 3-3 | 43-33 | 47-33 | -5 | 37-26 | 36-58 | Do weather |
| M | 22 | SbE | 142 | 141-3 | 13-9 | 45-11 | 45-11 | -20 | 37-06 | 37-10 | More Moderate & hazy Wly |
| T | 23 | NSW | 134 | 58-0 | 103-6 | 46-35 | 46-35 | 2-29 | 39-36 | 38-54 | Strong Breeze and hazy WSW |
| W | 24 | NbE | 75 | 27-0 | 44-7 | 47-2 | 47-2 | 1-05 | 40-40 | | Havy gails at W NW |
| Th | 25 | SyW | 92 | 90-2 | 18-0 | 45-32 | 45-32 | 0-25 | 41-05 | | Do weather |
| Fr | 26 | SwW | 85 | 93-4 | 16-6 | 44-8 | 44-9 | -23 | 41-28 | 40-38 | Calms & Variable |
| S | 27 | NSW | 135 | 6-6 | 134-8 | 44-16 | 44-16 | 3-8 | 44-36 | 43-31 | Fine Breeze and hazy at SW |
| S | 28 | NSW | 100 | 7-3 | 99-7 | 44-23 | 44-23 | 2-19 | 46-53 | | thick foggs and dead calm |
| M | 29 | SbW | 67 | 51-8 | 43-0 | 43-32 | 43-33 | 1-00 | 47-53 | 47-00 | Smart NW and foggs |
| T | 30 | SeW | 76 | 29-0 | 69-9 | 43-4 | " | 1-36 | 48-29 | | Thick foggs with Small rain N |
| W | 31 | NSW | 120 | 62-5 | 102-6 | 44-7 | | 2-22 | 51-57 | | Very thick foggs & rain SW |
| Th | 1 | SbW | 85 | 20-7 | 82-5 | 44-27 | 44-27 | 1-55 | 53-46 | 52-03 | Clear big great Many fishing Vessel |
| Fr | 2 | SbW | 74 | 3-6 | 46-4 | 44-26 | | 1-6 | 53-52 | | Light wind and rain |
| S | 3 | NbW | 144 | 73-0 | 73-5 | 45-39 | 45-42 | 1-44 | 55-36 | 54-5 | Strong winds and clear W |
| S | 4 | NbW | 102 | 53-9 | 86-6 | 46-36 | | 20-5 | 57-21 | | Strong W. and very thick NW |
| M | 5 | SbW | 34 | 1-8 | 33-9 | 46-3 | | 30 | 57-47 | | havy rain and thick SE |
| T | 6 | NbW | 62 | 13-3 | 60-0 | 44-16 | | 1-26 | 58-17 | 58.51 | Light wind & hazy Great Many |
| W | 7 | at Noon Entry Island NW dis 5 Miles Tacked | | | | | | | | | | to the SW wind WbSW hazy |
| Th | 8 | Strong W & N gails and Showers Noon Tacked | | | | | | | | | | close in with p'd Colar Islan |
| F | 9 | Light winds from the N and Clear in | | | | | | | | | | 46-51 Lh at 8 Am 62 34 W |

## Abstract of a Journal from St. John N.B. towards Sligo

In the Ship Swan — S. Graham Master Sailed 17th Sept 1844

18th at 8 Am Byng 30 laid N. E. by Et Dis 6 miles from whitch I take departure

| Week day | Month day | Course Pr to | Diff. of Lat. | Lat. if my act. | Lat. by bl. | Diff of Long Dr | Longt my bl. | Remarks on Board |
|---|---|---|---|---|---|---|---|---|
| Th | 19 | Light winds from N.E. | | | | Standing down the Bay Crew mostly Drunk | | |
| " | " | S3 E | 121 | 101·4 | 67·0 | 42·33 42·15 | 1·32 64·51 | 65·39 | Fine the wind W.N.W. Spoke a Schoo |
| Fr | 20 | N 84 E | 102 | 11·0 | 101·5 | 42·25 42·28 | 2·17 62·34 | 63·43 | Fine wind W.S.W. people clearing decks all Sail Set |
| S | 21 | S 72 E | 162 | 35·14 | 157·2 | 43·7 43·07 | 3·35 58·59 | 60·43 | Fine to Am Spoke the Mary of Shields from London Bound to St Johns |
| S | 22 | N 46 E | 180 | 43·5 | 122·4 | 43·50 43·50 | 2·48 56·11 | 57·35 | Fine the Wind S.S.E. |
| M | 23 | N 74 E | 104 | 28·5 | 100·2 | 44·18 | " 2·19 53·52 | | Thick rains wind at E.S.E. |
| T | 24 | S 60 E | 85 | 42·5 | 73·7 | 44·55 | 1·44 52·08 | | Strong Breezes and hazy with rain |
| W | 25 | S 82 E | 161 | 27·5 | 157·4 | 44·28 44·28 | 3·45 48·23 | 51·44 | Strong do. passed Several fishing Sounded in 45 fathoms on the Gr Bank |
| Th | 26 | S 75 E | 144 | 41·8 | 137·8 | 43·47 43·47 | 2·46 45·37 | | Moor Sounded in 28 fathoms |
| " | " | Sounded off the Grand Bank at 6 PM from whitch I take a fresh departure |||||| | the Log Line being marked 9 feet | |
| Fr | 27 | S 82 E | 48 | 25·9 | 38·2 | 43·17 43·14 | - 53 47·57 | 47·48 | Strong Easterly Breezes and Clear |
| S | 28 | S 82 E | 77 | 11·1 | 76·1 | 43·3 | " 1·44 46·13 | | Strong Breezes at and hazy |
| S | 29 | N 6 E | 158 | 38·4 | 153·3 | 43·41 43·41 | 3·30 42·43 | 41·39 | Moderate and hazy |
| M | 30 | N 8 E | 95 | 51·7 | 73·2 | 44·48 44·48 | 1·52 40·57 | 39·56 | Moderate two Brig in Sight Standing East ward |
| T | 1 | N 60 E | 192 | 40·5 | 169·3 | 46·18 46·21 | 4·04 36·47 | 35·45 | Strong Breezes and Clear |
| " | " | at 10 Am Exchanged Signals with the American Ship Partheon |||||||| |
| W | 2 | N 40 E | 207 | 64·9 | 193·0 | 47·26 47·26 | 4·40 32·07 | 31·35 | Fine Strong S.W. winds & hazy |
| Th | 3 | N 75 E | 175 | 36·6 | 186·6 | 48·23 48·23 | 4·11 27·56 | | Do. weather passed a Barque to the Eastward |
| F | 4 | S 8 E | 86 | 17·9 | 82·1 | 48·5 | " 2·5 25·51 | | Strong gales at East |
| S | 5 | N 8 E | 96 | 27·0 | 91·6 | 48·32 48·32 | 2·18 23·39 | 22·11 | Strong Breezes and Squalls |
| S | 6 | N 6 E | 142 | 54·3 | 131·2 | 49·26 49·26 | 3·30 20·18 | 18·14 | Squalls & flying Showers |
| M | 7 | N 8 E | 134 | 38·9 | 128·2 | 50·5 50·5 | 3·20 16·59 | 15·00 | Moderate and hazy |
| T | 8 | N 60 E | 193 | 36·6 | 184·7 | 50·53 | " 4·50 12·09 | 10·10 | Hard gales 7 PM close |

The crew may have been green hands and not used to such a threatening situation. In any case, the master's judgment was good; the vessel made a speedy crossing.

It is clear that *Perekop* was not completely rigged when she set out on her voyage. This seems to have been the rule of the shipyards. The lower and topmasts were set and rigged — sufficient for the vessel to be seaworthy. The topgallant and royal masts were sent up and rigged by the crew; otherwise, failing bad weather when such masts were unnecessary, there was no work for the crew aboard a new vessel.

An inexperienced crew, perhaps shorthanded, faced with pumping a leaky vessel, deckload to jettison, new rigging to set and damaged rigging to repair may have been overwhelmed by the magnitude of the task. They would have been clumsy and unsure aloft. Further, the dispute between the master and Mr. McCulloch would have set a bad example.

Reference to a steward, cabin bread and coffee for the cabin breakfast suggests that *Perekop* carried passengers. Assuredly, Mr. McCulloch was not a mate, who would have had little interest in retaining the deck load and who certainly would not have disobeyed the master in such a matter. McCulloch was, then, a passenger and the agent of the cargo's owner. From other information, it is quite certain that Annie Graham, the master's wife, was aboard.

Cabin bread was bread in the usual sense, not the hardtack fed to the crew. There would have been a great dissimilarity between cabin and forecastle food. The passengers would have taken cooked fowl, hams, bacon, bottled beer, reasonably soft biscuits and other luxurious foods aboard in hampers. It was the custom of the day. This may have proved too much for an undisciplined crew to accept.

The following letter from Dorchester, N.B., completely authenticated, provides a hint of conditions 12 years later.

Liverpool Feb 12th, 1867

Dear Brother:

I suppose that by this time you know that Charles was drowned. It was on the 18th of January when about half passage he was washed overboard from the bowsprit by a sea. We threw over lines and some deals but he was unable to reach them. And by the time we got the vessel around...he had sunk to rise no more. He was floating on the water about ten minutes. We had a very hard time coming across and have been here now about 12 days and are only half discharged I expect we will be here about a month longer and then go to Boston with a general cargo.

I expect to come home in the spring if I live and have my health if I do not call up to Dan Lowreys too often for I am as wild as ever...if I live and have my health to get across to the other side again Bill Hickman and old Hance Atkinson will not get me to cross the Western Ocean again in the Middle of Winter with half a crew and starve us to death in the bargain....I do not want you to preach Charles' funeral sermon till I come home for me and all the boys want to hear it.

From your affectionate brother,

"Isaac Smith"

# Simon Graham, Master Mariner

In the year 1850, by Act 13th and 14th, Vict. Cap. 93, all masters and mates of seagoing vessels were required, without exception, to obtain a Certificate of Service. Possession of such a certificate was intended as proof of competency. Before the certificate would be granted, applicants had to produce evidence of adequate experience. Simon Graham applied at Port of London, 4 November 1850, and in the space allotted to recording the number of his existing Register Ticket, he wrote "never had any." He was then 54 years of age and had spent 37 years at sea, all but four of them as mate or master.

Under the heading, Particulars of Service, claimants had to provide details of six kinds: Vessels' Names; Port Belonging To; Tons; Capacity — Whether Apprentice, Seaman, Master, or Mate; In What Trade; and Date of Service. The record set down by Simon Graham and attested to by one G.W. Morgan of London yields information about Simon's early career that might not have been found otherwise. Simon Graham's "Master's Claim for Certificate of Service" and his later "Master's Certificate of Service," No. 39777, 19 Feb. 1852, are both retained at the office of Mercantile Marine Records in Woolwich, England. Here is the data Simon set down, in his own spelling.

> *Druid*, Kirkcudbright, 35 tons, Apprentice, Costing,[1,] 11 July
> 1813 – 1817
> *Neptune*, Whitehaven, 30 tons, Mate, Costing, 7 months.
> *North Star*, Dumfries, 85 tons, 2 Mate, Foreign, 6 months.
> *Sarah*, Whitehaven, 75 tons, 1 Mate, Costing, 6 months.
> *Barbra & Margrate*, Dumfries, 45 tons, 1 Mate, Costing, 10 months
> *Alementina*, Dumfries, 50 tons, 1 Mate, Costing, 3 months.
> *Dusty Miller*, Kirkcudbright, 45 tons, 1 Mate, Costing, 3 months.
> *Elizabeth*, Kirkcudbright, 65 tons, Master, Costing, Jan 1819-1823.
> *Derwent*, Workingtown, 80 tons, Master, Costing, 18 months.
> *Matthews*,[2] Kirkcudbright, 153 tons, Master, Foreign, 1825-1830.
> *Colonial Yact Fort*,[3] Halifax, 153 tons, Master, Nfld. Stn.,
> 1830-31.
> *Sarah*, Halifax, 150 tons, Master, Foreign, 1831-1832.
> *Sybilla*, Halifax, 375 tons, Master, Foreign, 1832-1835.
> *Richibucto*, Richibucto, 400 tons, Mate, Foreign, 3 months.
> *Hirculas (Hercules)*, Richibucto, 800 tons, Master, Foreign, 6
> months.
> *Devonport*, Liverpool, 773 tons, Master, Foreign, 5 months.

*Caledonia*, St. John NB, 518 tons, Master, Foreign, 1837-1839.
*Ammy (Amy)*, St. John N.B., 458 tons, Master, Foreign, 1839-1840.
*Cambridge*, St. John NB, 328 tons, Master, Foreign, 1840-1841.
*Hannibal*, Richibucto, 583 tons, Master, Foreign, 1841-1844.
*Swan*, St. John, 800 tons, Master, Foreign, 6 months.
*Grampian*, Liverpool, 774 tons, Master, Foreign, 1844-1850.

"Directions" on the reverse side of the application told claimants to state where they would be from and after 1 December 1850 so as to be able to pick up their certificates or to renew their applications and have their certificates before 1 January 1851. Simon Graham was far from a British port 1850 through 1851 and couldn't take possession of his before January 1852. The Master's Certificate, about 4" x 7", was printed in duplicate on one sheet of paper. When properly completed, the two forms were separated with scissors. One was given to the Master and the other, stamped "Office Counterpart," was filed with Mercantile Marine Records.

Simon Graham's first nine vessels in the coastal service of the British Isles were likely schooners, possibly brigs or brigantines. Since he stated that the vessels were coastal and not fishing, it is not likely that they were hookers,[4] as he later referred to fishing craft. None of them, it may be observed, was anywhere near the burden of the modest schooner whose portrait adorns the reverse side of the current Canadian dime.

We see that Simon Graham worked his way up from the forecastle to the master's cabin. His climb was doubtless not made easier by the fact that he was apprenticed to the trade. Tradition has it that masters treated apprentices roughly. Seamen leaned towards a man who made his own way in such a fashion. They recognized that while earning the position of mate he had to be the equal of any man aboard his vessel and, most likely, the best among good men. They knew that throughout his apprenticeship and service as second mate, his position aloft was on the weather earing of the highest yard, – unless circumstances found an even more dangerous and difficult location demanding his skill. Officers who obtained their ranks by favour or schooling ashore, are said by sailors (deprecatingly) to have got them by way of the hawsepipe.

Simon Graham was a true seadog. He was six years at sea before he gained command of a 65 ton cockleshell manned by three or four men and was knocked about for 12 years by the vicious small seas around the British Isles before he acquired a vessel of respectable proportions in which to attempt the wide Atlantic Ocean. Seamen who survived such an education were competent beyond doubt.

Tradition in Richibucto relates that many of the early settlers were brought to that part of New Brunswick by Simon Graham. Edward L.

Gallagher reiterates this in a small book, *History of Old Kingston and Rexton.* He names the vessel *Dickes,*[5] its captain, Simon Graham, and some passengers, among them the first of the famous Jardines. The evidence of Simon Graham's application for a Certificate of Competency refutes Gallagher's belief. Captain Graham may have transported latecomers to the area, but not before 1825.

Lloyds Register provides some meagre details of his first foreign command, the *Matthews.* She was a brig of 152 tons and not at all well recommended. Her voyages are not clearly recorded but, if one may use the arithmetic of 2 x 2 yielding 5, Simon Graham's career between 1825 and 1830 may be summed up quite neatly.

For three years or so he voyaged regularly to a mysterious port known to Lloyds as Lgbrn. No harbour around the British Isles, in Europe or across the Atlantic has a name which will readily yield such an abbreviation. Nevertheless, Lgbrn must have been Liverpool (Richibucto) New Brunswick because in that place Simon Graham bought a parcel of land, registered on 3 September 1827. The grantors were James McClelland and his wife, he by his signature, she by her mark. The grantee was "Simon Graham, seafaring man at present in Liverpool." His wife was not mentioned. The parcel contained 100 acres and the consideraton was 45 pounds or $1.80 per acre. The land was situated adjacent to New Galloway burying grounds and appears to be the same which Simon computed so carefully in 1835.

In 1828 and 1829 Simon's pattern of voyages changed somewhat. *Matthews* called at Halifax and later at Port of Miramichi and Dublin, Ireland. Joseph and Henry Cunard were both in Miramichi at that time, indeed since 1820, and their brother Samuel was already a prosperous shipowner in Halifax. Considering the small populations of the day, the four men must have been acquainted.

Passing south of Newfoundland (the use of the Straits of Belle Isle to the north came later, with steamers), inward or outward bound from Miramichi in 1829, Simon must have put into St. John's and there parted company with *Matthews.* The brig, however, continued to call at St. John's, under another master, Donaldson, through 1830 and 1831. Simon found himself a command more attractive in St. John's. As master of Governor Sir Thomas Cochrane's Yacht, H.M. Colonial Brig *Forte,* loaded with 8 six-pound cannon, rum and rum-drinkers, he began another phase of his career.

Knowledge of Simon's new command begins with a letter addressed to Mr. Graham, Master and Acting Commander, H.M. Col. Vessel *Forte,* St. John's, Newfoundland. It is franked by Henry P. Steele and is dated (aboard *Forte* ) 1 June 1831:

Dear Sir, Having obtained leave of absence for four months from this date and His Excellency Sir Thomas Cochrane having sanctioned my leaving you in the temporary command acting for me until further orders, I write you these presents today. I will make your pay £10 currency or $40 per month during the time you continue to act for me — to commence this day and you will be entitled to the undisturbed use of my Cabin, and you will supply yourself at your own expence with such small stores as you may require, it being quite understood you do not make any use of the accommodation abaft the glazed door of my Cabin, at any time without leave from His Excellency Sir Thomas Cochrane to do so.

I am Sir, Yours very truly,

Henry P. Steele, Capt.

From *The Royal Gazette and Newfoundland Advertiser* it is learned that Steele assumed command: "1 December 1829. By Authority. His Excellency has been pleased to appoint Henry P. Steele, Esquire, Lieutenant of the Royal Navy to be Captain of His Majesty's Colonial Vessel *Forte*"

On the same day: "WANTED — immediately in the Service of His Majesty's Colonial Yacht, the *Forte*, a chief mate, who can be well recommended, and will engage for at least one year from 1st. December. Apply to Captain Steele on board or Messers W & H Thomas."

Simon Graham joined *Forte* on 1 December 1829 as chief mate (to Henry Steele) or, as sailing master. His application for a certificate, years later, says he was master of *Forte* 1830-31 although, as will be seen, he omitted reference to another command later in 1831. Certainly Graham was aboard *Forte* in some capacity before Steele's letter to him for, in May 1831, he drew up an account headed "Yacht's Disbursements May 1831." A quantity of rum purchased and, presumably, consumed seems also to have had its cost expressed in terms of cleaning and repairing the cabin, rehabilitating the furniture and providing new tableware. A goblet etched with Simon's signature is extant and may be one of those referred to as costing 15 shillings and sixpence for nine.

The accounts, taken with reports in the *Public Ledger* of St. John's, Newfoundland, make clear that the expenses were incurred in transporting government to the outports of Newfoundland and Labrador. They suggest that *Forte* was sheathed with copper, that her decks were holystoned (Bermuda stone) and that other woodwork was treated with seal oil.

Only one of Simon's copies of *Forte*'s logs has survived. It covers the return passage of a voyage to Cowes, England, made in the fall of 1831. It is headed "England to St. John's N.F.L. in the Brig foart Nov 9." It was a rough passage. *Forte* suffered considerable superficial damage and one potentially serious blow. On December 13, "a sea carried away our iron tiller." The happening and Simon's precise wording indicate that *Forte* may have had no wheel but was steered by means of a long bar on deck, working directly on the rudder. Such an arrangement was not unusual on vessels of *Forte*'s burden, 152 tons, of the period. Brigs of that burden lacked raised forecastles and poops.

Captain Steele left for Britain before Simon Graham took *Forte* to Cowes. A Captain Buchan replaced Steele in England and was in actual command on *Forte*'s return to St. John's. A personality conflict between Simon and the vessel, perhaps between Simon Graham and Buchan, may have arisen for, three weeks later, Simon was in temporary command of another brig, *Leander*,[6] bound for Oporto, Portugal.

*Leander* carried 10,393 gallons of cod and seal oil and 2,335 quintals of fish (dried cod), all contained in 196 casks. Oporto was then threatened with siege by Miguelite supporters. Three or four months later the siege began. It lasted for a year and 16,000 citizens died in defence of the city.

A tradition of receiving, aging and reshipping Portuguese wine from Oporto (Port Wine) had long been carried on at St. John's and it may be that the impending siege thwarted a plan to return with tuns of the rich red blood of the vineyards. In the event, *Leander* sailed from Oporto to Norfolk, Virginia, from thence to New York and, not delaying there long enough to load or unload, made for St. John's where she came to on June 4, 1832. Captain Graham omitted reference to *Leander* in the list of vessels on his certificate application.

Simon Graham is lost to record briefly but then, on 3 August 1832, he sailed from Halifax as master of the barque *Sarah*,[7] bound for Liverpool, England He made Queen's Dock, there, in 27 days. He had passengers aboard but in this log, the only one in which Simon recorded the names of his passengers, time and waterstain have all but erased his handwriting.

*Sarah* was owned by Samuel Cunard. She was either sold in Liverpool or left there in a different trade, because Graham immediately returned to Halifax aboard *Corsair*,[8] another brig, commanded by Captain Jenkinson. He may have been a passenger, he may have been mate, or he may have shared the master's duties. In any case, he kept a full log of the voyage, October 28 to November 24, 1832.

Again Simon Graham is lost for a few months. It is tempting to think that he visited Richibucto but, in his application for Certificate, he says he commanded *Sybilla (Sybylla)* in 1832. It is likely that his logs have been lost for, on 3 September 1833, he made a one-page, loose Abstract of a

"Jurnal: (corrected from Voyage), Sydney C.B. to New York." *Sybylla* was fast alongside the wharf at "Brookland" on September 17, 1833.

Simon Graham was then close to beginning his first major voyage, if one dismisses Atlantic crossings as something less, around Cape Horn to Nicaragua. In the intervening six weeks before leaving New York on that voyage, he made one trip indicated by some indecipherable scraps of log. Except for a period of three months when he was mate of *Richibucto*, Captain Graham's voyages appear all to have been recorded in his logs until 1855 when, without a crew to take his vessel the last few hundred yards, he landed at Liverpool.

Logs later than that of *Perekop* have been lost, but scraps of information show that Simon Graham continued at sea. A book, *The Mechanic's Bride*, U. Cambridge, Boston, 1857, bears this note on its flyleaf: "Simon Graham's Book Bought Charleston 1857 South Carolina." Another was bought in New York in 1859.

In 1863, the *Chatham Gleaner* carried this terse item under shipping news: "Cleared Richibucto, November 19, Bark *Janet Patterson*[9] (new vessel). Graham, for Liverpool, Lumber, J & T Jardine." Yes! It was the old seadog, 67 years young and bound to try his luck once more against the treacherous North Atlantic. A month or two later the ever-vigilant *Gleaner* reported this sad news under the heading SHIPWRECK.

> The Editor of the Halifax *Express* says he has been informed by letter dated Gros Isle Magdelene Islands, December 3rd., of the loss of the ship JANET PATTERSON of and from Richibucto loaded with deals and bound for Liverpool, G.B. The J.P. is a new vessel, 707 tons register, cost some £10,000, was on her first voyage and was wrecked 40 hours after leaving Richibucto. Crew all saved and were sent to the mainland by Lloyds' agent.

So Simon Graham returned to Richibucto more than a little crestfallen, it may be supposed; but wait a moment! Both Simon Graham and *Janet Patterson* may have made Liverpool safely. Lloyds' Registers carried the following records for 1864, 1865, 1866, 1867 and 1868: "JANET PATTERSON, ship, 708 tons, S. Graham, Master; built and owned by J & T Jardine, Port of Registry Miramichi; voyages Mir (sic) to Liverpool.

It is not now possible to know what happened after *Janet Patterson* was run aground. On the face of things Lloyds' Register has to be accepted. It is impossible not to admire a stout-hearted old bundle of rawhide like Simon Graham, still eager at 67 years of age to defy Davey Jones; and continuing to do so two years after his allotted three score years and ten have been used up in the same dangerous career.

A letter to his grand-daughter attending Mount Allison Academy in Sackville, N.B., shows that Simon Graham was in Richibucto in 1874. His hand and wit were both as firm as ever.

A book bearing the notation: "Simon Graham's Book, dublin, 1876" indicates that he was abroad at 80 years of age but he could not then have commanded a vessel. He died two years later[10] at Rexton (then Kingston) adjoining Richibucto and was buried in the Presbyterian Cemetery there. His tombstone bears the inscription:

> Simon Graham, Master Mariner, Native of Colvend, Kirkcudbright, Kirkcudbrightshire, Scotland, died 17 April 1878 aged 82 years.

His son James G. died at sea aged 2 years 7 months.

## CHAPTER 14

# From Stem to Gudgeon

Nudged by nostalgia upon the disappearance of canvas from the great oceans, writers immediately began to set down the record of the long age of sail. Many magnificently illustrated works, British, American and, more lately, Canadian, have followed. From them a clear picture of the evolution of sailing craft may be obtained.

Nevertheless, one finds some aspects of shipbuilding ignored or, at best, dismissed as lacking interest. For instance, most North American writers mention that design of a hull took the form of carving a half-model from which shapes were transferred, full-size, to a molding loft floor where patterns were then prepared but none provides reasons for such a procedure, assuming them to be obvious, perhaps.

Words alone are insufficient for conveying the concept of a particular vessel to be constructed. Drawings are not much better because many different views must be prepared to substitute for those presented when a model is turned before the eyes. Drawings also deny a craftsman use of the sense of feel which is a valuable interpretive aid when one is dealing with small objects in three dimensions. Models, then, were the natural manner of portraying the vessel to be built.

Design of a wooden hull comprised determining the precise shapes and dimensions of a great number of bits and pieces for assembly into a composite whole. This could not be done accurately on drawings at a scale of, say one-eighth inch on the drawing representing a foot on the hull. The ratio being 1:96, a vessel 200 feet long becomes 25 inches on the drawing and an ink line $\frac{1}{32}$" thick represents a quarter of a foot on the hull. Further, there being only one straight hull line, the longitudinal centreline, it was not possible to determine dimensions arithmetically. Nevertheless, a drawing had to be prepared before the shapes and dimensions of hull components could be determined.

This was done at full scale on the molding loft floor, all the hull lines being laid down one over another and marked with keel or ruddle, a hard, grease-filled ochre chalk. The dimensions were taken from the model but, being increased 96 times, they were wildly inaccurate. The skill of the master shipwright had then to be called upon, and he adjusted the sweep of each curved line so that all were relatively correct. This was called "fairing the hull." It was the actual process of fixing the lines of the hull for construction purposes.

To facilitate the layout of lines, a model was sometimes built up of flat laminations, their thicknesses being to a predetermined scale. They were pinned together to make up the hull shape but could be separated to yield scale plans at elevations about three feet apart. Since pieces made for one side could be turned over to yield those for the other side of the hull, only a half-model and a half-drawing were necessary. By reversing shapes, pieces were made identical but, right and left hand. The holding loft floor was of the best pine planks available so that marks could be removed later by planing. Its joints made useful reference lines.

On the loft floor a pattern or mold was made for each piece of timber in the hull, the keel, keelson and planking excepted, of course. The work was done with precision yet great accuracy was not achieved. This was deliberate and two examples illustrate the reason. They concern futtocks (foot-hooks), the individual pieces of curved timbers later joined together to form ribs.

A precise fit is necessary where futtocks butt one against the other. This was obtained when fashioning the futtocks by setting the ends, already shaped as well as possible, against one another and then sawing across the joint so formed. The kerf of the saw-cut made the two ends an exact match so that they fitted when moved in the width of the kerf.

The faces of ribs, inside and out, were not square, particularly at bow and stern. When erected in position they had to be dubbed by highly skilled adzemen to accept the curves of the ceiling and sheathing. In effect, these men finally faired the hull as they smoothed timbers to agree with their neighbours. The patterns or molds allowed for this extra work.

The stem, the forepost of the hull and its numerous pieces of strengthening timbers, deadwood, all had to be fitted in place despite the care put into the molds. Small pieces like gudgeons, the braces that project aft of the stern to hold the rudder, were designed and fitted as work progressed to their points of inclusion. Thus, although everyone knew what was to be done and how to do it, final design ran with construction.

Almost every piece of shaped wood that went into a vessel had its own name, usually descriptive of its position or function. A list of many hundreds of components could easily be set down for an ordinary merchantman. For a warship the list would run to thousands of items.

The term "planking" is, today, commonly used for the exterior wooden skin of a hull — the material, as well as the application of it. That usage of the word is somewhat misleading in that it suggests covering the ribs with planks which, compared with timbers, are only moderately thick but wide, like boards. Planks served in the construction of light craft but larger vessels required heavy dimension lumber which, owing to curvature of the hull, had often to be hewed to shape with axe or adze after being set in place. Such timbers could not be bent by steaming as is often claimed owing to lack of adequate boilers and machinery. Individual pieces were strakes, each being known by its location on the hull.

Strakes varied greatly in their dimensions and sometimes in the species of wood used from keel upward to the rail. The lowest or garboard strakes were sometimes ten inches thick and not wider. Those above the loadwaterline were thinner, the wales, heavier. The interior lining of a hull, the ceiling, used material more like planks in shape. Sheathing might be a better word than planking for the exterior skin, but for the fact that sheathing seems to have become associated with the application of copper plates outside as protection against the teredo, a kind of marine worm or, rather, mollusc that bores into wooden hulls and which is commonly called the shipworm.

Particular species and varieties of wood were favoured for certain locations and functions. Strength and durability were prime considerations but hardness, toughness, workability, availability, cost and even appearance had to be taken into account. Early records, ever scant, are rarely much help when taken separately but, when they are brought together, an acceptable picture may be assembled. Its view has been rendered obscure, nevertheless, by writers who have taken late records, accounts from various areas and oral tradition as indicative of all ages and practice.

Alex Monro, writing in *New Brunswick, Nova Scotia and Prince Edward Island*, in 1851, had this to say about shipbuilding materials: "The descriptions of timber generally used are Spruce, Birch, Maple, Ash, Oak, Elm, Beech and Hacmatac. Ships built of the latter are most durable and safe; they class for seven years while those built of the other materials only class for three or not higher than four years."

H.Y. Hind (and five others) in *Eighty Years' Progress of British North America*, went a little further in 1863. They reported: "The forests of New Brunswick supply timber of large size, in any quantity, for building ships of the first class. Such ships are principally built of black birch and larch or hackmatack. The black birch is used for the keel, floor timbers and lower planking; larch or hackmatack for all the other timbers, knees and upper planking. American live and white oak are imported for the stems and posts of superior ships, and pitch pine for the beams. White pine is used for the cabins and interior finishing and for masts. The black spruce furnishes as fine yards and topmasts as any in the world. Elm, beech, maple, cedar and spruce are used in construction of ships of the second class and for small vessels."

Stanley T. Spicer, in *Masters of Sail*, reiterates those species and adds others, some exotic, some vague. He mentions, quoting *The American Shipmasters' Association Instructions to Surveyors* but without a date: White and Red Oaks, Live Oak, Teak, Locust, Green Heart, Red Cedar, White Chestnut, Bayshore Spruce and Common Spruce. Spicer notes that the Instructions assign an A1 classification (underwriters' arbitrary life expectancy) of ten years for vessels or parts of Live Oak, Teak, Locust and Green Heart with fewer years granted for the other woods — down to only three years for Red Oak when used for planking "above the bilges."

Monro's comments are the more reliable with regard to early shipbuilding in Eastern Canada, supported as they are by Hind. The latter's reference to American oak and pitch pine, 12 years after Monro, shows two influences; the presence of Lloyds surveyors in New Brunswick and the growing shortage of native timbers. It may be inferred from Spicer's observations, since he was writing about ships of the Maritime Provinces, that the woods he mentions were commonly employed in construction there, but that was not so. The A.S.A. standard doubtless applied to vessels constructed anywhere under the watchful eyes of the Association's surveyors but that is not to say that materials used in one part of the world were representative of those in another. Shipbuilding in British North America was surveyed and classed almost exclusively by Lloyds of London. Before 1851, with some exceptions, the surveying was done on completion of the vessel and usually abroad, in an English port. In 1851, Lloyds surveyors were officially and permanently stationed in British North America.

Lloyds Registers reveal almost exclusive use of local woods in early vessels constructed in Eastern Canada, that is, through the era of our interest. The Locusts are not native to Canada though they are becoming naturalized in some localities. The Cedars and Oaks were never plentiful in the Maritimes, at least in useful varieties, dimensions and quantities. The situation was not quite so limiting in those parts of Quebec situated within the once-great St. Lawrence Hardwood Forest. Teak and Green Heart (Greenheart) are foreign woods, the former native to the Indian sub-continent and the latter, rarely imported to Eastern Canada, to South America.

The situation was different for Britain, which had to rely on foreign materials. Except for some parklands of fine oak safeguarded for the Royal Navy, Britain had exhausted her shipbuilding woods a century or more before Simon Graham entered upon his career. The situation had become so critical that in the eighteenth century no live timber could be cut for firewood. Hedge-row trees (especially compass-timber) were counted and the use of waterpowered sawmills was banned because of waste in the wide kerfs made by crude blades. (Later, when power mills were permitted, hand-sawyers rioted in protest.)

Britain had, then, to import all lumber required for her navy and merchant marine. Her main sources, often interrupted by wars, were in the Baltic States and British North America. At the same time, the East India fleet had vessels constructed in the far east of teak and other superior species and, doubtless, on occasion, for lack of a more valuable cargo, brought shiploads of teak back to British shipbuilders. Judge T.C. Haliburton of Nova Scotia tells us, in *The Attache*, that in 1814 he "embarked at Halifax on board the Buffalo, storeship, for England. She was a noble teak-built ship of twelve or thirteen hundred tons burden."

Soon after the end of the American Revolution British shipbuilders began to establish themselves in the remaining North American colonies.[1] The trade assumed such promising proportions in New Brunswick by 1825 that an act (V Geo. IV Ch. 14) then required that every shipbuilder employ two apprentices under indentures of four years for each vessel of one hundred tons or more constructed. A penalty of £50 — really a substantial sum considering the small cost of an apprentice — was to be levied for each contravention. The year marked the start of half a century of shipbuilding in New Brunswick not equalled anywhere throughout the history of wooden hulls, if the criterion used is tons of production per head of population.

Three species within the New Brunswick forests permitted the astounding production of ships. They were Larch, Pine and Birch. Although Pine, really the only material suited to mast use, by virtue of its great lengths and girths, was most highly valued it would not have, alone, enabled the growth of shipbuilding. Larch and Birch presented qualities lacking in each other and in Pine. None of the three was in the class of the most esteemed foreign species but they were plentiful, easily worked and adequate in performance.

Eastern Larch, *Larix laricina (Du Roi)* K. Koch, better known as Hackmatack, or Tamarack, and sometimes wrongly called Juniper, provided the general all-purpose wood for Eastern Canadian shipbuilding. It is moderately hard, heavy and oily for a softwood, strong and quite resistant to decay. It was once common in parts of the Acadian Forest where mature trees 18 to 24 inches in diameter and 40-50 feet in length were almost completely cut out.

Most forest trees were cut for the prime sawlogs in their trunks. Hackmatack was more fully utilised, however. The curved sections where root and trunk joined yielded a most valuable bracket, haunch or knee for use in seating a beam against a column. A typical application was in the attaching of deck beams to the ribs of vessels.

Several species of wood provide sufficient strength for such a purpose but Hackmatack, in addition to the properties noted above, is more easily worked than most woods of equal density and it is tougher than many dense hardwoods. Toughness may be considered as an ability to flex and redistribute stress, so delaying the reaching of a breaking load. Strength in wood is generally proportionate to density but toughness is related to fibre pattern.

A natural shape (compass timber) is valued in a curved wooden member, regardless of size, because the fibres which partly govern strength flow around the curvature without interruption. They may be regarded as being in tight bundles that separate far more easily along their length than across the bundles. Curved shapes cut from straight fibre bundles, straight-grained wood, present numerous parallel cleavage planes that constitute potential sources of failure by splitting.

Yellow Birch, *Betula alleghaniensis Britton (Betula lutea Michx,* f.) known in New Brunswick as Black Birch and elsewhere as Silver, Golden or Red Birch, was almost as important to shipbuilders as was Hackmatack. The wood is hard, heavy, strong and durable. Logs of 20 inches in diameter and 40 feet in length were not uncommon and they provided fine keel material.

Black Birch, to use the name of the period, accepted stain and oil well and the wavy fibre pattern found in many logs was quite handsome. It also found favour as show wood, therefore, particularly for panelling of cabins.

White or Paper Birch, *Betula papyrifera Marsh*, lacks the useful properties of Black Birch and it was not used in ships.

Eastern White Pine, *Pinus Strobus L*, the giant of the Acadian Forest, yielded spar materials. Alex Monro noted the common size of squared logs in 1850, after years of cutting, as 21 inches by 60 feet. The wood is light, not particularly strong nor decay-resistant but those faults gave way to the tremendous sizes not matched by other native trees. White Pine was adequately strong for three inch thick decking. This was a common use because the wood could be either holystoned to a near white contrast with painted bulwarks or it could be heavily oiled to resist the effects of continuous wetting.

Some modern writers suggest a difference between White Pine and Yellow, specifying different applications for their woods: White Pine for spars and Yellow for decking "because it does not swell and shrink with alternate wetting and drying." This is defective because all woods change dimensions owing to increased or decreased moisture content. This may be less pronounced in dense woods but White and Yellow Pines, if different, are so closely related as to have similar properties. Unless the writer implies the Yellow Pine to have been an imported variety he is misled by regional names. They include the following variants all referring to *Pinus Strobus*: White, Yellow, Soft, Canadian, Pumpkin, Weymouth, Quebec, Pattern and Cork.

Red Pine, *Pinus resionosa Ait.*, was useful but not favoured by British shipowners despite good properties of size, strength and durability above the waterline. Notwithstanding its lack of general popularity, the wood was often incorporated in British North American vessels as shown by Lloyds Register.

The three varieties of eastern Spruce, *Picea A. Dietr.*, were used interchangeably for yards, decking and, in small vessels, for planking, ceiling, beams and ribs. They include Red Spruce, White Spruce and Black Spruce. Although the woods of the three varieties differ, little attention was paid to the fact, size of particular specimens being more important to the user. More importantly, it is limber or flexible to an extent that made it valuable for spar use.

Only one of the Canadian Oaks, *Quercus alba L.*, White Oak, was useful to shipbuilders. Its wood is hard, heavy, strong, tough, rot-resistant and slow to take fire. White Oak was therefore much sought after and, being scarce in the Maritime Provinces, quantities were sometimes imported from Quebec or the United States for special purposes. Red Oak, more common, is not a useful wood, being so porous that air may be blown through lengths of several feet.

White Ash, *Fraxinus americana L.*, was plentiful in the Maritimes. The wood is tough, hard, heavy and strong, although coarse grained. It was useful in small construction but few references are found to its employment in shipbuilding. Oral tradition suggests that mast cringles, the sliding hoops that hold fore-and-aft sails to their masts, were one use. Black Ash, plentiful but not as strong, hard or durable as White Ash, had no value to the shipbuilder.

Only one of several maples occurring in the Maritimes offered worthwhile properties to marine construction. Sugar Maple, *Acer saccharum Marsh*, also known as Hard Maple and Rock Maple, yields a heavy, hard, strong wood suitable for many purposes which, however, were as well served by Black Birch or Hackmatack. No references to the use of maple appear in descriptions of vessels in Lloyds' lists. It appears to have had more popularity in the New England states.

Two of the Elms were suitable for boat construction and for certain small parts of larger vessels where toughness was required. The superior of the two, Rock Elm, *Ulmus thomasii Sarg.*, was not part of the Acadian Forest. White Elm, *Ulmus americana L.*, the familiar umbrella of the landscape, occurred in many areas not too remote from shipyards. The wood of white or American Elm substituted very well for the more desirable variety.

American Beech, *Fagus grandifolia Ehrh.*, once common but now rare owing to disease, provided a heavy, hard, tough, strong wood but one not especially durable in water. American Beech requires careful seasoning to render the wood dimensionally stable. Monro claimed many valuable uses for the wood but it was not extensively employed in shipbuilding.

Eastern White Cedar, *Thuja occidentalis L.*, not uncommon in limestone areas of New Brunswick but never really plentiful, is not hard or strong enough for incorporation into ships. The wood is light and resistant to decay and so served in areas where strength and ability to resist abuse were not important.

Eastern Red Cedar, *Juniperus virginiana L.*, is heavier and harder than White Cedar but the variety was not part of the Acadian Forest.

Foreign species of wood imported for special uses not served adequately by native species included Pitch Pine for spars, when White Pine had been exhausted; *Lignum Vitae* for deadeyes; American Black Walnut for trim and show wood; White Oak and Live Oak for rudder stock, stems and sternposts. The importation of Pitch Pine was to offset the need for the meticulous building of spars by the fitting together of numerous specially shaped pieces. Not so common a procedure as reported by some writers, that method was resorted to late in the 19th century. The Royal Navy earlier built masts in that manner when warships became so large as to demand spars longer and heavier than any available.

*Lignum Vitae*, an exceptionally dense, hard, oily wood, excels in durability and mariners would willingly accept no other species for blocks and deadeyes. Walnut is a stable, attractive wood which accepts oil so happily that it becomes practically waterproof. White Oak and Live Oak were the very best North American materials for that most important component of a vessel, the rudder, which could not be given strength by increasing its dimensions.

Three materials were possible for use as fasteners[2] but they were not always ready to hand for the builder's choice. They included wood, always available and, generally speaking, unchanging; iron, scarce at first but gradually becoming more plentiful, demanding more skill and cost in working than wood and assuming different properties from decade to decade; and copper, quite scarce and expensive until the supremacy of wooden vessels was on a decline.

Wooden fasteners took the form of treenails, sturdy wooden dowels driven to a snug fit in holes bored through one wooden member into another. Small iron and copper fasteners took the form of a true nail having both head and point but they, too, were seated in bored holes and were not nails in the sense of being forced into the wood. Often they acted in combination as a friction-held spike and as a bolt or rivet in tension by way of being clinched at both ends.

Treenails were true nails in that the wood into which they were driven gripped the treenail to hold it fast, an action made possible by a behavioural property of wood which shrinks as it dries and expands as it takes up moisture. This takes place across the grain but not along the length. The ends of treenails were usually split and further expanded by having a wooden wedge driven into the split.

The timbers and planks that went into a vessel's hull were never dry. One may be assured of that, regardless of much nonsense published to the contrary. No significant difference in water content exists between newly felled timbers, whether cut in the spring, summer, fall or dead of winter. An appreciable difference may be found in thoroughly dried timbers but to obtain such a condition elaborate kilns and procedures are necessary. They were not available during the eras of our interest. Lumber may have been seasoned, which reduces the moisture content but only to about the level of the surrounding air. This could have been achieved by stacking lumber off the ground in well ventilated piles, preferably with a rain cover, and leaving it so for a year or more to come to balance with the prevailing humidity.

Green timbers possessed maximum volume dimensions and, if construction took long enough, the timbers dried a little in the stocks and shrank somewhat. Seasoned timbers remained relatively stable in dimension because the air along the seacoast is quite moist and unchanging throughout the year. In any case, hulls under construction were drenched with rain and, in dry weather, by artificial soaking.

Treenails were not large — a fair-sized specimen being as long as the arm and as thick through — and so they could be made of bone-dry wood, or as dry as it is possible to render wood. Treenails were kept dry and then, when driven into snugly bored holes in the hull they took up moisture from the air and expanded, so they were seized securely by friction and held tightly the members in which they were seated. When the vessel took to the ocean the hull members swelled a little, which was desirable, but the treenails swelled even more and tightened the structure.

The merits of treenails lay with ready availability, low cost and ease of handling. One disadvantage ran with a tendency to rot and the pattern of this rot. Wood rots first just below the surface in contact with the air. Its heart may yet be sound. Such a condition may not greatly affect timbers or planks, but it is disastrous if rot occurs in the area of contact between timber or plank and treenail. The friction grip may thus be lost. To aid against this the holes to receive treenails were bored at angles to one another. It didn't matter if the holes converged or diverged so long as the treenails driven into them effected a wedging action.

Metal spikes, 6 to 16 inches in length, were always square and driven into holes with diameters a little less than the face of the nail. Thus the nail had to crush itself into the wood, particularly along its four corner edges, and so achieve a friction grip. The spikes were angled as well. A far more positive fastening would have been obtained had the spike been driven completely through both members and held inside by a threaded nut; but such an arrangement was not practicable for a number of reasons, among them, the great thickness of the ribs to which planks were attached.

Treenails and metal spikes served very well in futtocks, planking and ceiling, but for holding heavy timbers together only metal bolts and, with economy in mind, only iron bolts would do. Such bolts were expensive, especially large ones, owing to the taps, dies and labour required to turn on threads and cut them into the nuts.

The problem was overcome in this manner. Iron rods with one wide spreading head and one blunt end were prepared and the seating holes bored. The blunt end of the spike was then heated to a glowing red, the bolt rapidly driven home and its head end blocked solidly. A ring washer was dropped over the red-hot end and the end spread with rapid hammer blows, drawing the bolt into tension. It was then quenched with water which halted charring of the wood and also contracted the iron.

The same could be done with copper and even more easily since the metal is softer than iron but, having less strength, copper required a much heavier section. It was a more expensive material than iron and its use was made more so by the demands of thicker bolts. It was less popular therefore.

Metal fasteners might not quite fill their seating holes and, if that situation existed, little pipeways along the metal permitted water to seep into the wood. Precautions were taken against this. The first part of the hole was bored considerably oversize and the head of the spike, before it was driven, was dipped in tar or pitch (not the same materials) and wound with oakum or yarn around the shoulder. The spike was then driven home and countersunk. That was the function of the narrow-head spurs we so often see on adzes in century old photographs. The oversized bore was then stopped with a treenail plug. Countersinking the spike head had another value. It permitted working over the hull with adze and axe to shape and smooth the surface.

Copper spikes and smaller iron nails were sometimes clinched inside the hulls of smaller vessels. The evidence of intent of such use is presented by a flat, chisel end rather than a point. Such nails, driven or seated, entered the wood with the chisel end cutting across, not along, the fibre or grain of the wood.

When copper nails had been in use for some years, not before 1850 on Canada's Atlantic Coast, arguments began and continue to this day concerning the relative benefits of iron and copper fasteners. The issue was concerned mainly with material below the waterline. Higher on the vessel damage could be repaired comparatively easily. The bone of contention was whether or not the respective corrosion by-products of copper and iron were beneficial or harmful.

Copper corroding in saltwater acquires a slime in addition to the tight coat of green rust usually seen. Proponents of iron held that this made copper fasteners loose in their seats. Iron on the other hand produces the red rust with which we are familiar. In watersoaked timber a black colour is assumed by the products of corrosion which expand, locking the iron more securely into the wood. That was another view of those who favoured iron. It is the opinion of the authors who have knocked apart numerous boxes and timbers to recover their tightly seized nails, that the corrosion of iron was not harmful within the wood.

It is not possible now to know how early iron and steel nails (some were undoubtedly of low-grade steel) performed in saltwater. Too few specimens remain to permit a worthwhile study. The use of iron was deprecated in the last half of the 19th century but the fact that iron had its proponents suggests that its performance was not obviously bad. The conclusions of one study, rather small but important because it stands alone so far as we know, may be of interest. Some time prior to 1920, Armco Steel Corporation analyzed a number of very old American iron nails and compared findings with those of an earlier English study. It was found that badly corroded specimens contained a large amount of occluded gases, notably nitrogen, while specimens that were virtually unaffected contained little nitrogen. A collateral conclusion is of more practical value: the absence of nitrogen and resultant increase in iron density was likely a direct result of the repeated heatings and beatings associated with the production of wrought iron.

Wrought iron is not as strong as steel and lacks certain desirable properties possessed by the more sophisticated material. Nevertheless, wrought iron was entirely adequate for all purposes in the building of wooden ships, edged tools excepted. Moreover, wrought iron items could be improved, the outside case-hardened or turned into a kind of steel by heating in an iron chest or muffle containing charcoal. In the process the iron took up carbon from the charcoal and was so toughened. Doubtless the process was used, although diminishingly, throughout the era of wooden ships.

From about 1830 onwards improvements in the making of steel, more desirable generally than iron, began to follow more and more rapidly. Consequently, iron workers and ship builders had no constancy of material and certainly no assurance of quality. Impure and porous metal could have been used in one vessel and would have corroded quickly to the detriment of the hull while, in another, a high grade of wrought iron may have performed superbly. Questions cannot now be resolved, of course.

Bronze, copper with the addition of tin, might have proved a suitable material but its cost was greater than that of pure copper. Brass, a similar alloy of copper but with zinc was used extensively above the waterlines of vessels because of its handsome appearance. Brass is said to deteriorate quickly in salt water owing to removal of the zinc through the action of salts of several kinds. Regardless of the supposed dezincification action, galvanized (zinc-coated) spikes were used in ocean-going vessels towards the end of the 19th century. No record suggests better results than were obtained with wrought iron. The zinc, of course, was a sacrificial protection that had to be removed before the iron could rust.

In passing, a possible anomaly with regard to the supposed dezincification of brass in salt water may be noted. A spike taken from the French warship *Le Marquis de Malauze*, sunk in the Restigouche estuary in 1760, was recovered nearly 200 years later. It appeared to be copper but a spectographic analysis revealed the following constituents: main — copper; major — zinc; minor — lead, tin and magnesium. The spike is, in fact, brass. It was securely seated in an oak timber and its head still bears part of the original yarn and pitch seal. It may thus have been protected, of course, and may have been below the level of oxygenated water where dezincification of brass may be slowed.

## CHAPTER 15

# The Spread of Canvas

The term *spars* admits masts, yards, booms, gaffs, sprits and all the slender wooden components of a vessel's rigging. The largest members were the masts, of which two or three to a vessel were most common. Their names were descriptive of position: foremast, mainmast and mizzen, if there was a third. Towards the end of sail's golden era additional masts were added in a vain effort to compete with more efficient steamers. Their names are not certain today but that immediately aft of the mizzen seems to have been called the jigger, the next, the pusher and the aftermast, the driver. Only one seven-masted vessel, the American schooner *Thomas E. Lawson*, 1902, was ever constructed, its aftermast being dubbed the kicker. It seems also that the masts were referred to by the days of the week, starting with Monday, the foremast, and by numbers, one being the foremast.

A mast was a simple mechanical device, known ashore as a ginpole, one of three arrangements by means of which, employing blocks and tackle, heavy loads could be lifted. The others, of no interest here, were shears, two timbers meeting at the top from a spread base, and the tripod, three self-bracing timbers. A ginpole was a single timber of suitable strength and proportions, its foot stepped in a shoe and made stable, or stayed, by guys (stays) running from points selected with regard to slenderness, down to anchors in the ground.

Three stays from each point were sufficient, one working against the others distant $120^0$ on each side. One set sufficed for a short, sturdy ginpole but two or three were required for a tall, high-lifting device. A means of adjusting stays was necessary because, even if of iron chains or steel rope, they tightened or loosened with load, wear and weather. Chains were avoided because of weight and steel wire until comparatively recently because of cost. Hemp rope was common. This stretches greatly as it dries and tightens (5% or more) when wet because the fibre components swell when they take up moisture and relax as they give it up, the twist of the rope playing a part. Rope also creeps to a permanent lengthening.

A ginpole becomes a derrick (named after an early English hangman) when equipped with a load-carrying boom which can swing through about $120^0$ around the foot and the extreme end of which can be raised or lowered by means of tackle. From the end of the boom other tackle can raise or lower the load.

A vessel's masts worked in the same manner except that they were also equipped to raise gaffs, a type of boom, upwards along the mast and to raise, lower and hold cross-members, yards, for carrying sail on square-rigged craft. Yards were swung right or left of the line of the keel and held there by ropes called braces.

Masts were stayed in four directions, from the sides and from front and rear. The side stays, collectively called shrouds, were strongest and most numerous. They ran back slightly from the plane of the mast, so that they were partly backstays as well as side stays. This also permitted yards to be braced more sharply than $90^0$. Fore and after stays anchored to the foot of the mast or sub-mast next behind, to the stern or bow of the vessel. Each sub-mast was secured by its own shrouds and stays and the entire composite mast was similarly secured from the bottom of the lower mast to the highest masthead.

The lower and intermediate shrouds were tied laterally one to another with chain, wood and rope. This positioned the stays and at the same time provided a handy ladder (ratlines) by which men could scramble to points aloft.

The mast stays and those of the bowsprit were collectively known as the standing rigging. This had to hold the masts against the winds' efforts to snap those timbers or uproot them from the keelson. Ordinarily there was no great problem, for the sails could be trimmed to accept the wind from any direction except the bow, the shrouds and stays being arranged for any condition, and to a certain extent adjustable.

The forestays were required to hold the masts against whipping. If the wind suddenly dropped off, relieving the sails of pressure, or if the vessel ran aground under full sail, the mastheads, unless they were restrained, could spring back violently enough to break or crack the upper sections. It was also possible for masts to have to accept a windload from the bow against which shrouds and afterstays were practically useless. Occasionally mariners brought their vessels to, halted them, in a flamboyant manner. The wind being light enough, in the right direction, and the larger sails reefed, the helmsman put his wheel down smartly and brought the vessel around, whereupon the few sails still set filled with the wind and worked against the vessel's way or forward motion. Similar conditions were encountered when a vessel tacked against the wind. More often and more safely, vessels were brought to when they entered a harbour against the tide or current.

Wind pressure has to be factored by sail area and translated into stress taken by masts, rigging and hull; and even this does not provide a clear picture of what happens. A generalization may serve. If poor seamanship permitted the sails to take a sufficiently strong blow from the beam, perhaps because of their having been improperly trimmed, the vessel rolled on her beam-ends. The windward shrouds alone, in that event, had to accept the full displacement weight of the loaded hull. This might well have amounted to thousands of tons and one can see that the shrouds had to be most numerous and of the heaviest and strongest rope.

Shroud stays were single ropes and they passed from a fastener above to an adjusting arrangement below. The adjusting arrangement was nearly always a deadeye, a circular hardwood block with a groove around its periphery by means of which the deadeye was permanently lashed into an eye of the stay. The deadeye had three holes in its flat face, in the locations of eye sockets and nose opening in the human skull, from which macabre resemblance it took its name. Through these a lighter rope, a lanyard, passed back and forth to another deadeye, which was then secured at the chainplates. This arrangement was fixed and tampered with only when repairs were necessary.

Fore and aft stays required adjustment more often and their lower ends terminated in a block and tackle arrangement which permitted a quick snugging up or loosening of the stays. One block was attached to the stay and the other to an anchorage. The rope rove between could be pulled or slackened to shorten or lengthen the stay. Blocks might have one, two, three or even four free-running wheels, which arrangement greatly multiplied a man's pulling strength as well as changing the direction of pull.

The ropes that hauled yards and sails up and down or back and forth were called, collectively, the running rigging. Each had its own name, associated with a particular mast, yard and function. Running rigging typically fastened to a yard and passed through a block above, before or behind the mast and thence fell to the deck where, having been tightened or slackened, the fall (loose end) was secured to a belaying pin. The ropes that raised or lowered yards were called halyards, from haul-yard.

Masts occasionally reared 200 feet above the deck, but they were never, then, of one piece. Few timbers of such great length could be found and they could not be handled without even taller and sturdier lifting devices. If a part of such a tall mast became damaged the whole had to be replaced and, obviously, replacements of such size could not be carried aboard the vessel. Mast heights varied considerably but the tallest were made up of four sections. They included the lower mast, heaviest and strongest, stepped on the keelson and rising about 30% of the total mast height above deck; the topmast; top gallant and royal, rising in order one on the other, each a little shorter and more slender than the one below. Smaller vessels carried only a lower mast, topmast and topgallant. Masts raked, or leaned aft, by a carefully calculated amount. Masts were never uniformly round nor were they uniformly tapered. Each stood on a ledge or cheek attached to and behind the mast below. The adjacent parts were larger, generally square in section but with chamfered corners. Parts were specially shaped to accept a means of fastening to one another or to permit the attachment of such necessary appurtenances as crosstrees and trucks. The former topped the lower mast and spread the top-gallant shrouds. The truck was a circular arrangement through which halyards were reaved. Numerous other structural arrangements, trestle-trees, for example, adorned the mastheads for specific purposes. Together the components made up work and observation platforms, a way of reaching certain yards and the means of spreading and fastening stays.

Late fully-rigged ships usually carried six yards on each of three masts. Their names reflected the mast terminology. The mizzen, for example, carried the mizzen lower yard, the mizzen lower and upper topsail yards, the mizzen lower and upper gallant yards and the mizzen royal. Earlier ships carried only three or four yards on each mast and they had to be much stronger and heavier because, proportionately, they carried more sail area.

The yards were supported by ropes attached to blocks or brackets and they were secured to the mast by parrels, these varying in size and arrangement according to the demands made on them. Yards could rotate to a fore-and-aft position and, the lowest excepted, they could raise or lower in a vertical plane. Control was maintained by a system of blocks and tackle operated from the yard's mast, from the mast behind and from the deck. Lower yards were fixed with regard to vertical position but others, the upper topsail, the lower top gallant and the royal yard were regularly dropped from their sailing positions to relieve the mast section from undue stress when their use was not required. Sometimes, as when anticipating long periods of bad weather, the royal yards along with the royal mast were removed completely.

The longest yards on large ships could exceed 100 feet although this was by no means common. From their ends — the yard-arms — an additional yard could be suspended for the purpose of carrying a studding-sail. The studding-sail sheets tied to the extension on the yard below, these being known as studding-sail booms. The lowest sheets tied to bumpkins (little booms) projecting from the hull at rail level.

All vessels shipped replacement spars and those making two-year voyages around the Horn carried as many as three or four of those most susceptible to damage. They all demanded space and so very long spars were a nuisance. The largest were lashed securely to high cradles on the weather deck. Others were stored a deck below which, on naval vessels, assumed the name spar deck, which clearly indicates the importance attached to having replacement parts aboard.

Simon Graham was naturally interested in the building of vessels as well as the sailing of them. Masting information is found in his *Abstract of "Jurnal"* tucked away for future reference between records of the Barque *Devonport* from Liverpool, England, to Philadelphia, U.S.A., December 28, 1836, to March 4, 1837, and the Barque *Caledonia* from Saint John, N.B., to Hull, England, August 4, 1837, to September 15, 1837.

*To place the mast for a sloop:*
Draw the length of the loadwaterline, mark its centre below the fore part of the rabbet of the stem and sternpost, then one-seventh of the length before the middle is the centre of the mast or place it one-half between one-third and three-eighths of the length aft from the stem.

*For a Ship or Barque:*
Divide its length on the loadwaterline into eight equal parts and set the mainmast one-fourteenth of the length abaft the middle division, the foremast one-eighth of the length abaft the outside of the rabbet of the stem, the mizzenmast three-eighths of the distance between the centre of the mainmast and the outside of the rabbet of the sternpost. Set forward from the same the rakes abaft should be the foremast a one-quarter inch for every foot of the length, the mainmast one-half do, then the mizzen three-quarter do.

*For a Brig:*
Place the centre of the mainmast one-eighth of the loadwaterline abaft the centre of the same and the foremast one-sixth abaft the rabbet of the stem, the rake the same as a ship.

*For a Schooner:*
The mainmast one-eighth of the length of the centre and the foremast one two-nineths of the length of the loadwaterline abaft the rabbet of the stem. The rakes of the masts should be for the mainmast three-quarters of an inch for every foot of its length. The foremast three-eighths do.

*To find the lengths of Spars:*
To one-third the length of the loadwaterline including the main stem and sternpost, add three times the breadth of the midship frame inclusive of the plank and the housing of the mast from the main deck to the keelson, and half that same will be the length in feet and inches — for the main topmast the length four-sevenths the length of the mainmast, for the main topgallant mast do five-nineths do, length of the main royal mast from heel to peak four-sevenths of top

gallant mast, foremast the length fourteen-fifteenths of the main. For the mizzen mast when set on the same level as the main the length of the main royal pole is three-fifths the length from the heel to the rigging.

*To find the length of the bowsprit without the knighthead rules:*
To one-third of the length the loadwaterline add the ship's extreme breadth and half this same will be the length outside the knightheads — bowsprit and mainmast same on Brigantine and Barquentine do.

*Ships' Tops and Yards:*
The breadth of the main top is half the breadth of the ship adding the thickness of the mast. To find the length of the main yard — to the length of the loadwaterline including the breadth of the main stem and sternpost add the extreme breadth in feet and inches and four-elevenths of the length is the length of the main yard.

Main topsail yard seven-nineths of the main yard.

Topgallant yard three-quarters of the main topsail yard.

Main-royal yard two-thirds of the main gallant yard.

Diameter of main yard at the slings is one inch for every four foot of extreme length, outer end one-half the slings, yardarm one-twentieth of the full length.

"Spread the canvas to the gaills, it's time for us to gow." There's a touch of fine style in that line, but with deference due the poet's position as mate of the Barque *Caledonia*, one must find it strange advice, nevertheless. When the wind blows a gale it's time to take in canvas, not to shake it out. Simon Graham demonstrated that quite clearly in his logs.

"Single and duble reeft breezes" — that's what Simon Graham called them. The wind was strong enough that he had to reduce the spread of canvas by reefing. Across each square sail, on both sides, stretched two or three reef bands of reinforcing canvas and from them dangled short ropes called reefpoints. The strain was taken off and the canvas lifted by means of buntlines whereupon, by tying the reefpoints over the yard (with reef-knots), the sail was gathered and made smaller. In cold, wet weather reefing was a miserable job for all hands.

"Scudding under close reeft foresail," Captain Graham observed. A vessel scuds when all its sails have been taken in and yet it is still driven by the wind, that is, according to authorities today. Simon used the term differently. With all others furled (lashed tightly to their yards), the foresail was still drawing a little. It was reefed as much as possible, the next step being to furl, take it entirely out of the wind.

The least taking in of a square sail was achieved by merely hauling up its lower corners. Ropes, clewlines, were provided for the purpose. When the breeze freshened, as Simon put it, the sails were "clewed up." Similar lines, brails, decreased the sail areas of spencers and staysails.

The paintings seen today of a square-rigged vessel driving through a rough sea with billowing canvas exaggerate somewhat. A ship could carry all sail only when the wind was light and every stitch of canvas had to be called on for speed. In winter on the North Atlantic and when rounding Cape Horn, ships with a mast and yards above the topgallant usually sent them down and stowed them. This precluded damage to valuable spars and also helped against scudding.

Simon Graham sailed ships, barques (barks) and, early in his career, brigs. Those and three others, schooners, brigantines and barquentines made up the merchantmen commonly encountered throughout Graham's career.

Schooners were generally the smallest of the ocean-going fleet; however, the largest merchantman ever built, *Wyoming*, 6000 tons, a late vessel, was a schooner. In the first half of the 19th century most schooners were in the range 25 to 175 tons, although some were smaller and some larger. The smaller vessels were coastal fishermen and packets. The larger schooners were bank fishermen which, on occasion, peddled cargoes of dried salt cod in Europe and the Caribbean. They brought foodstuffs and rum back to the Maritimes.

Early schooners had only two masts. Later vessels, attempting to compete with steam, carried three or more. They were known as terns or tern schooners. Tern was a word that applied to things that came in threes and so it more properly referred to three-masted vessels.

All masts of a schooner were rigged fore-and-aft, the sails being in line with the keel when at rest. The foremast carried a fore-sail and jibs, lacking on the other masts. Staysails[1] were spread between topmasts to catch as much slack air as possible. A less common variation had small square topsails at the mastheads instead. The two types were differentiated as staysail or topsail schooners.

Schooner-rigged craft offered several important benefits. They could tack most quickly, making them well suited for coastal sailing under variable breezes, and they could be sailed with fewer men than were required for any other rig. Five men could handle a substantial two-masted schooner but twice as many were required for a brig, also of two masts but square rigged. Schooners could sail closer to the wind than any other vessel, a most valuable characteristic on occasion.

Brigs, somewhat larger than schooners, had an advantage over the fore-and-aft rig in that they sailed faster under a wind from the stern or quarter.

On the other hand they required a larger crew and they were less manoeuvrable. Brigs were favoured as small cargo craft for fast, low-cost ocean crossings.

Brigantines had two masts also. The foremast was square-rigged and like a brig, carried jibs. The main mast was schooner-rigged. The brigantine was designed to take the advantages of brig and schooner, being between the two in requirements of crew, speed and ability to tack quickly. Brigs and brigantines, quite common early in the 1800s, soon gave way to ships, barques and barquentines, larger and more efficient cargo-carriers, and then returned to favour late in the century when economy of operation became a more important factor.

A ship had three masts and some, late in the 19th century, four or even five. The four and five masted vessels relied heavily on steel construction. All masts carried square sails, the foremast sporting jibs as well. Staysails were spread between the masts and each square-sail could be extended laterally with small additions known as studding sails.[2]

The main feature of a fore-and-aft rig was the large spanker aft of each mast, the canvas being spread between a gaff above and a boom below. Nearly all vessels carried a spanker on the after-most mast. Ships and barques carried a variation of the spanker on the foremast and main as well. This sail was different only in that it was loose-footed, — it lacked a lower boom. It was called a spencer, taking the name from its inventor, a British naval officer.

Ships of the 18th century usually bore three large square-sails on each mast. From bottom to top they were known as course, topsail and topgallant. As ships became larger another sail, the royal, was added. It took its name from an over-size warship, *Royal Sovereign*, which required more canvas. Each of these sails was carried on a submast and yard bearing the same name, all related to the lowest mast. Thus we know a particular sail as the main topgallant, for example. The course was usually referred to as *the* sail, foresail, mainsail and mizzen — sail, the latter, sometimes, the crojack (crossjack).

Large sails were heavy when wet and they were difficult to reef, furl and hand. With the success of clipper hulls, about 1850, sails, except for the course, were divided into two, with more area added. From bottom to top they were: course, upper and lower topsails, upper and lower topgallants and royal. Fifteen years or so were required for the transition, whereupon a few vessels added a small uppermost skysail to each mast. Eager mariners also spread, in light breezes, a spritsail under the bowsprit.

Simon Graham pinpoints the start of the move towards more and smaller sails. On March 17, 1851, he recorded, with astonishment one may conjecture: "passed an American ship with two Top Gallant Yards on Eatch mast."

The largest wooden Canadian ship built for service as a merchantman was the *William D. Lawrence,* Maitland, N.S., 1874, 2458 tons. The heavyweight title of all wooden vessels was held by H.M.S. *Lord Clive,* 1866, 7750 tons displacement.

Barques were similar to ships except that the after mast, whether of three or four, carried no square sails. Instead, the mast was schooner-rigged. Barques were of the same general dimensions as ships but two, in Canada, were much larger. *Columbus,* 1824, 3690 tons, and *Baron of Renfrew,* 1825, 5294 tons, both of the Isle of Orleans in the St. Lawrence River, were record-breakers. They were not intended for merchant service, however, but rather to be broken up for timber in Britain, to where they sailed under Governor's pass. The first was broken up but the second was unwisely sent to sea again and was lost.

Barquentines (barkentines) had a foremast ship-rigged and two or more masts rigged fore-and-aft. Barquentines sacrificed some speed before a stern wind in favour of economy of crew and manoeuverability. They were also more economical of yards.

A minor variation of the brig rig, to do with the manner of carrying the spanker, may be of interest. When mounted aft of a mast bearing squaresails, as spankers usually were, the mountings sometimes got in the way of one another. Some brigs, therefore, carried their spankers on a short mast immediately (two feet or less of separation) aft of the main, square-rigged mast. The arrangement made for ease of handling the spanker. Brigs so adapted were known as snows (Dutch: *snau*). This was suited to brigs, which were intentionally small, but not to ships which were built as large as possible within economic limits. If a separate spanker mast was desirable for a three-masted square-rigged vessel, the hull could be profitably made longer and a trymast stepped aft of the mizzen, so changing the rig to a four-masted barque.

Spankers, but not spencers, were occasionally divided diagonally into two triangular pieces. The lower sail was then called the spanker and the upper sail, the gaff spanker. The main reason for carrying numerous small sails rather than fewer large ones concerned the economy of crew size. Fewer men were required to hand small sails and they could move from one yard to another quickly. As well, small sails permitted finer adjustment to the wind and torn sails could be patched together more easily.

Old and repaired canvas was spread to light breezes. The best was saved for strong winds and for show when entering port. Small sails receive less total wind force than large ones and this permitted use of a less strong canvas — another argument for smaller sails. From course to skysail lighter weights (and cost) of canvas were employed. When not called to more urgent tasks all hands reshaped and repaired sails. Scraps of light material were fashioned into work clothes. Sailors spent a lot of time sewing; nevertheless, press gangs of the Royal Navy had an expression: "nine tailors make a sailor."

The ropes used to haul sails and hold them were called sheets and so one sees some faulty terminology in the well-known limerick:

> One night a lady named Banker
> Sailing to Casa Blanca,
> Awoke in dismay
> To hear the mate say:
> Hoist up the top sheet and spanker.

Simon Graham scorned light winds as his logs show. Although Simon made abundantly clear that he was sometimes bedeviled by winds too strong for his taste, he did not use precise terminology descriptive of their force. Sometimes he noted single, double and close reefed gales but more often Simon referred to light and strong breezes and gales. Only occasionally did he mention hurricanes. Even at the end of his career Simon Graham ignored the Beaufort Scale of Force adopted by the Royal Navy in 1838.

## CHAPTER 16

# The Shipbuilder

Before starting each new vessel a shipbuilder, in theory at least, decided upon an actual construction site and a method of launching but, in practice, for continuing building, the decision was made only once: at the time the location for the yard was selected. With that decision the builder established work methods from which he could not easily deviate.

Many factors had to be weighed in the choice of a site and the best balance obtained. An ideal location for the building of wooden ships was at the mouth of a river leading from prime timberland. The river had to be navigable to the extent that woodsmen and their supplies could be transported on it and suited to the passage of log rafts down to the yard. Its mouth, of course, had to be open to the sea, yet protected from wave action.

The topography of the foreshore, the range of tides or floodwaters and the competency of the ground to support the dead load of construction were aspects not to be ignored. Finally, the depth and breadth of the water off-shore had to be adequate to receive the largest vessel likely to be constructed on the site.

Three methods of launching were open to the shipbuilder. His vessels could enter the water stern-to, bow-on, or broadside. The usual approach in British North America was to get the stern into the water first.

That form of introduction of a vessel to its new environment was favoured nearly everywhere. Bow entries were avoided because the prow tended to thrust deeply into the water, its subsequent uplift as a result of buoyancy aggravating the stern's thumping drop off the ways. The comparatively fragile rudder assembly under the over-hanging stern could easily be damaged at that critical moment.

Launching by the stern also provided a site benefit, somewhat more valuable than it may appear, related to the difference of configuration between bow and stern. The stern of a vessel steered by muscle-power and mechanical advantage should, for economy of space, overhang the keel by ten feet or more to accommodate the arrangement of rudder, wheel drum and tiller bar. The overhanging stern is known as the counter. When the stern was located close to the water, the counter over the water, perhaps, the lower part of the vessel was farther away from wave action and workmen could walk around it.

Broadside launching entailed extra effort to prevent a hull, especially one masted and top-heavy, from capsizing. Nevertheless, construction on the banks of narrow rivers or where space would not permit building at a right-angle, required that a vessel be launched sideways. The four-masted schooner *Harry A. McLellan*, 643 tons, was built and launched in that manner at Campbellton, N.B., in 1919 because the only construction space available lay parallel to the Restigouche River.

Despite the care given to a launching (Simon Graham wrote "lanching", doubtless as he pronounced the word) trouble could not be precluded. One of the better-known instances of embarrassment concerned the undignified baptism of *Marco Polo* at Marsh Creek, Saint John, N.B., on April 17, 1851. Rather unwillingly, after some nudging, she slipped her ways, only to knife across the creek and embed her stern deeply into the muddy bank opposite.

It is not easy today to grasp what was entailed in building an ocean-going vessel, say, for Simon Graham, unless one considers the technical level of the period. A few facets will show the picture well enough and it is not necessary to use precise figures.

Fifty thousand cubic feet of timber went into construction of a fairly substantial vessel. That is, a thousand trees yielding logs averaging a little less than two feet in diameter and sixteen feet in length had to be cut, transported to a creek, along the creek to the river and down the river to the shipyard. Moreover, many were select logs of diverse species which had to be sought among vast numbers of unsuitable specimens.

The task kept twenty or more men busy all year round. Axes and crosscut saws were the only cutting tools available. Pikes and picks of several kinds were all the lumbermen had for handling logs, except that teams of cattle provided power for twitching. Compass timbers and root sections for knees, and mast and keel logs, required in the longest lengths and largest diameters possible, were difficult to get out of rough timberland.

Green hardwood does not float well. It had to be taken down the river on rafts of buoyant softwoods. More men at the yard had to haul the logs from the river to stockpiles and from stockpiles to the construction site. There, some logs had to be hewed to shape by axe (along the grain) and by adze (across the grain) while others were pit-sawed into planks.

Midway through the nineteenth century there were no more than a dozen or so steam-powered sawmills in New Brunswick and few shipbuilders possessed such expensive equipment. Water-powered saws were far more plentiful and they provided a source of sawed lumber. In one location or another about 50% of the wood was wasted in sawdust, chips and short ends. Scaffolding, props, stock-timbers and ways could be used several times with small additions to their quantities and so were more economical of effort.

Some of the native timber and a small quantity of imported material went to the shops and yards of artisans who produced specialty items for sale to builders. The specialists spent their lives turning pieces on water-powered lathes or shaping them with hand tools and rarely saw the vessels they outfitted. Their produce included spars, belaying pins, marlin spikes, deadeyes, blocks, toggles, treenails, wedges and dozens of similar small artifacts.

Elsewhere in the shipbuilding community blacksmiths, sailmakers, ropewalkers[1] and numerous other skilled tradesmen fabricated custom requirements. The shipbuilders' men shaped only those items that required on-site fitting; otherwise a tremendous manufacturing complex would have been necessary at each yard. The specialists settled themselves in the larger industrial centres whence they could ship by packet to yards along the coast. Newspapers published in Saint John and Halifax regularly carried their advertisements.

It may be interesting to note in passing that, throughout the first half of the nineteenth century, tradesmen making blocks and deadeyes in Eastern Canada worked entirely by hand with only the most primitive tools.[2] Yet *Encyclopaedia Britannica* in 1824 noted that blockmaking machinery functioned in Britain as early as 1781. It described a sophisticated, steam-powered production line operative about 1808, turning out superior blocks, deadeyes and similar pieces. *Britannica* observed that the Royal Navy used at least 200 different sorts and sizes of blocks and possibly many more. The species of wood favoured were elm and ash.

Finally, with regard to technology, one should be aware that a green hardwood keel-log, before being shaped, might weigh as much as three tons. It had to be manhandled through every process with no more assistance than could be provided by rollers, block and tackle, simple winches and slow-moving oxen. Perhaps one may then comprehend the reasons behind construction periods of nine to eighteen months for each vessel. The actual time required in the shipyards was about 10 man-days per ton of registered burden. The days were of dawn to dusk duration.

The keel, perhaps 20" x 14", was the first component shaped and set in position except that, if a false keel, or shoe, were also required, it went into place at the same time — a three or four inch plank spiked to the larger member. The keel was made up of several pieces, each as long as could be obtained, scarfed end to end and bolted or riveted securely. It was laid on cribs of timber blocks spaced to accept the ultimate weight of the completed vessel. The blocks rested on the ground or, if the ground was not competent to take the load, on capped piles driven to bedrock or a friction grip. Some writers suggest that stocks, as the arrangement is known, always included piling as the basic support. This was unlikely owing to the difficulty of driving long piles. The main problem lay in the lack of a means of raising a heavy weight reasonably quickly.

The keel was set high enough for workmen to pass under and also to facilitate the building of launching ways later. Considering end-launching only, the keel blocks and the keel fell towards the water at a rate of 5/8" for each foot of run. Thus, stocks 200 feet long dropped off nearly 10-1/2 feet. The launching ways sloped even more — 3/4" to the foot. Usually the site sloped so that the hull was not too high. The elevation of the lowest end, nearest the water, was set precisely with regard to the topography of the foreshore.

After the keel had been most carefully fashioned, aligned, bolted up and set to grade, the stem and sternpost were bolted into position. In small vessels those members were backed up by the largest natural knees obtainable, their legs sometimes 8' long. Barques and ships of the sizes sailed by Simon Graham required tremendous quantities of precisely fitted deadwood to brace the stem and sternpost.

The ribs were then positioned, each timber in each rib being doubled so that joints between futtocks were staggered to achieve as much strength as possible. The central, lowest futtocks between the port and starboard ribs were set first and the upward-curving sections, fully assembled, were raised on them. The central futtocks were termed floors and above them rose the first, second and third futtocks, the uppermost sometimes extending into the bulwarks.

It has been shown that the vessel was faired on the holding-loft floor so that its lines could be examined critically and smoothed into flowing curves. To carry the fairing process further, in some areas of the hull, alternate ribs only were finished before mounting. In other areas every third or fourth rib was fully fashioned. Intermediate ribs were mounted rough-shaped on the faces that were to be planked. They were then dubbed to conform with the curves of limber ribbands of wood laid from one finished rib to another. The eye of the master shipwright so adjusted the curves envisaged by the modeller and developed in the molding loft.

The ribs were hoisted or tilted into position by ginpoles. Labourers supplied the necessary muscle to the accompaniment of many a "Heave-HO, and again SO" with an occasional injunction: "Handsomely does it!"

On the smaller hulls, ribs were positioned as complete frames of floor, port and starboard members.

The frames were doubled, one must remember, to offset the weakness inherent in the best of scarfed joints. The pairs were spaced apart from one another at about their own, uniform width. Spacing was controlled by the insertion between each frame of another piece of flooring. Thus the bottom of the hull, rising up on the cheeks a little, was solid. It was literally the floor of the vessel. Above the floor the spacing of ribs was apparent.

As frames were set, so they were held in position by lumber scabbed across inside and by scaffolding outside. Ribbands of substantial lumber, the clamps or clamping, were then run inside from bow to stern, on each side. The clamps were part of the ceiling but, because they served as support for the deck beams and as a means of distributing loads, they were of heavier material. Clamps were required for each deck.

At this point one might pause to reflect that, the entire structure being on a slope, spirit levels and plumb lines could not be profitably employed. Nor could the carpenter's square be of much service. Although many timbers lay parallel, none met another at a right angle. Vertical and horizontal control planes, found everywhere in construction of a building, were absent on a ship's hull. The sloping keel was the sole reference plane.

Several phases of work could be started as soon as the ribs were in place. Workmen could proceed with the installation of beams, knees, planking, ceiling and keelson all at the same time. The keelson, which ran the length of the hull over the keel, had to be introduced before the last frame was in place, otherwise the timbers had to be lifted high and lowered into the hull.

The floor timbers straddled the keel, seated alternately in shallow saddles cut in the keel and reversed saddles cut in the floor members. The keelson, which in large hulls could be comprised of nine grouped, twelve-inch timbers, ran the length of the hull over the floor and into the deadwood at bow and stern. The keelson components were securely fastened together, as was the deadwood, and fastened to the floor. The entire arrangement bolted through its central member to the keel. Ends were joined with scarfs as long as six feet and the scarfs were staggered and spread through the huge bundle of timbers. The iron bolts used could be 8' or 10' in length.

The keelson, more than the keel, was the backbone of the hull but, unlike a true articulated backbone, it was made as rigid as possible. A stiff keelson was the major safeguard against sagging or hogging of the hull. From the keelson, stanchions rose to meet the lower deck beams and passed through the between-decks to join to the main deck beams.

Both the lower and main deck beams joined to the ribs. All the connections were made as positive as possible. None was a mere spiked or hinged joint. The ceiling and exterior planking were attached just as securely and so one sees the shipbuilder's aim. It was to obtain a completely rigid box that could not flex, bend or deform.

The deck beams being in place and the interior ceiling applied, natural timber brackets (knees) were bolted to the ribs and to the beams. They were not required as load-supporting members but as a means of immobilizing the joints. Those with longer legs in a vertical position were called hanging knees and those with legs horizontal were lodging knees. Both were employed in large hulls.

Most vessels were built with ceiling and planking strakes horizontal, but a few, after Simon Graham's time, attempted a diagonal pattern. This was not at all successful for planking, but was effective enough for ceiling. The barque *Andromache*, 1048 tons, launched at Richibucto on July 20, 1856, is an example. A description, quoted by Louise Manny in *Ships of Kent County*, observed: "Her...'twixt deck ceiling...is of trusswork wrought diagonally fore and aft...."The advent of steel hulls halted experimentation of that kind.

Seppings' diagonal strapping, introduced to the Royal Navy early in the nineteenth century, was not commonlyemployed in Eastern Canadian hulls.[3] No mention of it can be found in early records, at least. The material was a low-grade steel band, 4" to 8" wide, 1/4" to 1/2" thick. Ends of the straps were riveted together to provide the necessary continuity. They paralleled one another 4 to 8 feet on centres, and served against hogging. All such devices were rendered obsolete when steel ribs were introduced in Britain midway in the nineteenth century. Diagonal stiffening was then easily worked between the ribs, connections being made by means of riveted gusset plates.

Planking strakes were installed as closely together as possible, but with a vee-shaped opening at the weather face. Tarry oakum was driven tightly into the groove and finished flush with the surface with putty. If seasoned planks were used — most unlikely, however — they squeezed the oakum more tightly when they became wet and expanded. Leaks resulted when the working of strakes in old hulls spat out the oakum. Simon Graham experienced this on one of his voyages and remarked the happening with such nonchalance as to imply that it was a commonplace occurrence.

Strakes varied in thickness, those in the bilge and the beam wales being heaviest. Strakes were applied from keel upward and from rails downward, closing sections being shaped to fit. They were held in place, before being fastened, by means of a timber dog, a steel device shaped like a flat "U". The legs of a dog were sharpened and at an angle to one another so that when driven into two planks they drew them closer together. Steel clamps and other tightening devices, some of great size, were also employed to draw members close.

As planking proceeded toward the bow a cutwater was attached to the stem. The planking was thickened and faired to produce a smooth transition from stem to hull. Nevertheless, early bows were quite bluff at the cutwater. They contained no knees but were braced with curved horizontal timbers called breast-hooks. Planking on larger vessels was almost always laid smooth, "carvel-fashion", with edges butting one another.

Seamen sometimes claimed that "clinker-built" hulls sailed better because of bubbles of air being trapped under their lapped planks. The planks could not be held as securely as when flush, however. Copper sheathing, which only became common about 1850 in Eastern Canada construction although developed a century before, demanded carvel hulls. Earlier, vessels were sometimes sheathed abroad.

Hulls were always painted before launching; thereafter, unless refitted, they saw no paint below the waterline. White was a popular colour, with wales and bulwarks in a contrasting scheme. Early shipowners and masters were fond of a deceptive pattern of false gunports painted along the 'tween deck level. Black was the colour for these pseudo-threats. The grinning row, always included by early portraitists, appears grim and sinister but one wonders if privateers and freebooters ever shied away from such a bluff.

Privateering was outlawed soon after the Napoleonic Wars and pirates quit the seas as modern navies sought out their lairs. Nevertheless, the practice being so well established, false gunports adorned merchantmen long after the midpoint of the century. Notwithstanding, some seadogs of the period could bite as well as bark. The brig *Pilgrim*, which carried R.H. Dana around Cape Horn in the 1830s, was armed. The swivel gun or falconet once owned by Simon Graham which survives is evidence that at some date he anticipated having to deal with boarding parties in small boats.

Most British North American vessels of the period of our interest were built with only one weather deck but with beams installed for another. An open hold was desirable for bulky cargoes such as lumber. Vessels so built were commonly called droghers, regardless of rig. Packet and passenger vessels required the second deck. Its headroom rarely exceeded 6 feet. The largest vessels, particularly those built after 1860 for passenger service, sometimes had three decks.

Deck beams were cambered. They fell off, that is, they were molded, in their depths towards the scuppers, to facilitate the run-off of water. An actual gutter arrangement does not seem to have been common on early vessels. What are pointed to as waterways on some old cross-sections are merely thicker, raised deck planks. Simon Graham had his carpenter fill in the waterways on one vessel, which suggests that, whatever shape they took, they were not an especially useful feature.

Deck planking was of the best quality, narrow, 3" or 4" deep white pine. It was spiked to the beams through bored holes plugged later with pine dowels. The deck was planed smooth after installation. Vee-shaped grooves between the planks were paid with oakum and a pitch obtained from pitch-pines. This kept the decks reasonably watertight and gave them a pleasing striped appearance. Although many references are found in modern texts to the use of holystone to whiten decks by removing the weathered surface, as many early records point to the use of oils and even varnish. Perhaps the decks were oiled for long voyages and cleaned for entry to the vessel's home port a year or two later.

With regard to the filling of grooves between planks, paying was always the term used with oakum and pitch, properly referring to the pitch, while caulking applied to the use of oakum and lead putty. Most landlubbers are familiar with the expression: "the devil to pay." Its use to indicate an awkward situation comes from the larger expression: "the devil to pay and no pitch hot!"

Having been advised by an old seaman that the devil was the central deck seam, difficult to keep watertight because it received most distress as planks worked, attempts were made to verify his statement. *The Oxford Companion to Ships and the Sea* has the devil between the keel and the garboard.[4] De Kerchov's *International Maritime Dictionary* has it bounding the waterway although allowing any seam below the waterline. A constant problem to do with terminology is so illustrated. On one voyage Simon sought long to find the source of a leak. When he found it, he dismissed it airily as "only the huddens." A century and a half later, it took more time to find what the "huddens" were than Simon required to find the leak. They were likely "whoodings" — planks rabbeted into the stem.

British North American vessels have sometimes been described as frigate-built. If the term means that the weather deck was practically flush from stem to stern it is meaningful only for early vessels. Frigates had a flush fore-deck but had also a raised poop extending beyond the mizzen and well toward the mainmast. Later merchant vessels occasionally exhibited such a profile. Simon refers quite often to stowing his anchors on the forecastle without, however, making clear whether the forecastle was partly above (a topgallant forecastle) deck or fully below. He seldom mentioned a poop but does refer occasionally to a deck-house, also known as a roundhouse, simply because it was possible to walk around it.

Too few written or pictorial records remain from the period to permit having complete confidence in any present day description of deck arrangements of British North American vessels. Nevertheless the following generalizations may be safely set forth with regard to ships and barques constructed at various times. First, it is necessary to differentiate between the drogher and packet vessels, the one built for carrying bulk cargoes such as timber and guano, the others designed for the transportation of smaller items of commerce, mail and passengers. Simon Graham's vessels were nearly all droghers, it may be deduced from logs.

Early droghers, identified by a pronounced beak and a shallow well above the cutwater in front of the hull proper, seem to have been built with a flush weather deck. The crew's quarters, termed the forecastle despite the absence of a raised area, were located in the bow, aft of a storage area. They were forward of the 'tween decks, no higher than 6 feet, reached by means of a steep companionway, almost a ladder, leading from a small sheltered opening on deck. The forecastle contained the end of the bowsprit, the ends of the catheads, the supporting knightheads and the samson (bowsprit back-up) post. Deck beams in the area were somewhat heavier than others and they were supported by substantial stanchions because the two anchors were stored overhead, the capstan being located in the same area. The capstan's pivot stood through the forecastle also.

The capstan was well forward for several reasons. Its use was primarily for raising the anchors, always at the bow, and then for hoisting upper masts and yards. Its bars and the men moving around the central pivot had to clear the companionway, the fore hatch and the foremast aft of the hatch. A jeers winch or windlass (for handling spars and heavy cargo) may have been located further aft on the deck although on early vessels this sometimes substituted for a capstan.

Between the fore and main masts, closer to the latter, was the main hatch to the hold. Timber droghers were usually loaded through stern ports and sometimes through the bow. The bilge pumps and their wells were positioned aft of the mainmast. A squat roundhouse for the cook lay aft of the pumps. It contained the galley (Simon Graham wrote "gelly"), small foodstores and, sometimes, quarters for the cook and steward. The ship's boats, at least two, were stowed on the roundhouse along with spare spars.

The after hatch lay between the roundhouse and the mizzen. Aft of the mizzen was the companionway leading to the 'tween decks, the after part of which made up the captain's private domain. The arrangement varied from vessel to vessel, of course. The main stores of food and water were locked up just forward of the companionway along with small, valuable items of cargo. The captain's steward, alone of the crew, had access to these compartments.

Aft of the companionway, their extent depending upon the vessel's size and whether it was complete drogher or partly packet, were quarters for the mate and for a few passengers, along with a living-dining area, the whole being known as the cabin. Occupying the full width of the stern, usually wider than deep, were the captain's quarters, dignified with the title of great cabin, regardless of size. When Simon Graham assumed temporary command of H.M. Colonial Brig *Forte*, he was authorized to use all the cabin but he was not to enter the great cabin without written permission. Returning to Britain from Charleston and lacking passengers, Simon filled the cabin of the ship *Laurel* with cotton. Even if the bales were smaller than was usual, there is the impression of considerable space.

Below the weather deck, the hold of a drogher was completely open save for beams for a second deck and conversion to a packet or passenger vessel.[5] The cabin area was sometimes quite minimal and, when it was arranged for passengers, the bulkheads or partitions were removable. The transom or square end of the stern had four large ports covered with top-hinged trapdoors to facilitate the movement of timbers into the hold. The deck was purposely kept as clear as possible for the purpose of storing additional timber there.

The great cabin may have been separated from the cabin by shallow cupboards for storage of small items such as clothing and weapons. Through that area passed cables or chains from the wheel-drum overhead to the great tiller bar immediately below the cabin. Ready access to these passages was necessary in case of breakage of a rope, block or pin. If the shape of the stern and the position of the rudder are visualized, it becomes apparent that economy of space dictates the location of the wheel and its differential drum as far aft as practicable.

The binnacle stood before the wheel. The helmsman steered from behind the wheel but to one side with the wheel-drum (housed against weather) on his right or left. The ship's bell was mounted near the binnacle,[6] from which position the wind carried its sound along the length of the vessel. Around the base of each mast at deck level a curtain of painted canvas, wood, rope, lead and caulking kept water from pouring through the mast opening. A foot or two from the masts, on three sides and about three feet above the deck, fife rails carried belaying pins to hold halyards securely. The water-cask or scuttlebutt[7] (scuttled butt, i.e. with a hole and cock in the bottom) was cradled close to the main mast.

Later vessels, usually larger, with a pronounced cutwater but with only a rudimentary beak and no well, were arranged similarly except that the forecastle and poop were raised four feet or more above deck level. A few steps led down to the areas whose floors were two or three feet below deck level. Steps or ladders led up to the forecastle and poop decks as well.

Packet ships nearly always had two decks and divided holds designed for better stowage of crates, barrels and boxes as well as ready conversion to passenger quarters. Their transoms were characterized by large, heavily ornamented and strongly built windows opening into the great cabin. Their hold hatches were somewhat smaller than a drogher's and the weather decks were comparatively crowded with structures.

Clippers, often bulk cargo carriers, lacked a beak and usually had a fully raised forecastle entered from deck level. The bowsprit was secured under the forecastle, which provided more space, and the foremast often stood aft of the forecastle. Headroom was still limited, nevertheless. The poop, too, was fully raised and on some larger vessels it took the form of a deck house around which one could walk. The mizzen rose through the poop area of large vessels with spacious poop deck. The wheel was aft of the poop, the helmsman steering by compass, by command and, of course, by feel of the vessel.

It would appear that, as freeboard decreased and tumble-home sides began to straighten, designers realized that deck houses were profitable space-savers. The change from top-heaviness necessitated a new configuration at the stern which had still, however, to lift above the rudder assembly. The huge quarter-timbers that characterized and shaped square sterns being no longer required, a rounded or fantail sweep of smaller, fitted timbers evolved. Massive quarter timbers could not have been removed from earlier vessels because they were required for strength in high sterns impossible of other framing. Nevertheless, it is interesting to observe that, in a flurry of building of wooden motorized vessels in the United States in 1918, some designs again incorporated quarter timbers.[8]

Vessels had to be constructed on stocks raised above ground otherwise it was not possible to plank their bottoms. The launching ways could not be constructed, therefore, until the bottom of the hull was finished. Ways had to be built up to meet the vessel's cheeks by an amount not necessary, had workspace under the hull not been required. This made the ways and the procedure of launching quite elaborate.

Nagging doubts arise as to the complete accuracy of accounts or descriptions written long after Simon Graham's era, of how a vessel was launched. Always there is a feeling that something is missing. Modern launching methods, of course, cannot be relied upon as being identical to those of a century or more ago.

To a certain point accounts agree, or their variances may be put aside as the differing of technique rather than of method. Many state that the vessel was first raised by wedging under the keel so that it could be caused to fall a small amount later by knocking out the wedges. Small craft could be so lifted, but the process would be slow and difficult, perhaps impossible, for large, heavy vessels. Nor is it necessary. The wedges could have been and likely were, installed when the keel was shimmed to grade. Provided that the vessel could be dropped quickly, absolutely no need existed for raising it at all.

Parallel to the stocks and on each side, judiciously located with regard to the vessel's tendency to overturn sideways when free of props, ground ways of large dimensions were anchored. Known as ground ways because they were immovable, those timbers could be well above ground level. They extended far enough into the water to ensure the vessel's later floating free without striking bottom. Their fall, as noted earlier, was 1/8 inch per lineal foot greater than that of the keel. Thus, in 200 feet, the ground ways dropped about two feet relative to the keel, an amount gauged by experience as sufficient to get the vessel moving, but not too quickly.

Sliding ways were then placed over the ground ways. The meeting faces of the timbers were smooth and the space between well larded with animal fats to reduce friction. The sliding ways were kept in alignment by means of flanges overhanging the ground ways. On the sliding ways and affixed to them was a cradle, sometimes divided into bow and stern sections. The cradle arrangement was built up tightly to the hull without, however, actually raising it.

At this point the weight of the vessel rested on the keel blocks with the cradles snug to the hull bottom but not carrying any weight. Accounts often stumble at the next step because either of two courses was then practicable. The cradle could be wedged upwards, at points above the sliding member, so that the vessel's weight comes off the keel blocks and onto the sliding ways. When sufficient weight has been transferred and friction lessened, the cradle and vessel shudder indecisively. As more weight leaves the keel blocks and comes to the cradle, friction is overcome. The vessel moves and quickly picks up momentum.

The other method of transferring weight called for the splitting out of wedges or blocks in the keel crib, so dropping the weight quickly because the cradle was already snug to the hull. Both methods demanded a large number of men at key points, wedging or splitting in unison. Raising cradle and hull seems to have been fairly common for the launching of small vessels but dropping the hull onto the cradle appears to have been necessary for large vessels.

One part of the cradle arrangement should be clarified. Timber flanges on the sliding ways, overhanging the standing or fixed ways, were not sufficient, alone, to keep the sliding ways from spreading. The two sides had to be joined under the cradled hull. Only one means was possible with large hulls — stout cross-timbers had to be installed between the keel cribs. Their presence accounts for reiterated references to splitting blocks, rather than wedges, to lower the hull. It must have been imperative to have the cribs well loosened to prevent blocks from fouling the spreaders.

In *Cape Breton Ships and Men* John Parker shows an alternate method. Chains join the ways and, when the hull is raised by wedging between hull and cradle, the chains clear the keel blocks. The technique appears more suited to the launching of small vessels than large ones.

Vague references are found to the use of a launching trigger, not described, which appears to have been a late development on the New England coast. No mention of such a device is to be found in descriptions of launchings in Canada's Maritime Provinces. In a fine, well illustrated text, *How Wooden Ships Are Built*, H. Cole Estep mentions (in 1919) "the usual trigger gear" but does not elucidate. Estep sets forth an alternative method which has two men sawing apart the sliding and standing ways at the critical moment, to effect the ship's movement but it is difficult to see how it could be done.

Estep's book shows very clearly that he was in command of his subject; nevertheless, sometimes his handling of it is inadequate for landlubbers. He has this to say about launching: "When the ship is ready...it is raised off the keel blocks by wedges. Then the shores and keel blocks are knocked out transferring the weight of the ship to the cradle." One sees something wrong in the last statement because, according to the first step, the vessel was already free of its cribbing.

However it was achieved, vessels were always successfully launched. At least, one finds no record of any being left to rot on their stocks. We know what was accomplished by so many months of effort and we may ask how the results were regarded. Almost always the newly launched vessel was described in press reports in the most glowing terms. An *Encyclopaedia of Illustration* (London, 1845) ventured: "A ship is unquestionably one of the noblest works of man. It is a distinguished masterpiece of human skill. To build and manage so stupendous a vessel as a first rate ship of the line gives us a very high notion of the power of the human mind."

Sometimes some of the finishing and, usually, much of the rigging was completed when the vessel was afloat. One necessary procedure was to trim the hull.

It is not possible to construct a vessel so that its two sides are in accurate balance. Trimming was accomplished by ballasting the bilges with stones or clean gravel, a little more to one side than the other until the hull floated on an even keel. A plumb-bob hung from the mainmast acted as a tell-tale. This device was used also whenever the hull was loaded with heavy, especially bulky, cargo.

Simon Graham, in keeping with other mariners before and after his time, often referred to a vessel as *she* or *hir (her)* — but never as *he*, *it* or *him*. The origin of the custom is obscure although *The Hants and King's County Gazette* (Windsor, N.S.) ventured an explanation, copied from *The Boston Post*, in its issue of 10 February 1834:

Ships are called SHE because,
- they are useless without employment,
- look best when well rigged,
- their value depends on their age,
- they are upright when in stays,
- they bring news from abroad,
- they wear caps and bonnets
- they are often painted,
- and because a man knows not the expense 'till he gets one!

## CHAPTER 17

# Winds of Change

British vessels were said to be, until about 1855, the least efficient, most dangerous, most uncomfortable and most generally avoided of all the bad vessels afloat. Many such dreadful assessments may be found in technical and non-technical statements of the nineteenth century and even earlier. Thomas Gray commented along such lines in a paper: "Fifty Years of Legislation (1836-86) in Relation to the Shipping Trade and the Safety of Ships and Seamen," a lecture to the Worshipful Company of Shipwrights (records of 1886-87) of Great Britain. He had this to say: "...naval architecture had received no adequate attention in this country; and the best models of ships, even in our Royal Navy, were ships captured from the French, or copied from them." Gray, a master shipwright speaking to shipwrights, must have felt secure in such strong statements for they were not at all novel.

William Cobbett,[1] redoubtable old Englishman that he was, went even further. Writing some fifty years before Gray he urged his fellow-countrymen to foreswear British vessels in favour of American craft when travelling west. He found as much fault with British master mariners and their seamen as he did with their vessels.

Gray supports Cobbett's views. He quotes a description of British masters and officers, excepting those of the East India Company and some better shipping firms, which stated that "they are incomparably below foreign shipmasters in every respect."

This may be a little dismaying to those raised on the tradition of the superiority of British colonial shipbuilding and sailing fostered by such writers as Wallace *(Wooden Ships and Iron Men)* and Spicer *(Masters of Sail)*. The majority[2] of British merchantmen traversing the Atlantic and working the coasts of South America throughout the period of our interest were built in British North America, most, it seems, in New Brunswick. Wallace, Spicer and others appear to have taken the evidence presented by good, late vessels built in the declining years of sail, as representative of the entire period of British North American shipbuilding.

British vessels of the nineteenth century may be compared with those built in the United States. The latter craft appear to have been more efficient for a period of about 25 years between 1830 and 1855. Thereafter the disparity began to drop away. One reason lay with the development of Clipper hulls, another with careless British legislation.

American shipping bore the same general defects as British merchantmen because it was subject to general laws and customs imported from Britain, even to the extent of using the same rules for determining tonnage. Defects were precisely similar until Clipper construction was started in Baltimore, Maryland, about 1832.[3] Thereafter, Clipper hulls gradually superseded older construction and American vessels outpaced the British in speed, safety and profit until about 1855.

The Clipper hull had cleaner lines. The beak and the heavy timbers at the bow were tossed aside and the bow was, as described today, hollow. The term hollow hull is often used with reference to the inside of the bow but that is incorrect. The hollowness was actually the new concavity of bow lines behind the cutwater, outside. The depth to beam ratio was decreased, the hull became slimmer[4] and the freeboard was lowered. The stern assumed a lower, more rounded configuration. Deckhouses were added between forecastle and poop for passengers and light cargo.

The Clipper is said to have taken its name from the hull's tendency to clip lightly over the waves rather than plow through them, wallowing like gravid garbage scows, as Simon Graham's heavy vessels did. Clipper construction was firmly established by 1845. A well-known designer was Donald McKay (variously MacKay) of Boston, Massachusetts, but native of Nova Scotia.

The greater efficiency of the Clipper hull permitted a better arrangement of masts and spars, particularly in the case of the bowsprit and its jib-sails. This was reinforced when wire rope, introduced in the 1830s, became readily available. Towering masts and huge spreads of canvas resulted. The use of wire rope is considered to have made possible the transportation of large numbers of immigrants to the west coast of the United States, so opening up that huge country.

Until 1830, when Sir Robert Seppings introduced diagonal iron bands to serve the purpose, vessels lacked components to work against wracking. The result was that soon after its first voyage, a wooden vessel started to sag. Since it spent so much time atop waves with bow and stern overhanging, the two ends drooped while the central part of the hull was raised. The deformation was called "hogging" and it was noticeable on most vessels. Seppings' innovation largely forestalled this destructive failure in better-built vessels for a few years but it was not overcome completely until the advent of steel frames and hulls about the middle of the nineteenth century.

The phenomenon of hogging limited the lengths of wooden vessels to about 200 feet and that dimension was reached only by the heaviest and strongest of warships. Seppings' diagonal braces permitted merchantmen to reach 220 feet although, before about 1855, 175 feet was more common.

Before the dredging of harbours became economically possible wooden sailing vessels often had to "take to the bottom" at low tide. A deep hull and especially one deformed by hogging was then greatly distressed. It came down on its bow and stern timbers and as the weight of the vessel, no longer buoyed by salt water, tried to straighten, its arched keel was heaved and twisted. Timbers worked to assume new positions and more damage occurred.

Many historical records refer to hogging and the only remedial action possible in an emergency. Chains were passed under the bow of the vessel and brought back diagonally to fasten to timbers further aft. Such relief was, of course, only temporary. It could not actually raise the sagging bow and bring it up to keel level but it could fend off, for a while, the moment when the vessel broke its back. The procedure was known as "undergirding" and one account is interesting. It may be read in the King James' Bible, in Acts 27. It is significant that English translators of the early seventeenth century understood what was done for St. Paul's vessel and had the right word at hand to use, one that would be understood.

Seppings' braces, then steel ribs and diagonal bracing and, finally, steel-plate hulls permitted longer and slimmer vessels to be built.

Although credit is generally given to Baltimore shipbuilders for the innovation of Clippers about 1832 the design is most likely older in its essentials. Britain, except by indifference when nominally the monitor and defender of the American provinces before 1776, was never greatly involved in the slave trade. After American independence, a strong feeling against slavery gradually peaked in Britain and the Royal Navy began to interfere with the slavers. So as to outrun warships which they could not hope to battle, American slave-traders early began improvements to the hulls and sails of their "Blackbirders". As well, slaveships had to be fast because it was not possible to carry and serve food to the tremendous numbers of miserable bodies packed in their holds.

One may trace the course of changing shapes of Canadian ships before and after Confederation by examining portraits of vessels bequeathed to posterity by proud masters and owners. That task has been made easy by the publication of Armour and Lackey's wonderful book, *Sailing Ships of the Maritimes*. Armour and Lackey brought together a large number of paintings and drawings of sailing vessels, along with much pertinent and valuable data.

Information of that kind is, unfortunately, scant with regard to the first half of the nineteenth century. Throughout that period most vessels built in British North America were immediately sold abroad. They comprised a commodity not generally considered worthy of recording beyond the most meagre details of dimensions and tonnage.

Shipbuilders, seeking the lowest possible costs of operation, transcribed proportions directly from a half-hull model, fairing these on a molding-loft floor without intermediate drawings. The practice must have continued very late, for few construction drawings may be seen today. Spar plans are more common, likely because a vessel would need many new suits of sails throughout its life.

One combination of hull drawings, spar plans and dimensions has been safeguarded in the New Brunswick Museum at Saint John. They belong to the ship *Oliver Lang*, launched at Saint John in 1853. The data presented illustrate many points of interest. Armour and Lackey reproduce the drawings and data in their work.

*Oliver Lang* is termed a "Clipper Ship" on the drawings. Her dimensions were:

| | |
|---|---:|
| Length between the perpendiculars | 185' (56.39m) |
| Length of keel for tonnage | 158'2½" (48.23m) |
| Breadth, extreme | 38' (11.58m) |
| Breadth, molded | 37'2" (11.33m) |
| Depth in Hold | 24' (7.32m) |
| Burthen in Tons | 1215$^{10}$⁄₉₄ |

The ratio of beam to overall length is 38:185 = 1:4.85 for *Oliver Lang*. An average for ships about 20 years earlier (from a sampling) seems to be about 1:4.3; for vessels late in the century, about 1:5.2. Thus we see that she was about midway between early ships and late clippers in slenderness.

Her depth-to-beam ratio was 0.63, – less than 0.7 which was more common before 1855, but greater than the (rough) average 0.6 of later years. In this vessel and others of about 1853, one may see that Moorsom's rule, widely discussed for at least a year earlier, was anticipated as law and was therefore influencing design.

*Oliver Lang* sported a prominent beak, a feature of early ships not to be observed on late clippers. *Marco Polo,* Saint John, 1851, had none, although her bow by later standards was old-fashioned and rather bulbous. *Oliver Lang*'s cutwater, too, is pronounced. The length between perpendiculars does not include beak or overhanging stern. The latter is high and square, clearly reminiscent of the 1830s.

The spar plan shows course, topsail, topgallant and royal sails. Doubtless studdingsails were also carried but the four-sail arrangement contrasts sharply with that of seven sails on each mast of *John M. Blaikie*, Great Village, N.S., 1885. Accordingly, *Oliver Lang* may be considered an early transitional vessel, midway between ships of 1830 and those of the end of the century.

The ship's burden, 1215-10/94 tons, may be related to Old Measure with confidence. Use of Old Measure at that date, 1853, is surprising, particularly so since Dr. E.C. Wright found the registered tonnage as 1236 tons (1236.31 on her Governor's Pass) which Armour and Lackey note as well. That burden may be related to New Measure, just as confidently. Dr. Wright's many problems with tonnage are illustrated in an account of the launching taken from a New Brunswick newspaper of the day by Armour and Lackey. The report provides tonnages of 1230 (NM) and 1275 (OM). These seem to be defective since no method of computation will yield such figures.

Inspection of registration data and of plans and portraits of sailing craft shows very clearly that British North American shipbuilders stayed abreast of changes in hull design, canvas and rigging. Indeed, they were leaders in some aspects. Nevertheless, their vessels were disparaged throughout the nineteenth century and it may now be appropriate to examine this contentious issue.

The scoffing revolved around the extensive use of softwoods in the construction of British North American vessels. This caused them to class at only seven years in contrast to twelve years granted to vessels built of the more durable hardwoods. That was relatively unimportant, being offset by lower selling prices in the marketplace. Of more significance was their handling afloat.

Experience had taught that softwood vessels were not as sturdy as their hardwood counterparts. Their hulls would not accept as much stress. Accordingly, in strong winds and especially in rough seas, skippers of British North American vessels had to take in canvas and start caring for the safety of their commands earlier than was necessary for the stronger hulls. Thus, more time was lost running before storms. That was an important factor, since time effected profit. It explains, in part, why so few softwood vessels were employed in the tea trade.

Midway through the 18th century, the date being uncertain owing to lost records, British shipowners found a pressing need to compile registries of vessels showing their degree of seaworthiness. The growth of that endeavour into *Lloyds Register of British and Foreign Shipping* is discussed by W.S. Lindsay in a *History of Merchant Shipping, 1774-1876*.

The earliest surviving registers date from about 1760. Vessels were classified by hull condition – A, E, I, O or U and rigging – G, M or B for Good, Middling or Bad. Lindsay found numbers substituted for G, M and B in 1775, so dating the first known reference to the historical designation, "A1". Nevertheless, the classifications A, E, I, O and U all appear in Lloyds

Registers until 1833. A rival register existed from 1779 to 1834, whereupon both joined to form the continuing Lloyds Register; and thereafter the more familiar designation of A1 for a period of years is found as the sole classification system.

Lindsay could not find that the A1 class was given for a specific period on merit of construction. Rather, it seemed that vessels retained their original ratings according to place of building, varying from twelve years for London (the homeport of the East Indiamen) to five or six years for "north country" ports. After that arbitrary period, no way appeared for reinstatement to an A1 category. He pointed out that the method encouraged inferior building and discouraged efficient repair.

The union of registers in 1834 removed "those and other mischievous tendencies." Unclassed vessels were gradually dropped from the new register and the following provisions were made for classification of wooden vessels.

Depending upon a surveyor's evaluation of materials[5] and workmanship, a new vessel was assigned a number of years through which, if "occasionally" surveyed, it might retain its A1 rating. The period was shown before the rating, 7A1 indicating seven years, the maximum for most New Brunswick and Nova Scotia construction, it seems. "Occasionally" was qualified as "annually if practicable," with the penalty of loss of rating if four years elapsed without survey. (The certificate of resurvey of a late Canadian barque, *Queen of the Fleet*, 941 tons, Dorchester, N.B., 1876, is appended to this chapter.)

If specially resurveyed a vessel might retain its A1 rating, then recorded in red ink, for a further period not exceeding two-thirds of the first period granted. The A1 rating permitted the carrying of dry and perishable goods to all parts of the world. A lesser classification, AE, was granted (upon annual survey and special survey within four years) to carry dry and perishable goods on shorter voyages and for non-perishable cargoes. An inferior rating, E, requiring annual and three-year special surveys, permitted the carrying of non-perishable cargoes only. The three classifications show how many vessels dropped from pride-of-the-fleet-status to end their days as colliers.

Lloyds Register was a non-profit enterprise truly devoted to the good of those who used seagoing transportation. Its use quickly spread abroad, where similar registers, most under Lloyds control but some under other guidance, were opened. All British shipowners and those from the colonies intending to sell or register vessels in Britain used Lloyds but, after Confederation, some Canadian vessels dealing with the United States used Bureau Veritas or The American Shipowners Register. Lloyds and other societies maintained a staff of surveyors at home and abroad who were available for inspection, on request, so that vessels under construction might "class" as well as possible upon launching. Registration with the classification societies was not synonymous with registration of nationality.

Armour and Lackey, in *Sailing Ships of the Maritimes*, point to registry of British (colonial) vessels at Canso and Annapolis as early as 1728, but they later seem to imply that enforced registration stemmed from a British law of 1786, *A Bill for the Further Increase and Encouragement of Shipping and Navigation,* (one of the famous "Navigation Laws"). They noted that vessels of 15 tons or more were to be registered but that no foreign craft, particularly those of the new United States, were to be permitted registry unless a prize taken in war. This law appears to have been directed towards British North America with regard to small coastal traders dealing with the United States. Actually, it only decreased the size of vessel, from 100 to 15 tons, required to be registered.

Two years earlier, in 1783, Governor Thomas Carleton, upon the erection of the province of New Brunswick and his appointment, had been directed as follows in "Royal Instructions to Governor Thomas Carleton," (18/8/84). "Fifth....You shall every three months or oftener...transmit to the Commissioners of our Treasury...a list of all ships and vessels trading in your government according to the form and specimen herewith attached." One sees that Britain was acting quickly to enforce the restrictive aspects of the Navigation Laws following the American Revolution.

Registry of vessels in Eastern Canada could be made at a large number of ports in New Brunswick, Nova Scotia and Prince Edward Island from the earliest days of the colonies. Vessels had to be registered, before sailing, at one of those ports unless intended for sale and registry in Britain, whereupon a single voyage was permitted by special leave. A "Governor's Pass" served the purpose before Confederation.

Throughout Simon Graham's career legislation was enacted from year to year in Britain, some of it valuable, some of it insignificant. Some points should be noted. In 1852, Simon Graham applied for and received a Master's Certificate of Service "pursuant to Act 13th & 14th Vict., cap 23". Before that enactment, his own word was a Master Mariner's reference; and anyone, even a porter, even a youth of 17 years, could be given command, actual instances of which were cited by Gray. This was the beginning of a move to prove the qualifications of officers.

In 1849, Britain's resources of mariners proving inadequate and this being aggravated by lack of worthwhile training programs, foreign seamen were admitted to British vessels. Tonnage rules were revised in 1854, following studies by Admiral Moorsom (see Chapter 3) who found British vessels so slow and unsafe as to be unable to compete with foreigners.

*The Merchant Shipping and Passenger Acts* of 1854 and 1855 finally set British shipping on the way to recovery of a leading position.[6] It is ironical that steam rather than sails prompted the resultant improvements. With steam and steel the British merchant marine entered a new era of dominance and prosperity.

LLOYDS REGISTER OF BRITISH AND FOREIGN SHIPPING

15TH AUGUST, NEW YORK

Bark *Queen of the Fleet* of Dorchester

Copy of survey report June 1881

This vessel was placed on Dry Dock on blocks of sufficient height so that keel and bottom were fairly exposed. Outside planking was scraped where necessary and found good. Hold cleared and proper stages made inside and out. All air courses and timbers cleared. Condition of frame ascertained by a new listing being cut out according to rule. Yellow metal stripped off and one treenail put in each timber from lower turn of bilge to about fifteen foot line or into lower deck clamp, so as to make her square fastened. Bottom thoroughly caulked, refitted and remetalled up to 14'6" line. Yellow metal bolts taken out of rudder braces and pintles, and renewed with copper ones. New foremast step. Condition of beam ends found good by boring. Yellow metal bolts, good. Caulking all good. All general equipments examined and found good and sufficient. Partly Retreenailed.

S.W. Langdon

## CHAPTER 18

# The Lutine Bell

The Lutine Bell at Lloyds, sounded whenever a vessel is reported overdue, would have been long worn out if struck for every mariner lost at sea. Proportionate to numbers engaged in Man's many endeavours, seafaring has always been by far the most demanding of life and limb.

The ship in which a seaman sails is his whole world. Any threat to it immediately renders the mariner's survival a chancy affair. Always in jeopardy, his life and well-being merely become factors to be flung onto the scales of fortune in hope of tipping them towards the safety of his vessel. Desperate men have to swallow both the bile of fear and the sour taste of selfishness, whereupon astounding feats of daring may be accomplished in the common weal. The dangers faced every day of their lives lead seamen to regard as ordinary those acts considered by landsmen to be heroic.

In Simon Graham's day the least a seaman had to fear was the early loss of all his teeth, an inevitable outcome of malnutrition and scurvy. More to be dreaded was the consequence of a gash that severed muscle tendons which, owing to lack of medical skills, could not be repaired. Seaports were full of seamen crippled in the pursuit of their livelihood. Deformed bodies, the result of inexpert attention to compound fractures, were so ordinary as to be ignored. Seamen actually hoped to fall into the sea rather than onto the deck when they lost a grip aloft.

Pestilence, too, was accepted as an unchangeable fact of life. The attention given incoming vessels at quarantine grounds of ports helped to prevent the spread of contagious diseases ashore, but once aboard a ship at sea, disease had to run its course unchecked. One of the consequences, seen on *Sybylla*'s return trip from the Pacific, was that more healthy and less-infected crewmen worked to exhaustion to keep the vessel safe.

Hunger and thirst, aggravated quite often by extremes of heat and cold, were accepted. Being wet to the skin, above deck or below, were conditions to which, like the stink of a forecastle, seamen had to become inured. Illnesses, acute and chronic, were set aside in a seaman's mind because, even in the best hospitals of the era, little could be done for them.

Early in the nineteenth century, impressment by Royal Navy officers was a fate to be avoided at all costs. Life in a warship was harder than in a merchantman and, having taken the King's shilling, a seaman might not see his home for a good many years. Mutiny was often thrust upon the best of seamen and the chances of unwilling involvement or false accusation were always great.[1]

A hazard faced constantly was that of the vessel foundering. Storms were the common cause. Steady pounding by heavy seas could break the stoutest of hulls. Leakage, whether by storm action or the rot of old age was a great harrassment for a crew. Manning the pumps killed ailing men and left the strongest worn out even if their vessel remained afloat. Foundering under an unexpected great wave of origins not fully understood even today, sent many a vessel to the bottom.

Capsizing in heavy seas was an ever-present danger. In addition to being topheavy by design, vessels were often overloaded and the cargo poorly stowed so that it shifted under the rolling of the hull. Dismasting by hurricane force winds predisposed a vessel to capsizing. This danger was often aggravated by carrying more sail than prudence advised. Impaired navigation and seamanship, whatever their origins, resulted in the loss of many a sound vessel.

Collision with other ships, icebergs, even flotsam and jetsam, sank many vessels. Shipwreck was to be expected and written off lightly, as many logs reveal. Stranding on a shoal from which the vessel could not be dislodged was always a possibility. Slim chances of survival were in prospect for the best provisioned small boats that left a stranding, although such conditions were preferred over shipwreck on a rocky shore.

Destruction by enemy action caused tremendous losses of vessels. Until about 1835, piracy and mutiny[2] played parts in the disappearances of many ships.

Fire at sea was dreaded. Once flames took a strong hold on a wooden vessel they could not be doused because pressure pumps were not available before the advent of steam power. Lightning often split masts as it set them afire. Careless use of cooking fires, oil lamps and candles were less a factor than spontaneous combustion of cargo. Bucket lines would handle a small fire between decks if it were caught quickly, but they were useless on a smouldering cargo. As soon as hatches were opened to attack the problem, draughts so created fanned the fire into flames.

The causes of many losses at sea remain a mystery. In founderings attributed to ordinary storm action, rotten hulls must be considered to have contributed frequently.

Throughout the era of sail, adversities suffered by wooden vessels not owing to the negligence of men, were blamed on the unavoidable risks of seafaring. The exercise of normal prudence in the management of a vessel having been demonstrated, liability for damage could not be assessed and insurers assumed the financial burden. When a vessel failed to complete its voyage for reasons unknown, that is, having simply disappeared with its crew, its loss was attributed to "the perils of the sea."

Such a stand appears necessary as a legal device and reasonable in view of the harsh environment in which a vessel passed its days. Nevertheless, insurers such as Lloyds knew that in many cases negligence was more to blame than the ferocity of the ocean. More particularly, they knew that faulty construction and deterioration of the vessel's hull, one or the other or both, were often causative factors when a vessel foundered.

Lloyds, to limit the horrifying losses of merchantmen, and the Royal Navy, in its own interests, initiated standards relating to the building of wooden vessels, their materials and regular inspections. What was missing was a knowledge of the processes of decay in wood.

Writers for 200 years or more have attributed the deterioration of wooden vessels to a mysterious malady they call dry rot. Some, more recently, have expressed the view that if a hull did not succumb to dry rot it was eventually ruined by becoming waterlogged! That makes the situation very puzzling indeed. It sounds as though wood, to remain sound, should be neither dry nor wet. The truth of the matter is that the term is faulty. Dry rot takes its name, not from the process of decay, but from the appearance of seriously affected wood — ashore, however, not at sea.

It is the result of micro-organisms (fungi) feeding on the cellulose component of wood. Intercellular moisture between 18% and 25% has to be present for such activity. Below a moisture level of about 18%, fungal spores are dormant or, at least, less voracious. At a level above about 25%, when the cells begin to fill with moisture, the wood becoming waterlogged, activity is precluded by lack of necessary oxygen.

In damp basements wood rots quickly but, in dryer rooms, panelling and furniture may last for centuries. Timbers on an ocean floor or piles driven into wet ground, unless destroyed by worms, may last for even a thousand years.

Decay could have begun in a ship's timbers even before they were set into position. Regardless of whether they were green or well-seasoned to start with, this could have come about through faulty storing of the material having permitted the wood to remain or become suitably moist. Infected material would have continued to decay as it was built into a vessel, although the process might have been temporarily arrested by hot dry weather. It was hastened by rains and by filling the hull with water to reveal poorly caulked seams, which practice was not unknown.

When the vessel was afloat the exterior planking took up moisture and passed it to the inside. The surface in contact with the sea may have been too wet to rot but the inside face and abutting timbers were suitably damp. Poor housekeeping practices which allowed debris such as chips and residue of cargo to accumulate, fostered rot. Lack of ventilation aided the growth of fungi. Failure to clean and dry holds after discharge of cargo and to seek and replace decaying timbers ensured that rot never left the hull. Reasons for the short lives of some vessels and the longer lives of others, well cared for, are then apparent.

Few records to do with early British North American shipbuilding activities make reference to materials. No exhortations for the proper seasoning of lumber may be found and no owners' complaints against the use of green timber are of record. Consequently it might be argued that shipbuilders knew all about dry rot and seasoned their woods properly. That may have been the case but it is to be doubted. Throughout its long career as the world's largest owner, builder and operator of wooden vessels, the Royal Navy never learned to season its construction lumber. Had it been otherwise one would surely find Lloyds also insisting on the use of seasoned timbers, which is not the case in early years.

The Royal Navy's experiences and struggles with rotten hulls are set forth in a wonderfully interesting and erudite address presented on 20 March 1937, to the Essex Nature Society by its president, John Ramsbottom, O.B.E., and published in the *Essex Naturalist* that year. Its title was, of course, "Dry Rot in Ships," but its author had his tongue in cheek. Ramsbottom seems to have been a mycologist. He was preparing an account of Essex fungi when he found a number of old records relating to fungi in the naval dockyard at Deptford near London. Puzzled by research having been performed in such an unlikely location, Ramsbottom studied Admiralty records and produced a valuable report.

He found that a Commission of Inquiry appointed by James I recommended, in 1609, that timber be "seasoned in water to sucke out the sappe and after dried by the ayre and sonne and pyled uppe till thear be fit use of it." Ramsbottom then proceeded to trace the Royal Navy's concern with dry rot which always recognized that fungi seemed responsible but which never quite accepted the cooperative role of unseasoned timbers.

Ramsbottom says that, up to 1804, only four species of wood were employed to any extent in the hulls of the King's ships — oak,[3] in by far the largest proportion, then elm, beech and fir. The others were accepted only because of a chronic shortage of oak. Ramsbottom stresses a constant endeavour to use only the best timbers, yet he finds an astounding range in the useful lives of Royal Navy warships not lost in battle.

*Royal Sovereign,* built slowly between 1635 and 1637 of oak barked in the spring and left standing until it was felled in the winter had a long life. Fifty years after construction her timbers were sound and so hard that a nail could hardly be driven into them. She was burned by accident or negligence in 1696. *Achilles,* built of such material in 1757 was sound after twenty years, but, needing repairs in 1784 when the navy was not engaged in hostilities, she was broken up. *Victory* was 45 years old at Trafalgar although extensively repaired three times during the period.

On the other hand, Ramsbottom observed, *St. Domingo,* 1809, and *La Hogue,* 1811, were both in a state of decay by 1812. *Rodney,* 1809, had scarcely put to sea when she had to be recalled and paid off. *Dublin,* 1812, was paid off after only one voyage. She was subsequently rebuilt at great cost. The first-rate ship *Queen Charlotte,* 110 guns, launched in 1810, rotted so quickly that she had to be rebuilt before she could be commissioned! Many attributed this to the great quantities of Canadian oak and American pitch-pine worked into the hull. After extensive rebuilding, the *Queen Charlotte* remained afloat until 1892.

Ramsbottom reports that "the duration of a ship was estimated at twenty-five to thirty years in the seventeenth century, about twelve years from 1760 to 1788, about eight years during the Napoleonic period, dwindling to no duration immediately after Trafalgar." He also observed that in 1759 several Thames shipbuilders unanimously stated that English river-built ships would remain serviceable about sixteen years and the French only seven.

Many writers, including Ramsbottom, refer to generally accepted views that French vessels were better designed and built than British ships. Indeed, they were considered real prizes when captured and they were immediately refitted under British colours. Ramsbottom notes that sixty-six Royal Navy warships foundered during the American Revolutionary War, in striking contrast to the few lost in action. He makes clear that many consultants to the Royal Navy understood how conditions could have been greatly improved but that dry rot in the Admiralty itself precluded acceptance of their arguments. Poor maintenance played such a large part in the decay of vessels decommissioned and at anchor in harbour that in some, fungal growth had to be cut away before lower decks could be inspected.

Ramsbottom wryly observed in a footnote to his account that there was often misunderstanding because the term dry rot was not used in early days. Its introduction dates from 1775 and a paper: "Some observations on the Distemper in Timber called the Dry Rot."

Merchantmen built in British North America had a life expectancy just as unpredictable as for the Royal Navy's warships. That may be ascertained from inspection of lists compiled by Manny, Parker, Spicer, Wallace and Wright as well as those in Lloyds Registers and in the census of Canadian vessels taken soon after Confederation. Examples of extraordinary longevity may be found side by side with instances of vessels being erased from the record after a few years at sea.

Unfortunately, contemporary observers did not leave as much information to do with the shortcomings of merchant vessels as they did of warships. Circumstances differed and those concerning a humble merchantman found with a rotten bottom were hardly comparable to those that attended discovery of a mighty man-of-war unfit for service. Reading between the lines of Lloyds Registers one gets the impression of wooden hulls deteriorating quite quickly, but the Registers list only vessels considered seaworthy; they do not indicate the numbers of vessels considered too rotten to repair or to present to Lloyds for resurvey. Only brief reports remain outlining how inspections were performed, their findings, and, sometimes the improvements deemed necessary. No records exist by means of which one may estimate the extent to which founderings were brought on by rotten hulls.

It may be an astonishing statement but it appears that experienced seamen did not bother to make regular inspections of their ships' hulls to determine the state of seaworthiness, upon which their lives might well depend. Here is an example of the discovery of a weak spot that should have been noted much earlier. It is described (although in a way hard to accept) by John Ledyard in *A Journal of Captain Cook's Last Voyage, 1776-79*, published only five years afterwards.

> The gale was very severe and was the means of opening a defective place in the Resolution's bottom which was of an alarming nature. We did not meet with an opportunity of repairing it until some time later when we found that the complaint originated from a hole eat (sic) through the bottom of the ship as far as the sheathing by the rats, and the sheathing being old gave way when the ship strained. We were surprised to find the aperature stopped up by some old shakings of yarns and oakum, that by some accident was washed into it.

Early in the nineteenth century, the Royal Navy, or rather, some innovators connected with the Navy's marine architecture, experimented unsuccessfully with chemicals in a search for a timber preservative. No record of similar endeavours is to be found in reliable accounts of shipbuilding in British North America through the same period. Some writers refer to the custom of packing rock salt between the ceiling and planking but research fails to find support for the practice in the first half of the century. In fact, the only dependable references appear very late in the era of sail. Rock salt contains compounds other than sodium chloride. It is hygroscopic but does not dissolve readily. Rather it assumes a different chemical form which, coupled with its void-filling bulk, does inhibit fungus growth.

Throughout the nineteenth century, particularly as the use of copper sheathing became more common, increasing attention was given to the ventilation and drying of wooden hulls. The practice originated in the Royal Navy. By means of sails erected on deck, dry air was forced down companionways and deep into the hull as the vessel sped along. In harbour heaters of the type called salamanders were positioned throughout the lowest deck.

As improved pumps became available, bilges of sound hulls were kept free of water and when the vessel was in harbour, as soon as it was free of cargo or ballast, the holds were scraped and whitewashed. Pumping, drying, cleaning, ventilating and whitewashing added greatly to the longevity of ships' hulls. One may judge the practice to have been common because Simon Graham refers to such work on *Sybylla* in 1834 and on his other vessels later.

## CHAPTER 19

# Master and People

Even the most casual examination of the relationship between master and crew in the merchant service must inquire into the laws and customs of seafaring. Reference must be made to them if affairs of more than a century ago are to be interpreted.

The master's position of command was on the weather side of the quarterdeck. All authorities agree on that but without providing a reason. One was sought from a seagoing acquaintance. His reply indicates that interpretation is indeed a problem:

"The master did not have to stand on the weather side of the quarterdeck. He did so only because it was the safest and most comfortable location. An unfortunate seaman dropping from a yard fell to the lee, well away from the master's position. The heaviest seas came over the lee rail and so, by being on the weather side, the master avoided constant drenching."

That cynical explanation may be sound but custom assigns the weather side of the quarterdeck to the master for better reasons. The master exercised his authority indirectly through his mate. A long tradition demanded such an aloof stance and the mate insisted on its observance for practical reasons. When the mate became totally involved in a particular action he had to rely on the master to keep an overall watch and to direct the mate's attention as necessary. The weather side of the quarterdeck was the best position for scanning fore and aft, on deck and aloft. On the few occasions when the master was permitted to give a general command — tacking the ship was one — the mate commanded in the bow and the master on the quarterdeck[1] from the weather side.

The master broke the unwritten code of indirect command only at the risk of having his mate insist that thereafter the master assume all the mate's obligations as well as his own.[2] The master had a mate and second mate, not to assist him but to function within certain prescribed limits in the operation of the vessel.

The master's responsibilities were twofold. On the one hand the master was charged with the safe and expeditious conduct of his vessel and hence, its cargo and crew, from port to port. On the other, he was the owners' representative and ship's husband to an extent depending upon the size and strength of the organization for which he worked. The master had to deliver his cargo, at least. Sometimes he had to negotiate its sale at a profit and obtain a return cargo under the best possible terms. Always he had to seek and accommodate as many cabin passengers as space permitted. Occasionally he was required to act in the sale of the vessel itself.

The master hired the crew, including the mate and second mate, signing them to the articles of agreement negotiated.[3] He saw to the provisioning of the vessel, the rule appearing to be that he took aboard a little less food than would likely be required. It is easier to get the master's other duties in perspective if those of the mate and second mate are described first.

The second mate was only a seaman, but one who had ambition and who showed potential for the rank, later, of mate. The qualities that set him apart from other seamen included youth, eagerness, agility, ability to read, write and comprehend. His level of education was of no importance because no one cared how long it took him to acquire the knowledge that would see his promotion to mate if, indeed, he ever were mate.

The second mate worked as an ordinary seaman but was expected to excel in all ways. He had to be first aloft and always in the most demanding and dangerous of positions. He had to set a vigorous pace for others to follow or he did not hold long to his leading rank.

All officers had to be tough mentally and physically and those qualities certainly had to be demonstrated in a second mate. Master and mates were lonely men owing to the demands of their positions, but the second mate's lot was most unenviable. He was not one of the crew although he messed with them; and he was not one of the important officers although he had, on occasion, to command in the waist of the vessel.

The first mate's duties differed sharply. He had actual supervision of all work performed aboard the vessel. The mate was expected to be a fully competent mariner, lacking, however, the years of experience or else possessing another fault that held him from a command of his own.

The mate kept the log-book, a double-leaf slate, and made a fair copy on paper to the master's satisfaction. The mate commanded one watch — the larboard — but his authority was confined to minor adjustments to the sails. He could not change their set or undertake any manoeuver without the master's permission. The mate succeeded to the master's position in the latter's incapacity but the second mate was not automatically promoted.

The master selected the vessel's courses, performed the work of navigating (although often joined by the mate) and determined the spread of canvas required by conditions. He commanded the starboard watch but under ordinary circumstances he left the deck to the second mate, always on the master's watch for that purpose.

The daily log was kept on a slate and in it the officer of the watch recorded all noteworthy happenings. Each day the mate transcribed the record into a journal. An oft-repeated if apocryphal tale recounts that the master, fed up with the mate's habit of warming himself with rum, once wrote: "The mate was drunk today:" whereupon the mate, a day or two later, entered: "The captain was sober today." It can be seen that the master's prior entry was not possible if the mate had actual control of the journal. As a matter of fact, although many contemporary authorities state the mate's responsibility for the log, little support can be found today for that contention.

The journal, often referred to as the log or log-book, was turned over to the port marine superintendent on the completion of each voyage.[4] It was awarded almost irreproachable status if produced as evidence in court of law. Since they never again saw the journal unless upon search at a records office, both master and mate[5] made abstracts for their own purposes. A third copy was often made ashore for the owners' files.[6]

In the case of Simon Graham's "abstrack of jurnal," except where he noted specifically that he was master on the voyage, as he usually did, it is not possible today to be sure that he was not the mate. That possibility is reinforced, on occasion, by finding in Lloyds Registers that another is of record as master. No law existed to prevent a master sailing as mate but, as a general rule, it would appear to have been below his dignity to do so.

The master and his mates were expected to refrain from familiarity with crew members. Many quasi-authorities, among them, Dixon's *Law of Shipping*, New York, 1859, state that quite positively. The reason is apparent. Seamen were thus protected from taking liberties with their officers who were all-powerful at sea. This was in the general interest of all and the particular interest of individuals. Questions or quibbles could not be tolerated at moments when action was required and the best prevention was to keep seamen at arm's length from the master and mate at all times.

Before about 1840, a master had practically unlimited authority at sea. Perhaps the only measure denied him was capital punishment. Notwithstanding, a master could kill a seaman and, provided that he could demonstrate at least a confrontation with the man, he could claim an incipient mutiny stopped short, with little fear of more than rebuke in court of law. Moreover, a master could flog a man or have him flogged for a comparatively minor misdemeanour with small chance that his judgment would be questioned.

The important turning-points in the course of events that led to improvement of the situation may be noted. They concern American seamen and, though similar instances to do with Great Britain cannot readily be discovered, a sympathetic reaction may be imagined in that country.

In 1840, R.H. Dana published *Two Years Before the Mast*, an account of a voyage he had made as an ordinary seaman around Cape Horn a few years before. His narrative illustrated the hard and often unfair treatment seamen had to endure. Of particular repugnance were the details of a flogging administered by an unstable master. Dana had, in the meantime, become a lawyer, and he appended a well-reasoned appeal for consideration of the mariner's plight. This seems to have generated a number of successful court actions against brutal masters, all building on precedence.

In 1842, the rights of the U.S. Navy to flog a seaman and the commanding officers' privilege of being able to sentence a man to death on their own judgments were removed. Flogging was abolished as a form of punishment and the sentence of death was reserved to courts-martial. Those actions followed the hanging of three seamen by Cdr. A.S. MacKenzie of the U.S. brig *Somers*. MacKenzie, claiming to have apprehended a mutiny, had acted without recourse to trial.

By Act of September 28, 1850, flogging and all other corporal punishment was made illegal in the U.S. merchant service. An earlier Act of Congress (3 March 1835, Chap. 40 Sec. 3) had made it an indictable offence for a master to inflict punishment of any kind from malice, hatred or revenge and without justifiable cause" but the qualification rendered the law inoperative.

More than a century was to elapse before Great Britain passed similar legislation. Nevertheless, the practice of flogging began to diminish at the same time, although it lingered for twenty years after the U.S. enactment of 1850. Records of the Royal Navy are full of accounts of extreme brutality by commanding officers, including the flogging of men to death, until about 1850. Merchant masters, on the other hand, were subject to civilian courts and could not as readily evade responsibility for their actions.

There is no evidence whatsoever of brutality on the master's part in Simon Graham's logs. At the same time there are many references to gross misconduct by his seamen.

Graham had three of his men locked up in jail on the west coast of South America and he was in high dudgeon when Lord James Townshend had them removed and pressed into the Royal Navy. Merchant masters often had certain high-spirited, valued seamen — those who might desert or, by way of intemperance, might fail to sail with the vessel — locked up for safe-keeping while in a foreign port. By 1850, such action was indefensible in court but, by the time of return to the home port where a charge might be laid, the incident had lost all meaning to the injured seaman.

Lord Townshend's behaviour lay within his commission, although a civil court in Britain, Nova Scotia or New Brunswick would not have allowed it. Civilians had always feared and hated the naval press gangs and the Admiralty had surrendered some years earlier to loud public declamations against the practice. Britain had no means of conscripting military or naval forces at that time and the Royal Navy's reputation for brutality militated against its getting all the volunteers it needed.

The chronic shortage of hands became acute when a man-of-war was on foreign station. To ease the situation the Admiralty empowered its commanders to seize any able-bodied British subject found abroad, being a deserter of any kind, a miscreant in jail or merely a vagabond in another nation's service. In fact, *Dublin*'s commander did not take three of Simon Graham's seamen. That was not permitted. He merely rescued three British subjects from durance vile abroad and then, being able to spare some hands, gave three others to Simon. "Yousless!" that worthy spluttered.

When *Grampian*'s crew became alarmed at the leaky state of their vessel they advanced as a deputation and requested that the master abandon the voyage and put into the nearest port for repairs. The seamen were well within their rights as conceded by maritime law, provided that the consensus included the mate and the majority of the crew. By the same law the master was required to comply with the request.

*Perekop*'s crew was in an entirely different set of circumstances. The seamen had actually mutinied and their position was indefensible. Each man faced a long jail term if apprehended. As well, the men named by Simon Graham were soon blacklisted by all reputable shipping firms. Although they may well have had legitimate grievances, no court would have condoned such actions on a short voyage, even had there been very great aggravation.

The law of the sea, maritime law as it is more commonly known, is tremendously complex. In the nineteenth century it was often ponderous and sometimes quaint. Many volumes of court cases set forth precedents with regard to the master's responsibility for his cargo, yet one of them established that he could not be blamed for damage by rats if he had shipped a cat on board!

The rate of pay for a master during Simon Graham's active period was ten pounds sterling or forty dollars per month. Almost certainly he received commissions as well, but they were not large. Simon Graham, for instance, never became wealthy.

The mate received five pounds sterling or twenty dollars per month and no share in the profits. Seamen's wages varied from about six or seven dollars for a boy to twelve dollars for an ordinary hand. The second mate, carpenter, boatswain and steward were paid from 12 to 17 dollars per month, depending upon their skills and value to the master.

Those rates seem to have applied aboard vessels up to a thousand tons burden through most of Simon Graham's career. The masters of larger vessels, and especially the stewards of passenger ships, received somewhat higher pay. Their food was much better as well. By 1880 wages had doubled but another fifty years were to pass before they had doubled again.

The crew were "The People." The usage is old and yet it is recognized today by east coast Canadian seamen, even by young people. The term is not cold but it is remote. It smacks of paternalism and points to the custom of the master holding himself aloof from those with whom he shares the perils of the sea.

Under any circumstances the master must be obeyed and obedience is fostered if he is not close to his seamen. Such routine behaviour sets a pattern to be followed in emergency when the slightest delay in executing an order may endanger the vessel and its crew. However, that simplistic view is equally aloof from the actual conditions of the early nineteenth century.

Seamen were a tough, hard-drinking, unruly, often rebellious lot. Simon Graham did not waste words describing his people but occasional references to the crew being drunk and the account of near mutiny aboard *Perekop* speak quite loudly of the kind of men he had to deal with. Clearly, a master had to keep them at arm's length if he expected to control his vessel.

When hard men come together no room is left for weaklings and men of moderate behaviour are squeezed out, no matter how tough they may be. It simply is not possible to be part of a small, closely-knit, hard-living body of ruffians and yet be different. Nevertheless, the selection of seamen for his crew being one of the master's functions, it would appear that to a certain extent at least, he alone was responsible for lack of harmony that might develop aboard.

That view, too, may be naive. Much depended upon where the crew was made up. A master could not expect to hire the kind of men from a lumbering area that might be found in an older, more sedate seaport. Obviously, a more tractable group might be signed on in a fishing town than could be found by searching the docks of New York, London, or Glasgow. The small ports provided crews of relatives and neighbours accustomed to working together.

Liquor, nearly always rum, played a part in some disturbances at sea but it was then more likely to have been a fault of the master or his mate.

Unless they were extremely careless, the pair in positions of authority made certain that all liquor that came aboard went into their own cabins or was safely secured in the hold. On the other hand, there appears no reason for believing that temperance vessels some of which are of record, were any happier or more trouble-free.

The main sources of friction between master and crew, if those cases in which the master was abnormally brutal are set aside, would appear to have derived from the ethics of the period and greed on the part of shipowners and masters working on commission. Labourers of any kind at that time expected discipline and, in fact, actually preferred stern overseers, but they would not permit infringements on the few rights they had. Most of Simon Graham's seafaring took place through the period of abuse of labourers described so often by Charles Dickens. Ashore, children from the age of eight were working twelve hours a day in sweat-shops and coal mines. At sea, grown men considered themselves fortunate to be removed from the situation.

Work hours ashore were from dawn to dusk, six days a week with Sunday reserved for self-denial and the singing of praise to God. Only a few religious holidays were allowed throughout the year. At sea the same rules were followed, with emergency work demanded at any hour on any day. Difficulties arose when greedy masters tried to get extra work out of seamen on Sundays and the few holidays observed. The dissatisfaction that resulted was compounded by shortages of food, generally of the poorest quality and often in a state unfit for consumption owing to having been kept so long. Variety was almost always lacking and, from the seamen's point of view, the quantity was always insufficient.

Dana draws a sad picture of seamen in a cold, wet, dark forecastle, in wet clothes, squatting around a kid of boiled but cold salt-horse, gnawing alternately on chunks of meat and hard-bread. That comprised the main meal of the day. A quart of tea sweetened with molasses was served once through the day, not necessarily at the same time as the meal.

Salt-horse or salt-junk was the sailors' name for beef, pork and, often enough, horseflesh, pickled in brine and taken aboard in casks. The hard-bread was, of course, the infamous ships' biscuit or hardtack. When asked about it an old seagoing acquaintance remarked that hardtack was indeed hard and almost impossible for anyone, without good teeth in strong jaws, to eat. There was a way around that problem, he advised: "You carried a couple of biscuits around with you, inside your clothes and close to your body, where perspiration and body heat softened them."

After storage for a few months, particularly in a hot, humid climate, hardbread provided protein as well as carbohydrates. It became the home of wriggly weevils that could, of course, be picked out during daylight hours. At night, the heart could not grieve over things the eyes didn't see.

Fresh meat and vegetables were taken aboard when possible but they did not keep well in the absence of refrigeration. Many masters provisioned their vessels with onions, dried beans and peas, especially later in the century, when good cast iron stoves were readily available.

Spicer, in *Masters of Sail,* finds the daily diet more plentiful, more varied and of better quality, but he appears to take twentieth century conditions as representative of the early 1800s. No records or accounts that are available for the earlier period support Spicer's generous view.

The ship's day afloat, considered as starting at noon, was broken into five four-hour watches and two two-hour dogwatches taken alternately by the starboard and larboard watches. The dogwatches together made up the second watch of the day from 4 p.m. until 8 p.m. and they were the means of progressing the watches so that all hands had a share of day and night duty. Since the watches had to carry through a seven-day week, the minimum amount of time a seaman spent on deck was 84 hours per week. That amount could be greatly increased in periods of bad weather.

Daylight hours for a minimum of two watches for larboard and starboard men were spent in maintaining the vessel, unless in rough weather or when tacking often. Periodical maintenance included greasing the masts with fat from the galley; tarring the standing rigging; painting inside and out; whitewashing the hold; oiling rails and certain other exposed woodwork.

Daily duties included handling the sails and sheets; protecting running and standing rigging from chafing; serving rope and parcelling spars; caulking as it became necessary; polishing brass; chipping ironwork free of rust and daubing it with a mixture of tallow and lampblack. Keeping openings and hatch covers watertight required constant effort.

When nothing more important demanded their attention the seamen picked old rope apart. The poorest pickings were set aside as oakum for use in caulking. Better material was spun into yarn and turned into light line for serving ropes. The best was spliced into long lengths of rope for light work. All seamen had to be able to sew and the neatest hem-stitchers (4 stitches per inch) were assigned to patch sails or to make new ones out of old or new material.

A good master had his men air and dry their blankets and clothes in good weather. On rainy days he had them collect rainwater in readiness for the weekly personal clean-up on Sunday. In their own time the men fashioned workclothes and wet-weather gear from old canvas. Waterproofing was achieved by use of tar, boiled linseed oil or even fish oil. Tar applied to a straw hat made it into a passable sou'wester.

Many seamen were accomplished at knitting and made their own stockings, sweaters and mittens. Some of their produce was sold to less adept seamen or traded for boots and dress clothes. Many seamen whiled away their free time, although there cannot have been much of it, making objects of art to sell ashore or to take home as gifts. Scrimshaw on whalebone, ivory or powderhorns was popular. The carving of elaborate walking sticks and wooden curios was not at all uncommon. Furniture was made on some vessels by the carpenter, doubtless for the master.

The ship's carpenter maintained the wooden parts of the vessel, calling on the crew for assistance in times of urgency. When he had nothing more pressing to do, he worked at improving the vessel or even at making spars and oars for sale.

The cook cared for livestock, often carried to provide fresh meat, butchered it and ensured that the best cuts went to the cabin. Simon Graham's accounts, scant though they are, indicate that he favoured "swine cattle." The steward was a servant on small vessels. He carried meals, served in the cabin, made beds and cleaned up. He weighed food for the cook and saw to it that the seamen got no more than their allowance.

The seamen carried their own food to the forecastle, sending a couple of their watch to ensure that a fair share was measured out and to bring it back. If the ration were lost owing to an unexpected pitch of the vessel, no more would be doled out and so, in bad weather, the messenger had extra hands to steady him. The helmsman had to wait until he came off duty when he could eat with his own watch.

Those hands who never went aloft were known by the seamen as the idlers. Nevertheless, in an emergency or when staying ship in rough weather, all hands were called to the deck. The captain, alone, did no hard labour. Work was done to singing or chanting which Dana called "cheerily." Most of the chanties were work cadences, the men putting their weight onto ropes or bars at certain times. Thus, with a song that followed an a, b, a, c phrasing, which has a weak, strong, weak, very strong repetitive rhythm, the men gathered rope and took a secure hold on weak phrases, leaned their weight into strong phrases and gave a little extra on the very strong phrase. An old seaman would be given the position of soloist unless a joint effort was entailed, whereupon he assumed the responsibility of leading or singing parts.

Singing brightened many a forecastle when conditions were right, and a seaman with good voice and repertoire was a highly valued member of the watch. Somewhere in research, a reference to "Fiddlers' Green" — the place where seamen go to besport themselves when they die — was discovered; but nowhere could the words to this old sea song be found. Upon this being remarked to a researcher he promptly sang it in a fine tenor voice, as he had done fifty years ago in a forecastle:

> I walked to the dockside one evening so fair,
> To view the still waters and to taste the salt air,
> I heard an old seaman there singing a song,
> Let them take me away for my time is not long.
>
> Wrap me up in my oilskins and jumper,
> No more on the docks I'll be seen,
> Just tell my old shipmates I'm on a long trip mate
> And I'll see them some day in Fiddlers Green
>
> Now Fiddlers Green is a place I've heard tell,
> Where old seamen go if they don't go to Hell,
> Where the weather is fair and the dolphins do play
> And the cold coast of Cape Horn is far, far away.
>
> The weather is fair and there's never a gale,
> And the fish jump aboard with a swish of their tail,
> You can lie in your hammock, there's no work to do
> And the Skipper's below making tea for the crew.
>
> I don't need a harp nor a halo, not me.
> Just give me a breeze and a good rolling sea
> And I'll play the old squeeze-box as we sail along,
> With the wind in the rigging to sing me a song.

Among Simon Graham's effects are two interesting musical items. One is an exceptionally fine concertina and the other is a well cared for manuscript-book of tunes. Each note is carefully set down without, however, the key being assigned. Many of the tunes are dated. One of the earliest is "Yankee Doodle Dandy," with a date almost one hundred years before Simon Graham could have been playing it at sea. What a history of forecastles that book could tell!

A seaman's life was possibly a happy one but it was by no means easy or pleasant, as witnessed by this remark casually ventured by an old seafarer. "You could identify a man who had spent a full life under canvas by the state of his knuckles. They were inevitably deformed as a result of pounding frozen canvas with his fists to break away ice and to make the sail flexible enough for reefing or furling."

Seamen carried small clubs for the purpose of beating the sails but, if caught without one or if it were dropped, the knuckles had to substitute.

If the urgency of taking in sail wasn't overpowering, the seamen might be aloft all day or night; but if emergency action was necessary they were luckier. If a sail wouldn't then reef or furl quickly it was cut away with knives.

## CHAPTER 20

# Polishing the Gilded Penny

One cannot discuss shipbuilding in the British North American provinces without an unpalatable amount of rationalizing simply because the figures necessary for the presentation of an unequivocal picture have not yet been assembled. This is true also for Great Britain and the United States where, for reasons to do with more dramatic facets of history, merchant shipping of a century ago excites a lot less interest and where much of the information required is stored.

The data will some day be brought together through the use of sophisticated computers, it may be supposed. In the meantime, one has to be content with generalizations of the kind that are, unfortunately, found in this book; and in that vein it may be argued that, throughout Simon Graham's lifespan, the economy of New Brunswick rested almost completely on shipbuilding and its subordinates, lumbering and sailing. Indirect comment in the press of the day shows how closely concerned were the province and the industry.

*The Gleaner,* 26 April 1862:
Ships building in the Province....

| RIG | TONS | LOCATION | BUILDER |
|---|---|---|---|
| Ship | 1500 | Courtnay Bay | Gass, Stewart & Co. |
| do | 1250 | do | James Nevins |
| do | 640 | do | do |
| do | 1420 | do | George King |
| Bark | 370 | do | do |
| Ship | 1500 | do | John McDonald |
| Bark | 520 | Portland | Wm. Howard |
| Ship | 1100 | do | Alex Anderson |
| Bark | 500 | do | do |
| Ship | 1100 | do | do |
| do | 1300 | Straight Shore | Thos. Hilyard |
| do | 1050 | do | do |
| do | 940 | do | A. McDonald |
| do | 1450 | do | F.& J. Ruddock |
| do | 1200 | Indiantown | Henry Rowan |
| do | 800 | Kennebeccasis | T.E. Milledge |
| Bark | 400 | do | do |
| Ship | 1250 | Carleton | McL. & Stackhouse |
| do | 990 | do | do |
| Bark | 350 | do | J.S. Thompson |
| Brig | 380 | do | J. & S.W. Olive |

| RIG | TONS | LOCATION | BUILDER |
|---|---|---|---|
| do | 300 | do | do |
| do | 200 | Rothsay | Mr. Maynes |
| Ship | 1650 | Clifton | W.P. Flewwelling |
| Bark | 450 | Musquash | H. Garbutt |
| Ship | 1400 | Quaco | J.H. Moran |
| do | 1000 | do | J. Bradshaw |
| Bark | 500 | do | H. McQuiston |
| do | 500 | Dorchester | A.L. Palmer |
| do | 500 | Salisbury | Mr. Pitfield |
| do | 550 | Kingston Kent | J. & J. Jardine |
| Ship | 900 | do | do |
| do | 1050 | do | L.P.W. DesBrisay |
| Bark | 500 | Weldford Kt. | Robert Brown |
| do | 389 | Kouchibouquac | W.S. Caie |
| Ship | 1100 | Chatham | Wm. Muirhead |
| Bark | 320 | do | do |
| do | 320 | do | Jacob Gough |
| Ship | 600 | Newcastle | Peter Mitchell |
| Brig | 220 | do | do |
| Bark | 320 | Rose Bank | John Haws |
| Brig | 220 | Douglastown | James Henderson |
| Ship | 900 | Beaubairs Is. | John Harley |
| Brig | 300 | Bathurst | F. Rankin & Co. |
| do | 290 | do | John O'Brien |
| do | 290 | do | John Mcahan |
| Bark | 600 | do | G. & A. Smith |
| Brig | 260 | do | do |
| Brigt. | 100 | Bay Chaleur | John McNair |
| do | 140 | Shippegan | W. Fruing & Co. |

So it appears that 35,888 tons of vessels were on the stocks in New Brunswick at one time in 1862. According to Alex Monro's data in *British North America*, 48,719 tons of vessels were launched in the province that year and the total value was $525,175.00 or about $10.77 per ton. Assuming that 40,000 tons were sold abroad at that price (which appears to be only the cost) about $430,000.00 new money was generated in New Brunswick. If the dollar of the day is taken to represent $40.00 of current buying power, the province was enriched by more than seventeen million dollars. The population of New Brunswick was then a little over 252,000 bodies. The value of lumber produced that year was 6-1/2 times as great as the assumption for vessels sold abroad.

Monro's figures appear to indicate a great drop in the value of vessels. *Eighty Years of Progress* sets the value per registered ton at £8-0-0 sterling — about $24.00 currency – for vessels produced in 1854 in the Colony of New Brunswick. The total value that year was £795,408.

The following advertisement from the *Gleaner*, 29 April 1843, illustrates the impact on the labour force in a period of slow movement of people about the province: "WANTED. 4 Shipmasters to take charge of new vessels immediately; 20 riggers for the season; 4 moulders for the Chatham Foundry...apply to J. Cunard & Co., Chatham." Four shipmasters for Joseph Cunard's current needs meant that at least fifty other seamen were required. The population of the Miramichi area around Chatham and Newcastle was then less than 15,000 men, women and children; and Cunard was only one of several builders.

The importance with which shipbuilding was regarded is shown in the following comments which were appended to the list of vessels under construction.

During the months of May, June, and July, nearly all the vessels in the city yards will be launched. It is a general complaint among builders that they are compelled to launch about July, in accordance with Lloyds' Regulations — the consequence of which is that a large number of vessels are placed in the Home Market at the same time, causing a glut, and lower prices. This rule is applicable to all the other Colonies and appears to have been framed for the benefit of ship-owners in England, who are thus enabled to purchase our vessels at almost their own prices. Another disadvantage which it places upon builders is this; when a builder enters into a contract for a ship, he bases his price upon the cost of timber, and the rates of wages current at the time. With respect to the latter the workmen well know that according to Lloyds' Regulation, the vessel must be completed (so as to be registered) by the month of July, plus the builder must be at considerable expense or delay; consequently we frequently hear of "strikes" for higher wages, to which the builder must submit — no alternative being left, as the contract must be completed at the time specified. By such strikes, contracts for ships have been rendered almost worthless. We have a case of this kind in our mind at the moment.

This is a matter that should be taken up by the Chamber of Commerce, if that body has not again fallen through. Representations respecting the injustice of Lloyds' Regulations should be made in the proper quarter. We know of no good reason why a builder should not launch his vessel at any period of the year, just as suits his convenience best. As matters remain at present, there is great activity in our yards during a few months of the year and during the others only stagnation.

We have made some enquiry into the subject spoken of by our contemporary, and from those who are well able to give an opinion, we have collected the following information:-

The Regulations issued by Lloyds', respecting the launching of ships in July, was intended rather to be beneficial than otherwise to shipbuilders; and it is entirely optional with them whether they avail themselves of it or not. We have obtained from the proper authority here, the Resolution of the Committee of Lloyds' upon this important point, which is as follows:-

"Lapsing of ships classed A. — It having been represented to the Committee, that much inconvenience and detriment is occasioned by the regulation at present in force, under which ships classed A lapse from that character on the 31st of December; and as the class commences from the date of launching, it is alleged an inducement is held out for Builders to launch their ships at a period of the year considered the most unfavourable, (namely, on the 1st January, or as soon after as practicable,) the Committee have given this important subject an attentive consideration, and it has this day been Resolved -

"That all ships launched on and after the 1st July, 1859, shall retain the characters respectively assigned to them, until the issuing of the Register Book for the year commencing on the 1st July next ensuing after the period for which they have been classed shall have expired, provided they undergo the surveys required by the Rules and are kept in an efficient state of repair. Thus ships launched on the 1st July, 1859, or on any other day between that date and the 1st July, 1860, and classed A.1 for 10 years will lapse on the 30th June, 1870.

"The existing tonnage, and all ships launched previously to the 1st July, 1859, shall remain under the present rules."

It will, we think, be apparent from this, that the glutting the Home Market, low prices, strikes, or other inconvenience to which shipbuilders are represented as being subject, as well as the want of employment by the workmen during the inactive portion of the year, ought not to arise, as it is stated it does from the operation of Lloyds' Regulations.

Shipbuilders are no doubt anxious to have their new vessels in the market as early as possible in each year after the 1st July, so as to avail themselves of all the intervening time before the 1st July next, as not until then do the years of Classification to which they have become entitled, begin to expire and it is probably owing to this the evils complained of exist. We think it is an error to state that vessels must necessarily be launched in July to be Registered at Lloyds, as they may be and are launched and registered in every month of the year.

We do not think the evils complained of have existed in this section of the Province and it is frequently the case that Builders send their new vessels, built for sale for a voyage before placing them in the market without interfering with the time for which they are classed, or being any essential detriment to them when they come to be sold; an advantage we take it, not formerly enjoyed. — With this view of the subject we cannot endorse the recommendation to represent an injustice which we do not think exists.

The continuing loss of vessels to perils of the sea appears to have been a factor just as important as the expansion of trade and emigration in placing a demand for new construction on British North American shipyards. The *London Illustrated News* carried this not at all unusual brief item on 16 June 1849.

> Shipwrecks on Ice in the Atlantic: The immense field of ice that has been encountered in and near the Gulf of St. Lawrence this season has not been equalled for many years. In addition to the melancholy loss of the *Maria* (200 perished) and the *Hannah* (111 perished), which foundered near the same bearing, two other vessels were lost, viz, the barque *Gleaner*, 500 tons, and the ship *Torrence* of Glasgow.

The traffic in and out of ocean ports indicates the size of the market in which British North American shipbuilders were selling their products. As many as 100 timber droghers congregated at a time in the Miramichi River and that was by no means uncommon. On April 28, 1852, the *London Illustrated News* reported: "On Sunday and Monday a fleet of merchant ships numbering 346 sail, of all classes, came up the Thames and were entered at the Custom-house, the aggregate tonnage of which amounted to upwards of 61,500 tons." London was the world's largest port at that time and doubtless the passage of so many vessels up the Thames within, presumably, about ten hours of daylight, was a result of favourable winds and tide. Still, 346 vessels stemming one river (smaller than the Miramichi) in such a period of time, conjures up a picture of a thousand or more docking at other British ports and tens of thousands at sea, anchored in other European ports, across the Atlantic in North America or elsewhere around the world.

The age of sail may return when fossil fuels are depleted and if nuclear energy cannot be employed safely. The shapes of vessels and their operation will then be greatly different from those of Simon Graham's era. One visualizes huge steel hulls almost entirely below the surface of the ocean. Buoyancy is greater there; wind and wave resistance is less. Masts, yards, sheets and sails will all be of steel or perhaps of a lighter metal. They will be actuated by numerous electric motors drawing energy from the wind, sun and waves. Taking information from sensors and converting it to the needs of the moment, computors will direct the spread and orientation of sails as well as the cant of the rudder. There will be no one aboard to grumble about the lack of roast goose for Christmas.

# NOTES AND GLOSSARY

## Chapter 1

[1]H.M.S. *Falkland*, a frigate, 54 guns, was launched at Portsmouth, New Hampshire, in 1696.

[2]Manny refers, in *Ships of Kent County, New Brunswick* to the *Miramichi Advance*, 25 September 1890, finding *Ellen Douglas* to be the first square-rigged vessel built in Kent Co., giving the date 1819 and the builder, John Jardine. Research fails to support this. Lloyds Register shows a brig, *Helen Douglas,* built by Walter Neilson in Richibucto, N.B., 1825, 237 13/94 tons, owned by Robert and John Jardine (32 shares) and Benjamin Nicholson of Anan, Scot., 32 shares.

[3]Other New Brunswick privateers are noted by John Leefe in *The Atlantic Privateers* (Petheric Press, Halifax, 1978).

[4]Many builders favoured iron, which is comparatively soft, over the harder metal, steel. The reason appears to be that iron plates yielded more readily than steel, placing less stress on riveted seams.

[5]A full-rigged ship, *Savannah*, 350 tons, used *some* steam crossing from Savannah, Ga., to Liverpool, Eng., in 1819.

## Chapter 2

[1]In 1818, Captain John Cleve Symmes, an American, claimed that the earth was hollow and open at the poles 12 or 16 degrees. American seamen held a belief for many years that Captain Symmes had been to the North Pole and had discovered a vent from which the cold Northwest winds issued. They also held that Captain Symmes could have closed the hole by stuffing it with his jacket which, unfortunately, he had discarded in his climb to the location. *(The New England Farmer*, Aug.1856.)

[2]A slate bearing a description of the bars at the entrance to Richibucto Harbour, in Simon Graham's hand, survives to this day.

[3]*Sybylla*, two decks, three masts, length 105' 3½" (32.095m), breadth taken below the main wales 28' 5½"(8.687m), height between decks 6' 10½" (2.1m) ship-rigged with a standing bowsprit, square sterned, carvel built, no galleries,* a Billet Head, built at Can Point, P.E.I., in 1829, owned by Samuel Cunard and chartered to Barclay and Livingstone of New York in 1833. (Lloyds Register).

[4]Graham would have been used to square sterns. This brig was of a transitional form leading to elliptical or fantail sterns.

[5]H.M.S. *Dublin*, the third of four warships of the name. Dana mentions a Captain Terry visiting the brig *Pilgrim* and spinning a four-hour yarn about (among other topics) "the Dublin frigate and Lord James Townshend." The latter was a

---

*Galleries were actually exterior walkways at the sterns of naval vessels but in merchantmen the term seems to have applied to large windows, especially those projecting, in the cabin area.

strict disciplinarian and it is ironical that *Dublin*'s Latin motto translates as "Obedience is Happiness." The motto on Simon Graham's signet ring was "Such is Life."

[6]An able seaman had to be able to hand (take in a sail completely), reef (take in partly) and steer a course.

[7]The bowers were the bow anchors *said* to have been both of the same size, the "best bower" being that on the starboard in the Northern Hemisphere and on the port below the equator, the reason laying with prevailing winds and their tendency to twist an anchored vessel around its cable. Nevertheless, Simon Graham referred to the "best" bower and the "small" bower.

[8]One the master and the other, the owner or his representative, not competent to command at sea.

[9]Bodies were usually sewed in a shroud of old canvas starting at the feet, the last stitch often passing through the nostril of the corpse with the intent of evoking signs of life, should there be any.

[10]*Benjamin Shaw*. Lloyds Register shows a barque of that name, commanded by Watkins, 284 tons, built in Sweden (no year) of pine, teak and spruce. (A brig, schooner-rigged on its foremast, was called a Benjamin.)

## Chapter 3

[1]*Richibucto*, barque, 400 tons, built at Richibucto, N.B., by John Jardine in 1835 of spruce, red pine and hackmatac. (Manny)

[2]A Governor's Pass, before Confederation, permitted the taking of a vessel abroad for registry at a port other than the closest official port of registry (Miramichi for Richibucto vessels).

[3]*Hercules*, ship 757 tons, built in N.B. of black birch and spruce in 1836, (Lloyds); 757 tons O.M., 132' keel (40.23m), 152' overall (46.33m), 3 masts, square stern, carvel built at Richibucto, N.B., by John Jardine in 1836 (Port of Miramichi Records).

[4]Likely St. Pierre of St. Pierre and Miquelon, still known to many Newfoundland fishermen as St. Peters although, possibly, Graham meant the very small port of St. Peter's, Cape Breton.

[5]To warp a vessel is to move it from one position to another by means of a hawser attached to an anchor, buoy or object ashore and taken in by hand or by the capstan. Warping is not synonymous with towing.

[6]The generally accepted rule in design was that freeboard (from loadwaterline to upper deck) should be ¼ of the vessel's depth. Lloyds, in 1835, put this as 3" (0.076m) for each foot (0.3m) of depth. Thus, four times as much hull lay below water as above. This does not include the bulwarks, of course.

[7]Beam means breadth, which may include the vessel's planking, i.e. "extreme breadth" or out-to-out of ribs, i.e. "breadth moulded," the latter being the measurement used before 1854 to determine tonnage. Dimensions quoted are those of record, e.g. 29.4'; but this may actually mean 29'4".

[8]*Gubbins' New Brunswick Journals 1811 & 1813*, ed. H. Temperley, New Brunswick Heritage Publications. 1980

[9]*The Gleaner*, 11 Oct. 1856, reported the launch of the brig *Alnwick* and her tonnage as 155 tons Carpenter's Measurement, 105 tons "by the Merchant Shipping Act," i.e., Moorsom's Rules; and *Clarendon*, merely as a fine ship of 760 tons, Carpenter's Measurement. On 28 January 1856, *The Gleaner* reported: "Launch. From the building yard of Messrs. Holderness and McLeod, on Sunday the 21st ult., a ship named the *McLeod*, measuring 1521 tons O.M., 1418 tons late register and 1365 tons by the New Register Tonnage."

[10]Admiral George Moorsom, R.N., was chairman of a committee set up by the Admiralty at the request of the Board of Trade to study "vexatious" problems to do with determination of tonnage. The recommendations of the committee were made part of the Merchant Shipping Act of 1854. Moorsom had formulated his proposals several years earlier (the Oxford *Companion to Ships and the Sea* states that the rule was in force in 1849) and this has led some researchers to attribute shallower hulls developing in British North America (e.g. *Oliver Lang*, 1853, ratio 0.65+) to Moorsom's rule. Such vessels may have been only following the trend that accompanied development of the clipper hull.

[11]Briefly (and coarsely), 307 vessels registered at Saint John 1834-1852 averaged 0.71; 314 vessels 1853-1865 averaged 0.61, ratio of depth to breadth.

## Chapter 4

[1]*Devonport*; Lloyds Register, 1837, spells the name *Davenport*, barque, 723 tons, built Nova Scotia 1836, black birch, spruce and pine. Graham's logs showed the vessel carried a spencer on the main mast.

[2]A shelf standing out from the hull and secured by brackets below, to which the shrouds fastened. Such an arrangement was necessary to permit the shrouds to clear the topgallant bulwark, to preclude stress on the bulwark and to prevent chafing of the shrouds.

[3]Starboard from steerboard, the right side to which the steering blade was attached before rudders were located astern. Larboard is from ladeboard, the loading side away from the steering side. Larboard was already out of favour by 1837 and was generally changed to port in 1844.

[4]Bending was to attach a sail to its yard. Bends were rope knots used in the process. Unbending was to remove the sail completely by untying the knots.

[5]Graham's usage is uncertain. *Devonport* was a barque which, by definition, carried a spanker (with boom and gaff) on the mizzen. A similar sail on the foremast or mainmast would have been called a trysail. Sometimes a trysail was carried on a trymast, a short mast immediately behind the mast carrying other sails; but Graham elsewhere referred to a spencer, a sail identical but loose-footed, i.e. lacking a boom, on *Devonport*'s mainmast. Perhaps *Devonport* had a spencer on a trymast immediately aft of her mainmast. This would have prevented the trysail/spencer from interfering with the operation of the mainsail.

[6]To tack by letting go an anchor and hauling the vessel around on its cable while resetting the sails. Often it was necessary to cut the cable with an axe, thus losing the anchor.

[7]For instance: 1064 vessels in the first 7 months of 1859, according to *The Gleaner* 15 August 1859.

## Chapter 5

[1]Simon Graham had 3 children: James, who died at sea, aged 2 years, 7 mos.; Ann, born in Scotland in 1821, who married James McAlmon (son of David McAlmon, M.P.P.) in Richibucto in 1839; and Simon, born Scotland 1826 who married Martha Girvan at New Galloway, near Richibucto, 1853, and had one daughter, Mary Ann, who married James Jardine of Rexton.

Simon Graham, Sr., "a seafaring man at present in Liverpool" (later Richibucto), purchased land near Richibucto in 1827. The deed does not mention Graham's wife, Annie, but her name occurs in a conveyance in 1837. Their daughter, Ann, is referred to as Captain Simon Graham's daughter in a newspaper account of her wedding in 1839 but Graham's wife is not mentioned. In 1855, Annie accompanied her husband to Britain aboard *Perekop*. Masters' wives often shared their husbands' sea life and this may have been the case with Mrs. Graham. Simon Graham simply did not mention her in his logs.

Tradition in Richibucto states that Simon Graham's wife, Annie, never lived in New Brunswick. No record of her death has been found in New Brunswick.

[2]*Caledonia*, barque 486 tons, built at (Black River) New Brunswick in 1837 of black birch, pine, hackmatack and spruce. (Lloyds Register).

[3]Symbols for sun and moon.

[4]*Brothers*: possibly the barque, 368 tons, of that name, built in Boston, Massachusetts, in 1831 and registered that year in Liverpool, England. (Lloyds Register)

## Chapter 6

[1]*Amy*, ship, 458-48/94 tons, one deck, three masts, length stem to stern 114'9" (34.98m), main breadth 29'10" (9.1m) depth 17" (5.18m);* owner/builder George Thompson, Saint John, N.B.; registered at Saint John 16 Aug. 1833, as No. 56. (From her certificate) (The fractional tonnage indicates Old Measure.)

*Depth in the hold.

[2]Fowler's *Modern English Usage* argues that "under way" is right and "under weigh," wrong. Both are found in old logs. Dana's *Seaman's Friend* uses "under way."

[3]A strong gale is as much wind as a vessel could take carrying any sail at all. All canvas had to be furled for a whole gale. The Beaufort Scale with observations for landlubbers follows:

| Calm | Force 0 | (Less than 1 kph., smoke columns vertical) |
| Light Air | Force 1 | (1-5 kph., smoke columns angle) |
| Light Breeze | Force 2 | (5-11 kph, tree leaves stir) |
| Gentle Breeze | Force 3 | (11-19 kph., tree leaves move) |
| Moderate Breeze | Force 4 | (19-29 kph., paper blows around) |
| Fresh Breeze | Force 5 | (29-39 kph., saplings sway) |
| Strong Breeze | Force 6 | (39-50 kph., large branches sway) |
| Moderate Gale | Force 7 | (50-61 kph., difficult to walk) |
| Fresh Gale | Force 8 | (61-74 kph., very difficult to walk) |
| Strong Gale | Force 9 | (74-87 kph., shingles blow off) |
| Whole Gale | Force 10 | (87-101 kph., uproots trees) |
| Storm | Force 11 | (101-120 kph., damages structures) |
| Hurricane | Force 12 | (120 plus kph., collapses buildings) |

[4]Lighters were towed barges or scows used for handling cargo to or from a vessel not fast at dockside. In this case the cargo was almost assuredly sawn lumber.

[5]*Calcutta*, ship, 706 tons, built 1836 in Quebec of oak and elm. (Lloyds Register.)

[6]*Cambridge*, barque, 327 tons, built in Nova Scotia of black birch, spruce and red pine in 1841 and registered in Glasgow, Scotland. (Lloyds Register). Simon Graham indicates that the vessel was built in Londonderry which means the township and not the inland town. No tradition of *Cambridge* was found at Great Village, Londonderry Twp., N.S., the main shipbuilding centre.

[7]Brier Island, N.S., the last landfall on leaving the Bay of Fundy.

[8]Departure, in the navigator's usage, means something more than leaving a landfall. It is the point through which a meridian passes, to which progress at 90⁰ is related. Thus, a vessel sailing due East or West makes maximum departure from the meridian while one sailing due north makes no departure at all.

## Chapter 7

[1]Notwithstanding the introduction of iron chain about 1800, this was likely a rope of large diameter known as cable. Seamen used chain and cable interchangeably (as Graham did) to mean the anchor rope although, later, steel chain became the material of use for large vessels. The rule for cable diameter was Beam in feet x 0.5/3.1416=inches.

[2]Roads; more properly, roadstead: water suitable for safe anchorage of vessels off the shore or in a port area.

[3]An open sighting arrangement. On the compass it took the form of a ring that encircled the compass proper and which could lock at any position. From the ring rose two vanes, separated 180⁰, one having a fine vertical vision slot and the other, a coarser slot to take in the point sighted.

## Chapter 8

[1]*Hannibal*, ship, 580 tons, built Richibucto, N.B., 1844. (Manny) (This may be a later vessel.) Port of Miramichi records show: *Hannibal*, ship, 383 tons, built

at Buctouche, N.B., in 1841. The vessel could not be found in Lloyds Register.

[2]Cape Tormentine, N.B.

[3]The Green Man was a fertility symbol in the West Country of England (J. & C. Bord, *The Secret Country*, Grenada Pub., St. Albans, Eng.) and so was hardly appropriate for use by ladies of the evening. On the other hand, public houses in Britain have carried the name. Graham, however, could hardly have been hypocrite enough to criticise McKay's public house, for it is quite certain that Graham not only enjoyed drinking alcohol but also selling it, in later years at least.

[4]Benjamin Franklin credited, in his autobiography, one Thomas Godfrey, a Philadelphian, with the invention, calling it a quadrant.

[5]Tradition relates that the Merriam family of Advocate and Parrsboro, N.S., which gave six or more sea captains one after another to maritime service, taught and used the technique with molasses in a saucer.

[6]An account may be found in the *Telegraph-Journal*, Saint John, N.B., 22 April 1938.

## Chapter 9

[1]*Swan*, ship, reg. #83, 2 Sept. 1844, Saint John, N.B., 859-679/3500 tons, length 141' (42.98m), breadth 29.7' (9m), depth 22' (6.7m). (From her certificate of registry. The fractional tonnage is unusual. Her depth to beam ratio was 0.74! It may even have been greater because the depth 22' was likely that in the hold.)

[2]*Grampian*, barque, 723 tons N.M., 774 tons O.M., built in Dalhousie, N.B., 1842. (Lloyds Register 1845, Appendix: *Vessels classed by the Liverpool Committee of which John Lockett was chairman.*)

*Grampian* was carvel built, square-sterned, registered at Miramichi, 12 Aug. 1842. (Port of Miramichi records.) She was later rigged as a ship with course, topsail, topgallant and royal on each mast as well as spanker, main spencer, studding sails and jibs. Her boats were gig, pinnace and longboat. She carried only one capstan and no jeers windlass. (Simon Graham logs)

[3]*Atlantic*, ship, 1042 tons N.M., launched Richibucto, N.B., by John Jardine, 16 May 1846. (Manny)

[4]The meaning of the word could not be ascertained. In addition to suction pumps, vessels of the period sometimes had a narrow, caulked, vertical shaft leading to a bilge sump. In this a long slender timber bearing leather cups around it was plunged up and down until the cups filled and eventually spilled water out of the top of the shaft. This may have been the "weegie."

[5]Parcel: to wrap with tarred canvas. Rope was wormed (cord laid in its grooves), parcelled with the lay of strands and served (wrapt very tightly with cord in the opposite direction) against chafing. Tar was not the asphaltic or coal varieties but the residue of the distillation of turpentine from pine trees.

[6]The allotment of space to passengers on British vessels was not firmly fixed at this time and masters had to steer between British and American rules. Very

early in the century one passenger or crewman could be carried per ton and half of registry. Later, 2 tons were required. Thus, if *Grampian* (723 tons) carried 274 passengers and 26 sailors she appears not to have been overloaded. However, rules were complicated by different allotments of space to cabin and steerage passengers. As well, *Grampian* may have carried many small children, not counted. The basic law a few years later *An Act Relating to CARRIAGE OF PASSENGERS BY SEA, 1855:* 18th & 19th VICT Cap. 119, 14, (1) ), reads, "No ship propelled by sails only shall carry a greater number of persons (including every individual on board) than in the proportion of one statute adult to every two tons of her registered tonnage." Two persons between 1 and 12 years of age constituted one statute adult.

[7]"Ruther," from the Anglo-Saxon *rother*, may have been pronounced as rudder.

[8]Graham usually wrote "motherate" which, however, has a Latin root and so may refute the pronunciation of ruther.

[9]"Foul-Weather Jack" Byron, Capt. R.N., grandfather of the more famous poet, referred to his seamen as "the people" in his dispatches reporting the Battle of Restigouche River in 1760.

## Chapter 10

[1]Likely *Irvine*, since Irvin could not be traced; possibly *Irving*, an antecedent of K.C. Irving, the New Brunswick industrialist whose family hailed from Richibucto, N.B.

[2]*Albion*, barque, 575 tons, built Richibucto in 1837 of black birch, hackmatack and spruce. (Manny)

[3]One has to wonder who got repaired first: the patient or the assistant.

[4]Eyestones come in pairs. Several (at least) are safe-guarded in the Maritimes. They are said to be the tips of small seashells of a certain kind and they are regarded as being alive and requiring feeding. Accordingly, they are kept in a small box on a bed of sugar, white or brown, depending upon the owner's views to do with relative nutritional values. Introduced to an eye irritated by a speck of foreign material, the eyestone moves around to cover the speck, whereupon both may be removed together.

## Chapter 11

[1]Lather: ladder. Like rudder this word comes from the Anglo-Saxon but, unlike rudder (rother), seems never to have been spelled with a "th."

[2]*Lady Blaney*, ship, 912 tons, built by F. & J. Ruddock, Saint John, N.B., 1850; lost 1864. (Wright)

[3]Spencer: Simon Graham may again be using the term carelessly in place of spanker.

[4]*Laurel*, ship, 808 tons, built Saint John, N.B. by John W. Smith, 1840; sold to Greenock immediately and from there to Liverpool and to Quebec in 1846. (Wright)

[5]Sprung: split or cracked.

[6]Whiskers are short horizontal booms on the bowsprit to spread the stays. The crance is a steel or iron ring around the bowsprit which holds the jib-boom in place and also seats the whisker booms and a downward-running spreader known as the dolphin striker.

[7]*Highland Chief*, brig, 192 tons O.M., 170 tons N.M., built New Brunswick in 1840. (Lloyds Register)

## Chapter 12

[1]*Perekop*, ship, 856 tons, built in 1855 in New Brunswick of tamarack, sheat'ed (sic) in yellow metal. (Lloyds Register). (Perekop was the name of an obscure village on the isthmus connecting the Crimea peninsula to the Eurasian Continent.)

[2]*Enterprise*, brought from England by J.W. Holderness for packet work along the North Shore of New Brunswick in the summer of 1852. She was 140 tons and operated at 7 or 8 knots by means of two 45 hp. steam engines and side wheels. *(The Gleaner)*

[3]This must mean that neither shrouds nor stays were in place.

[4]The use of parrals was an old-fashioned means of holding the yards to the masts even in 1855. Better found vessels employed iron or steel brackets from which the yards were suspended by chains.

[5]The meaning could not be found but the weigher may have been a horizontal windlass with a boom to permit lifting the masts and spars.

[6]Bowsprit shrouds hold the jib boom firm as well as the bowsprit itself.

[7]Brails are ropes from the edges of loose-footed sails that permit hauling the sail up and into the mast and gaff.

[8]Smith was likely the second mate. The steward usually found a private corner away from the forecastle – a privilege granted also to the cook and sometimes to the second mate and the carpenter on larger vessels.

[9]Pickled beef; possibly close to spoiling in the summer heat.

## Chapter 13

[1]Coasting; costing is not a misspelling, rather, it is an antiquated form of the word.

[2]*Matthews*, brig, 152 tons, built 1817 at Workington, England, sheathed (yellow metal), drew 12' (3.66m) loaded. (Lloyds Register)

[3]*Forte*: Among Simon Graham's papers are three pages of expenses in connection with a vessel he called "*The Yacht.*" They reveal that *The Yacht* was partly square rigged, was armed, flew a vice-regal pennant and was once on the Labrador Coast with passengers who consumed a tidy amount of rum. The cabins were carpeted, the tables were set with china and glass, the passengers ate well and used towels.

Later, a single page of log records was found recounting a voyage by the brig *Foart* from Cowes, England, to St. John's, Newfoundland, December 1831-January

1832, Simon Graham, Master. An overlapping time period suggested that *Foart* and *The Yacht* were one and the same vessel. In the log of *Leander*, Simon Graham noted shortly afterwards that a number of vessels were waiting to get into Oporto Harbour in Portugal whereupon "the *Foart* raised her flag and we all got over the bar." Nevertheless, not one piece of data concerning *Foart* could be uncovered in Lloyds Register or in harbour records at St. John's, Newfoundland. *The Yacht* and *Foart* proved to be H.M. Colonial Brig (variously, Vessel) *Forte*, the Treasury Yacht of Newfoundland. The *Foart* which hoisted her flag was the harbour fort of Oporto and the flag had to do with tides and depths of water at the harbour mouth.

Numerous references to H.M. Colonial Brig *Forte* are to be found in St. John's newspapers of the period but they reveal nothing of her size or origin. Colonial Records and Transactions contain letters dealing with the acquisition of *Forte* but they provide more intriguing hints than solid facts. This is a brief and partly conjectural history of the vessel.

Sir Thomas Cochrane (1789-1872) was appointed Governor of Newfoundland in 1825. Earlier, as a captain in the Royal Navy, he had served off the North Atlantic Coast where, from 1820 to 1825, his command in the famed North Atlantic Squadron was H.M.S. *Forte*, a 54 gun frigate. Upon becoming governor he acquired a brig, her earlier name unknown, which he renamed *Forte*. Being the King's vessel, *Forte* was not registered as a merchantman and not being a man-of-war, was not held in the navy lists.

*Forte* was chartered from Samuel Cunard of Halifax who was then providing a similar vessel, *Chebucto*, for Nova Scotia and who had also supplied transportation for Cochrane's predecessor at St. John's. *Forte* was about 160 tons. That was the tonnage Cunard had contracted to put into service. He first offered a cutter, *Vandeleur*, much smaller, which Cochrane rejected. Cunard seems to have obtained *Forte* from Plymouth, England, where she was rebuilt by Messrs. Hawkes of that port.

Correspondence on the subject shows the Colonial Office not anxious to be generous with either Cochrane or the supplier. Cochrane did not want a cutter, which the Admiralty and Colonial Office tried to foist upon him. He pushed for acceptance of Cunard's tender (in response to newspaper advertisements) to supply the required vessel for £2500 yearly charter. The Colonial Secretary, Lord Bathurst, balked and his civil servants finally persuaded Cunard to lower his price by £200! That worthy then tried to reduce his costs by supplying *Vandeleur*; but Cochrane would have none of it.

*Forte* remained in service until 1834. Throughout the period she was a busy brig. Her armament, approved by the Colonial Office to be eight brass six-pounders, never spoke in anger although one night her guns alerted St. John's to a fire ashore. In his accounts Simon Graham records payment of two shillings and sixpence for hauling two guns from "the dockyard." A small-bore iron falconet, less than a six-pounder, now defends the back yard of a house in Richmond Hill, Ontario. It is undoubtedly associated with *Forte* but it must also, later, have served one of Graham's other vessels.

The costs of maintaining *Forte*, estimated by Sir Thomas Cochrane's staff, may be of interest. They read:

| | |
|---|---|
| Master | £120 annum (£1 = $4 U.S.) |
| Mate | £60 |
| Carpenter | £60 |
| 17 Men | £612 |
| Victualling | £547 — 10 |
| Insurance | £300 |
| Wear and Tear | £225 |

£1924 — 10/ annum

*Forte* was always commanded by a Royal Navy officer, except for the period when Simon Graham took temporary command. Coupled with estimated costs for a master, this suggests that *Forte*, in common with most Royal Navy vessels of the time, carried a civilian (Warrant Officer) sailing-master as well as a naval commander.

[4]*Hooker*, any fishing vessel but, around the British Isles in Simon Graham's day, hookers were short, wide-beamed craft resembling the brigantine. The foremast had one or two fairly large square sails and carried a fore staysail and jibs as well. The after mast was spanker-rigged.

[5]A brig, *Dyckes*, did indeed trade into Richibucto, but Graham cannot be associated with the vessel.

[6]*Leander*, brig, 149 tons, one deck with beams for another, built Greenoch, Scotland, 1824. (Lloyds Register) A Captain McAusland was master of *Leander* before and after Simon Graham who, it appears, took temporary command while McAusland was otherwise occupied.

[7]*Sarah* (Certificate #50) 151-20/94 tons, one deck , three masts, length 80' (24.38m), breadth 20'10" (6.35m) depth of hold 12'1" (3.69m), schooner rigged with a standing bowsprit, square stern, carvel built, no galleries, a "Woman Bust," built at Cocagne, N.B., 1829. By Certificate #57, 2 Nov. 1830, Certificate #50 was surrendered: "said vessel having been altered from that of a three masted Schooner to a Barque." Registered de novo, Certificate #125, Halifax, N.S., 4 April 1832, barque rigged." (From her certificates of registry.

Of considerable interest is that this vessel appears to be the earliest tern schooner of record in the Maritimes.

[8]*Corsair*, brig single deck, 281 tons, drew 15' (4.57m) loaded, built in Nova Scotia in 1826. (Lloyds Register)

[9]*Janet Patterson*, ship, 653.9 tons under deck, 53.82 tons under poop, 707.72 reg. tons, one deck, three masts, carvel built, round stern, length 156' (47.55m) width 31.2' (9.5m), depth 20.5' (6.25m) from her certificate of registration, Port of Miramichi, 27 Nov. 1863, which also bears the note: "WRECKED A.L. 1863."

[10]Simon Graham left no formal will. His estate was comprised of his home and numerous personal effects but no cash or investments. His reward for so many hard years at sea was meagre and it is clear from some correspondence extant that he was not comfortable in his last few years.

Simon's wife, Annie Graham, appears to have survived him, although no record of her death has been found. She remains a vague figure and one of great mystery in the old seafarer's life.

## Chapter 14

[1]Nova Scotia may have had a substantial shipbuilding industry even earlier. Settlers at Chebucto (later Halifax) in 1749 included at least 300 mariners, 55 carpenters and 15 shipwrights. Numerous auxiliary trades, such as rope-maker, edged-toolmaker, joiner and smiths of various kinds were also represented. Four of the shipwrights had male servants who may have been indentured tradesmen. One, William Vernon, brought his wife, two female servants and ten male servants, which surely suggests intent to engage in industry. (Records Comn., Documents in Province of Nova Scotia Archives: *List of the Settlers who came out with Governor Cornwallis to Chebucto in June 1749.*)

[2]Chatham *Gleaner*, June 9, 1855:

> We are indebted to the New Brunswicker for the following important information...for...parties engaged in shipbuilding.
>
> We have been informed by John Tucker, Esq.,* Lloyds Surveyor at this Port that, in pursuance of a resolution passed on the 15th of February last by the Committee of Lloyds Register of British and Foreign Shipping, the Rule Section 46 has been amended and will stand in future as follows.
>
> *Fastening.* The treenails to be of good quality and of a description of wood equal to the best material through which they are to pass. They are to be circular being either engine turned, compressed or planed. In all cases in which planks above twelve inches in width shall be used, they must be double fastened and those above nine inches in width must be treenailed double and single except where bolts intervene and if less than that width then to be treenailed single.
>
> In such cases at least one half of the treenail must go through the ceiling, all the outside planking to be fastened with at least one bolt in every butt, the bolt through and clenched.
>
> The bilges to be secured with bolts so placed that from the foremast to the mainmast in Ships under 300 Tons there shall be at least one bolt through and clenched in each first foothook; and that in Ships of 300 Tons upwards there shall be at least two bolts through and clenched for each set of timbers in one or other of the thick bilge strakes.
>
> All the bolts of the knees, breasthooks, crutches,** riders, transoms, pointers, keelsons, shelfpiece, waterways, heels of timbers against fore and after deadwood and all other material fastening are to be driven and clenched on rings of the same material as the bolts. The up and down bolts in the

---

*It would appear from a number of references to his activities that John Tucker was an intelligent energetic man, devoted to the improvement of shipbuilding in New Brunswick, Nova Scotia and Prince Edward Island.

**Crutches are stanchions incorporating a natural wye-crotch. Many early vessels, particularly small ones, were built with ribs entirely of natural curvatures hewed somewhat to shape them and to rid them of excess weight. The French warship *Le Marquis de Malauze*, c. 1755, 96' overall, 28 guns, whose skeleton rests ashore at Reserve Church, Restigouche, N.B., is an example. All her bow frames are one-piece, natural oak crotches. Her stern frames are similar, those inboard having standing legs, all of one piece, that make up a composite stern-post.

knees to the beams are not required to be through the deck but, whether clenched upon the beams or upon the deck, they must be clenched on rings of the same as the bolts.

The two bolts nearest to the crown of the pintles and braces of the rudder are also to be through and clenched; those through the braces to be in the main piece of sternpost; the limber strakes to be bolted down to the floors and one bolt in every floor on each side to be through and clenched.

When the heels of the first futtocks (either with full moulding or with butted chocks) meet at the middle line on the keel under the keelson, the through bolting of the limber strakes may be dispensed with.

Ships otherwise entitled by their materials to stand higher than the six-year grade in which the flat of upper deck, poop and forecastle are fastened with nails or bolts of copper or yellow metal and the whole outside planking of which is fastened with treenails and copper or yellow metal bolts to the entire exclusion of iron bolts are used in any part of the vessel except the frame bolts and short bolts of inside planking, up and down bolts of knees which clinch upon the upper deck, poop, or forecastle beams when the flat of deck is laid over them.

Up and down bolts of hold and lower deck beams, fore and aft in arms of knees to beams, bolts of the coaming, windlass or bowsprit, bitts, deck fixtures athwartship, bolts in knees afore the stem, bolts or fastening incidental to the rigging or any fastening above the respecting planksheers of the poop, waist and forecastle, such ships will be allowed a period of one year and, in addition thereto, a further period of one year will be given to ships so fastened in which the outside planking above the floor-heads is also fastened entirely with bolts of copper or yellow metal in lieu of treenails. In all such cases of substitution the number of bolts must be the same as is already prescribed as above for treenails. The proportion of through bolts must be one half and all through bolts must be of malleable metal and clenched (sic) on rings of the same metal inside.

Whenever metal fasteners are used in place of treenails, this proportion must be observed. The sizes of copper or mixed metal bolts must be as under, viz:

| | |
|---|---|
| In ships of 150 tons and under 200 tons.... | ⅝ ins. |
| In ships of 200 tons and under 350 tons.... | ¾ ins. |
| In ships of 350 tons and under 500 tons.... | ¹³⁄₁₆ ins. |
| In ships of 500 tons and under 700 tons.... | ⅞ ins. |
| In ships of 700 tons and under 900 tons.... | ¹⁵⁄₁₆ ins. |
| In ships of 900 tons and above.... | 1 inch |

Smaller sizes must not be used and the length of the short bolts not less than as follows, viz:

When used in planks of 2½" to be 7 inches long
When used in planks of 3" to be 8 inches long
When used in planks of 4" to be 10 inches long
When used in planks of 5" to be 12 inches long

and so on in planks of other thicknesses. The size of bolts required in the several other parts must not be less than is shewn in Table 'D' following Page 28 of Rules.

## Chapter 15

[1]Staysails, as their name suggests, ran along the fore and aft stays.

[2]"Studding sails" is said, today, to have been pronounced "stuns'ls" but Simon Graham wrote "studdensails", doubtless as he pronounced the word.

## Chapter 16

[1]A moderately large vessel required 5 miles of cordage of various diameters and 5000 square yards of canvas.

[2]A "trunnel machine" was offered for sale in *The Gleaner*, July 1863. This would have been a lathe incorporating adjustable blades by means of which a billet of wood was reduced to round shape. It could have been powered by steam, water-wheel or even by hand. The process was known as engine turning.

Treenails were also fabricated by hand by clamping a billet of wood in a vise and rounding it with draw-knives and spoke-shaves.

"Compressed," mentioned in note 2 Chapter 14, has a connotation somewhat different from what is implied. That is, no weight was brought to bear on the wood. Rather, a square billet of dry wood was placed in a metal container allowing as little tolerance as possible. The wood was then thoroughly soaked in water. It could not expand outwardly as it would normally, by reason of being tightly contained, and so expanded internally. This reduced the dimensions of cells and voids in the wood and increased the density. The wood was then dried and the process repeated until increased density and strength were pronounced, whereupon the billet was turned to a round shape. The procedure was slow, expensive and likely not common; nevertheless, at least one specimen of such material is to be seen in New Brunswick although it may not be native to the Province.

[3]Estep demonstrates the method in his work *How Wooden Ships are Built*.

[4]The strake next to the keel.

[5]A vessel could carry up to 16 passengers before being marked as a passenger ship.

[6]That was the practice on most merchant vessels. Nevertheless, navy vessels and large passenger ships often carried the bell forward in an elaborate belfry and sometimes had two bells.

[7]If permitted, seamen would congregate there and exchange gossip while quenching their thirst; hence the term "scuttlebutt," meaning rumour.

[8]The port and starboard sides of the stern of a vessel are still known as the quarters.

## Chapter 17

[1]A prolific writer, champion of the underdog and activist for social improvements, who resided briefly in New Brunswick at the end of the 18th century but who returned to England and there published many books of a radical nature.

[2]Several counts for various years have been made for Liverpool, ranging from 50% to 85%. Stuart Trueman in *An Intimate History of New Brunswick* counted

150 ships of 500 tons or more at that port in 1843, of which 70 came from New Brunswick and 58 from elsewhere in British North America.

[3]*Ann McKim*, built that year, is often called the first Clipper but *Rainbow*, New York, 1845, has a better claim.

[4]The Chatham *Gleaner*, Nov. 30, 1855: "Of interest to Shipbuilders, Ships of 1000 Tons in Great demand while those of 600 tons in moderate demand. The Model of the great bulk are acceptable though not suitable to present requirements. *They should not in length be less than five times their width.*"

[5]Two items taken from *The Gleaner* reveal the relative merits of different species of wood used in shipbuilding at the time but they should not be construed as indicating that British North American shipbuilders ever hewed to the lines laid down. The superior foreign woods may have been used late in the 19th century but records suggest that most British North American shipyards contented themselves with native products classing lower than the most desirable 12-year rating.

November 30, 1855:

The New Brunswicker furnishes the following news to Shipbuilders. Extract from Lloyds Shipbuilding Rules. We learn that the practice of using Black Birch for the main pieces of Rudder, Stem and Sternpost in Ships of 6 Years grade having recently been under the Committee of Lloyds consideration is reported to be unsuitable for that purpose. Greenheart, Moria and Ironbark for main pieces Rudder, Stem and Sternpost, Knightheads and Windlass in 12 years ships.

March 8, 1856:

Important to Shipbuilders. We have been informed by Lloyds' Surveyor for the Northern District of New Brunswick that the following is the amendment of Table A of Lloyds' Rules by which are exhibited the number of years assigned to the different descriptions of Timber used in Shipbuilding for Main Pieces of Rudders and Windlasses; referred to in the Committee's Minute of 1st January 1856.

| | |
|---|---|
| English, African and Live Oak, East India Teak, Morning Saul, Greenheart, Moria and Iron Bark | 12 years |
| Mahogany of hard texture, Cuba Sabien and Pencil Cedar | 10 years |
| Red Cedar | ineligable. |
| Adriatic, Spanish and French Oak, South American and Australasian Hard Wood | 9 years |
| Other Continental White Oak and Spanish Chestnut | 7 years |
| North American White Oak and American Sweet Chestnut | 7 years |
| Larch, Hackmatack, Tamarac and Juniper | ineligable |
| Pitch Pine | ineligable |
| Second hand English or African Oak and East India Teak | 5 years |

187

| | |
|---|---|
| Cowdie, Baltic and American Red Pine | ineligable |
| English Ash | 5 years |
| Foreign Ash | ineligable |
| American Rock Elm | 4 years |
| European and American Grey Elm | ineligable |
| Black Birch | 4 years |
| Spruce Fir | ineligable |
| English Beech | 4 years |
| Yellow Pine | ineligable |

[6]The business of sailing rotten hulls, unseaworthy, over-loaded, over-insured, was not abandoned in Britain until about 1876 when, as a result of agitation by Samuel Plimsoll, (1824-98) Parliament passed adequate controlling legislation. Plimsoll seems to have coined the phrase "coffin-ships" to describe merchantmen of the day.

## Chapter 18

[1]See Dudley Pope: *The Black Ship,* J.B. Lippincott Co., New York, 1964.

[2]New Brunswick had a Piracy Court until Confederation. Its members included the Lieutenant-Governor, the Chief Justice and Judges of the Supreme Court, Members of the Executive Council, the Judge of the Vice-Admiralty (court of maritime law), the Provincial Secretary and Treasurer, flag officers, captains and commanders of ships of war on station in New Brunswick.

[3]English oak is more resistant to fungal attack than other species of wood of the north temperate zone.

## Chapter 19

[1]The after part of the weather deck, not the poop or forecastle as sometimes supposed.

[2]Dana reported such a situation.

[3]Shipping Agreements were, in fact, contracts which were signed by each seaman. They recorded data concerning the vessel, its owners, master, crew, diet, the proposed voyage, liquor, leave, wages, advances, ports visited and so on.

[4]Unfortunately, owing to the great bulk of paper accumulated, early journals and shipping agreements were often destroyed at port record offices after a year or so. See a paper: "Memorial University acquires Imperial Shipping Archives," Keith Matthews in *We Have News For You*, Newfoundland and Labrador Provincial Archives, Vol. II, No. 10, Oct. 1971.

[5]Simon Graham's records show clearly that he did not make an abstract of journal while mate of *Richibucto*.

[6]*The Halifax Mail,* Feb. 21, 1928. Dr. Archibald MacMechan:
"I learned that all the firm's (Cunard Co.) papers had been destroyed. The attic of the old warehouse had been full of them. It took three months to burn them on the wharf. Norwood Duffus remembered a chest full of the whaling papers done in neat packets, each voyage by itself, with wooden panels and carefully docketed."

# BIBLIOGRAPHY

Allaby, Eric. *Shipbuilding in the Maritimes*. Ginn and Company, 1970.

Armco Inc., *Research and Methods of Analysis of Iron and Steel*. Middletown, Ohio: The American Rolling Mill Company, 1920.

Armour, Charles A. and Lackey, Thomas. *Sailing Ships of the Maritimes*. Toronto: McGraw-Hill Ryerson Limited, 1975.

Atkinson, Rev. Christopher W. *A Guide to New Brunswick*. Edinburgh: Anderson and Bryce, 1843.

Baker, William A. *American Colonial Shipbuilding*. Massachusetts Institute of Technology.

Belliveau, John Edward. *Running Far In*. Windsor, N.S.: Lancelot Press, 1977.

Blunt J. *The Shipmaster's Assistant*, New York: E. & G.W. Blunt, 1837.

Bowditch, Nathaniel. *The Practical Navigator*. New York: E. & G.W. Blunt, 1851 and later years.

Chapelle, Howard I., *The Search for Speed under Sail 1700-1855*. New York, Bonanza Books, 1967.

Cooney, Robert A. *A Compendious History of...New Brunswick....* Halifax, N.S.: Joseph Howe, 1832.

Cornell, Felix M. and Hoffman, Allan C. *American Merchant Seaman's Manual*. Cornell Maritime Press, 1942.

Dana, R.H. *Two Years Before the Mast*. New York: Grosset & Dunlap, 1927.

— *The Seaman's Friend*, London: Geo. Philip and Son, 1841.

Dixon, Francis B. *The Law of Shipping*. New York: Henry Spear, 1859.

*Encyclopaedia Britannica*. Editions 1797, 1824 & 1956.

Estep, Harvey Cole, *How Wooden Ships are Built*, Cleveland, O.:The Penton Publishing Co., 1918.

Fisher, Alexander. *A Journal of a Voyage To the Arctic Regions*. London: Longman and Company, 1821.

Forbes, Eric G. *The Birth of Scientific Navigation*. Greenwich, Eng.: National Maritime Museum.

*The Gleaner*. Chatham, N.B.: 1826 and later years.

Goldenberg, Joseph A. *Shipbuilding in Colonial America*. Newport News: University Press of Virginia, 1976.

Hannay, James. *A History of New Brunswick*. Saint John, N.B.: John A. Bowes, 1909.

Hind, H.Y., et al. *Eighty Years Progress in British North America*. Toronto: L. Stebbins, 1863.

Hosie, R.C. *Native Trees of Canada*. Canada: Department of the Environment, 1969.

Kemp, Peter. *The Oxford Companion to Ships and the Sea*. London: Oxford University Press, 1976.

Kerchov, Rene De. *International Marine Dictionary*. New York: Van Nostrand Reinhold Co., 1948.

Kochiss, John M. *The Deadeye, How It Was Made in Lunenburg, N.S.* Mystic, Conn.: Marine Historical Assoc. Inc.

*London Illustrated News.* London, England: 1840 and later years.

MacNutt, W.S. *New Brunswick.* Toronto: MacMillan of Canada, 1963.

— *The Atlantic Provinces.* Toronto: MacMillan of Canada, 1965.

Manny, Louise. *Ships of Kent County, New Brunswick.* Sackville, N.B.: Tribune Press, 1949.

— *Shipbuilding in Bathurst.* Fredericton, N.B.: Brunswick Press.

— *Shipbuilding on the Miramichi.* Fredericton, N.B.: Brunswick Press.

Milner, Dr. W.C. *An Early History of Dorchester, N.B.* Sackville, N.B.: Tribune Press, 1932.

— *A History of Sackville, N.B.* Sackville, N.B.: Tribune Press, 1934.

Monro, Alex. *New Brunswick...Nova Scotia and Prince Edward Island.* Halifax, N.S.: Richard Nugent, 1855.

— *British North America.* Montreal, P.Q.: John Lovell, 1864.

Parker, John P. *Sails of the Maritimes.* North Sydney, N.S.: private publication, 1960.

— *Cape Breton Ships and Men.* North Sydney, N.S.: private publication, 1967.

Rees, A. *The Cyclopaedia.* London, England: Longman, Hurst, Rees, Orme & Brown, 1819.

Saul, J.W. *Norie's Epitome,* London, Eng.: Imray, Laurie, Norie & Wilson, 1917.

Smythe, W.H. *The Sailor's Word-Book: An Alphabetical Digest of Nautical Terms.* London: Blackie and Son, 1867.

Spicer, Stanley T. *Masters of Sail.* Toronto: Ryerson Press, 1968.

Stammers, M.K. *The Passage Makers.* Brighton, Eng.: Teredo Books Ltd., 1978.

*Steel's Shipmaster's Assistant.* London, 1832.

Thompson, Marjorie J. *Jardine Shipbuilders of Kent Co., N.B.* Miramichi Historical Socy., 1963.

Underhill, Harold A. *Masting and Rigging the Clipper Ship.* Glasgow: Brown, Son, and Ferguson, 1946.

Wallace, F.W. *Wooden Ships and Iron Men.* London, Eng.: Hodder & Stoughton, 1924.

Worcester, Joseph E. *A Dictionary of the English Language.* Entered 1859 in the District of Massachusetts.

Wright, Esther Clark. *Saint John Ships and Their Builders.* Wolfville, N.S.: private publication, 1976.